Advance Praise for

How to Build with Grid Beam

Grid beam is a revolutionary building system that enables anyone to build a variety of structures without expensive wood shop services or equipment. Flexibility in design is yours! The photos and diagrams make it so simple. You can even make your own grid beam if you want. Now that's local sustainability at it's finest!

— JOHN SCHAEFFER, founder and president of
Real Goods and the Solar Living Institute

I have been a grid beam builder for over a dozen years. Reusability and modularity are keys to good design. Making grid beam provides students with experience in material selection, measurement, toolwork and finishing. Grid beam allows for rapid prototyping, flexabilty for changes, easy documentation with camera and sketches. Projects can be dismantled, components put away, ready for the next project. Artifacts are stored in the computer as photographs, diagrams and materials list. We are rarely more than a day away from resurrecting a former project.

— DR. JACK MARTIN, Appropriate Technology,
Appalachian State University

The Jergenson Brothers are the masters of grid beam construction. Their amazing technology is the stuff that rigid, rectilinear, realistic dreams are made from.

— RICHARD PEREZ, publisher of *Home Power* magazine

What I liked about the book is its ability to get all of us interested in being designers, inventors and builders. It could start a movement.

— JOHN TODD, PH.D., Research Professor and Distinguished Lecturer,
The University of Vermont; Principal, Todd Ecological Inc.

Grid beam amounts to an adult Erector Set that enables ordinary citizens to "wrench-build" a variety of machines and structures without expensive engineering and machine shop services .... Working prototypes can thus be constructed quickly right from crude sketches, without even a modest home shop. The principle seems obvious, but — as with all modular systems — there are tricky, subtle details that must dance compatibly for the system to work. The authors have everything dancing very smoothly indeed.

— JAY BALDWIN, Adjunct Professor of Industrial Design
at California College of the Arts, and author of
BuckyWorks, Buckminster Fuller's Ideas for Today

This book will inspire you to invent! As we enter the post carbon age, *How to build with Grid Beam* will provide useful techniques and projects for amateurs and experts alike to make quick and sturdy structures without the use of power tools. This is a fun and practical guide with which to foster a culture of reuse and enable the process of relocalization — living locally with much less energy.

— JULIAN DARLEY, President Post Carbon Institute

HOW TO BUILD WITH
GRID BEAM

HOW TO BUILD WITH
GRID BEAM

A FAST, EASY, AND AFFORDABLE SYSTEM
FOR CONSTRUCTING ALMOST **ANYTHING**

Phil Jergenson,
Richard Jergenson
& Wilma Keppel

NEW SOCIETY PUBLISHERS

Cataloging in Publication Data:

A catalog record for this publication is available from the National Library of Canada.

Cover design by Diane McIntosh.
Cover images: Phil Jergenson, Richard Jergenson, Wilma Keppel, Reinhold Ziegler.

Printed in Canada. First printing May 2008.

Paperback ISBN: 978-0-86571-613-1

Inquiries regarding requests to reprint all or part of *How to Build with Grid Beam* should be addressed to New Society Publishers at the address below.

To order directly from the publishers, please call toll-free (North America) 1-800-567-6772, or order online at www.newsociety.com

Any other inquiries can be directed by mail to:

New Society Publishers
P.O. Box 189, Gabriola Island, BC V0R 1X0, Canada
(250) 247-9737

New Society Publishers' mission is to publish books that contribute in fundamental ways to building an ecologically sustainable and just society, and to do so with the least possible impact on the environment, in a manner that models this vision. We are committed to doing this not just through education, but through action. This book is one step toward ending global deforestation and climate change. It is printed on Forest Stewardship Council-certified acid-free paper that is **100% post-consumer recycled** (100% old growth forest-free), processed chlorine free, and printed with vegetable-based, low-VOC inks, with covers produced using FSC-certified stock. Additionally, New Society purchases carbon offsets based on an annual audit, operating with a carbon-neutral footprint. For further information, or to browse our full list of books and purchase securely, visit our website at: www.newsociety.com

NEW SOCIETY PUBLISHERS
www.newsociety.com

To everyone who wishes to build,
and needs to find a way.

Contents

Acknowledgments

Our deepest thanks to Ken Isaacs — visionary, builder, teacher, and author. In inventing grid beam, he made an immense contribution to people everywhere.

In creating this book, we were greatly assisted by many people and organizations:

- Grid beam system development: Tom Conlon, Ken Isaacs, Reinhold Ziegler.

- Project information and pictures: Dave Beard, Tom Blinks, Brad Booth, Ed Burton, George Buono, Eileen Chang, Michael Hackleman, Ken Isaacs, Alan Kearney, Howard Letovsky, Jack Martin, A. Nonymous, Jean Tantra, Larry Todd, Reinhold Ziegler, and the members of the Electric Moose Club and Terman Middle School Electric Car Club.

- Parts, labor and encouragement: Amp King (San Francisco), Ed Burton, General Electric, Howard Letovsky, Monty Levenson.

- Technical data: Tom Blinks, BuildItGreen.org, Ecohome Improvement (Berkeley), Allied Tube and Conduit, 80/20 Inc., Northwest Pipe Company, S-Square Tube Products, Wilson Swilley, Ultimate Highway Products.

- Technical support: Tom Blinks, Michael Hackleman, Chris Koveleski, Scott Service, Jean Tantra, Reinhold Ziegler.

- Additional support: Barbara Keating, Richard Perez, Jean Tantra.

We deeply appreciate the many years of support and encouragement we've gotten from our families and friends. Thank you!

Part 1

Grid Beam Basics

What is Grid Beam?

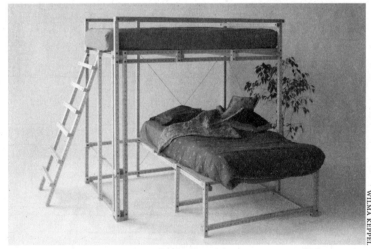

Grid beam is a simple, reusable system for building things. It is so simple that almost anyone can use it. Even if the limit of your mechanical aptitude is using a screwdriver, you can construct amazing stuff.

Yet grid beam is a real building system, not a toy. With it, ordinary people can create strong, durable, real-world projects ranging from furniture and sheds to vehicles, full-size buildings, and industrial equipment.

WILMA KEPPEL

PHIL AND RICHARD JERGENSON

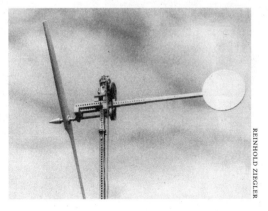

REINHOLD ZIEGLER

1.1: *Bunk bed, trade show booth with Vanda electric micro-van parked in front, and windmill and tower — all built from grid beam.*

1.2: Eighth-grader Jordan Bismuth racing a grid beam Moose car he designed and built in school. "It's a really good experience," he says. "Building a car isn't something I thought I could do before."

WILMA KEPPEL

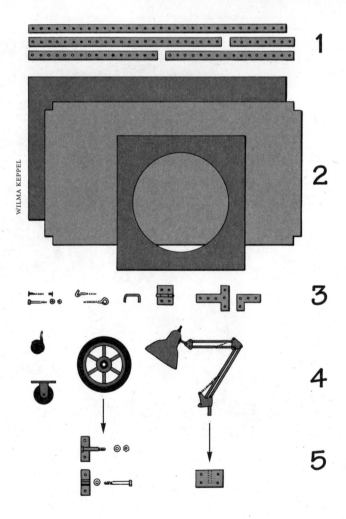

WILMA KEPPEL

The basics

The grid beam system includes five kinds of parts, and methods for putting them together. The parts (see picture) are

1. **Sticks** of wood, aluminum, or steel.
2. **Skin** such as plywood, sheet metal, or fabric.
3. **Hardware,** mostly nuts and bolts.
4. **Accessories** such as wheels, lights, sinks and drawers.
5. **Adapters,** which let you bolt odd-size accessories right into the system.

Depending on your skill level and budget, you can combine some or all of these pieces to build beds, shelves and workbenches, or more adventurous projects such as lofts, garden tractors, houses, and windmills. The University of Hawaii even built a remote-controlled grid beam submarine for deep-sea exploration. With grid beam, the possibilities are virtually unlimited!

How it works

Like Buckminster Fuller's geodesic domes, **grid beam is a completely new way of assembling things.** Unlike geodesics, grid beam looks a lot like older systems, so people don't notice the differences. A box is a box, right? Well, not quite.

Grid beam seems obvious, even simplistic, but it is neither. Many of its advantages are invisible until you actually use it. After over 30 years of using and introducing people to this system, we feel that **you will understand grid beam only after you have built projects with it.** Bear this in mind as you read.

The best way to understand grid beam is to build with it. Ideally we'd include a project's worth of beam with every book, but that's not practical. Instead we'll use photographs to take you through the process of assembling a simple workbench.

REINHOLD ZIEGLER

1.4: Steel-framed HELIOS helical rotor. Designed by Reinhold Ziegler and built by students in 1985, it uses Filon fiberglas rotors to pump water.

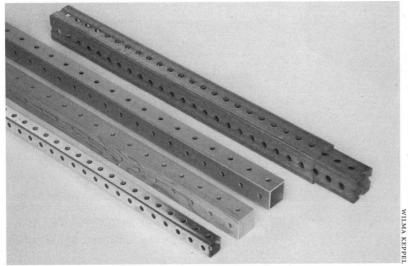

WILMA KEPPEL

1.5: Four types of commercial grid beam. From bottom: 1-inch (25 mm) steel, 1½-inch (40 mm) wood, 1½-inch aluminum, 2-inch (50 mm) steel double-hole with a 1¾-inch (45 mm) insert. You can also drill your own.

The Twelve-Minute Workbench

The key to grid beam's fast assembly is the bolted **tri-joint.** Three bolts fasten three beams tightly together. Each beam is bolted twice, from two different sides. The bolts squeeze the flat sides of the beams together, making a joint that is tremendously strong, rigid in every direction and automatically square. Speed-assemble a project, and when you tighten the bolts at the end of the process, the frame will square right up.

Now the materials: Those pictured here are already cut to size and ready to go.

1.6: *Tri-joint of aluminum sticks fastened with hex nuts and hex bolts. For a stronger joint, use washers on both sides of the sticks. Press-fit end caps are plastic.*

1.8: *Basic tools and fasteners for metal-frame projects. The nut driver and gear wrench at the bottom of the picture really speed assembly.*

1.7: *Wooden tri-joint uses fasteners that lie flat on both sides of the joint.*

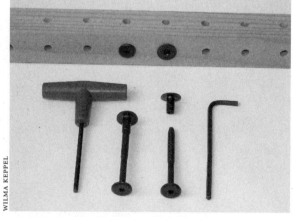

1.9: *Tools and fasteners for wooden grid beam. The T-handled Allen wrench at left is easy to use; the L-shaped wrench at right is better for tight spaces.*

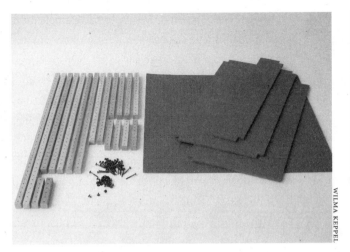

1.10: *Workbench materials.*

1.11: *The Twelve-Minute Workbench. The small shelf can also go on top.*

Grid beam is a modular system: parts are interchangeable and come in standard sizes. With a modest collection of components you can build dozens of projects.

Sticks and panels of various sizes and materials match whatever job you need to do. Our workbench frame is 1½-inch (40-millimeter) wood. You could build a heavy-duty version of the same project using 2-inch (50-millimeter) steel.

Two wrenches, or a wrench and nut driver, are enough to assemble most metal-framed projects. For wood, you only need an Allen wrench. We're ready to get to work.

1. The easiest way to begin building a grid beam structure is to build a tri-joint into it. This instantly gives the project shape. Installing an upright post on an outside corner seems to work the best. Do not tighten the bolts yet. You should have a bit of flex in each joint.

1.12

1.13

2. From this point on you only have to add a single piece at a time. This single-stick technique is invaluable in saving time and your back, especially with larger structures. Support uprights with your hand or shoulder until you have them fastened with two bolts. Uprights held by only one bolt can fall over and pinch or hit someone.

3. If you're designing a project as you build, establish your corner verticals and the main level, such as your work surface, as early as possible. Build up and down from there until your frame is complete.

4. Once the frame is assembled, tighten the bolts. As the joints get tight, your project's frame will straighten and square itself. Use between five and ten pounds of pressure on the wrench. Beginners often over-tighten bolts.

5. The rear panel attaches over the frame bolts. Tighten its bolts.

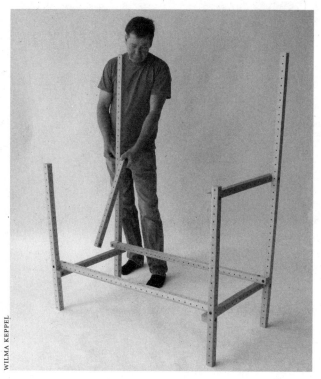

1.14

1.15

6. Add the shelves and work surface. Presto, you're done! Total assembly time: twelve minutes.

Yes, grid beam really is that simple. And with this simple system, you can build just about anything! Since 1976, we've used grid beam to build hundreds of projects, ranging from shelves, desks, and beds to vehicles, small buildings, and even complete industrial assembly lines.

Grid beam is faster than welding, carpentry or fabrication. It's also goof-proof: just unbolt the problem area and rebuild it the way you want. And because you can re-use the same components again and again, grid beam helps the environment while saving you money. Every way, you win!

Sources

Where do you get grid beam? You have three options:

1. Buy a kit. (See the Suppliers chapter for sources.)

2. Buy specialty components such as sticks from a vendor, and supply the rest of the pieces yourself. Grid beam is designed to work with standard, widely available sheet materials such as plywood and hardboard. Most grid beam components are available as off-the-shelf parts. This approach gets you exactly the right parts for your special project.

3. Drill your own sticks. While time-consuming, this can save you money, and is the only way to go if you need a

1.16

1.17: *Steel-framed stand for a chop saw that cuts bronze bar. Built in 1980 as part of an industrial assembly line, it is still in use.*

kind of stick that no one manufactures. Basic shop skills are required.

The easiest way to get plans is to copy designs from photographs in this book — just count the holes. Standard-size parts make it easy to build features from one project into another.

We encourage you to experiment with designing your own projects. It's a lot of fun, and a great way to get exactly what you want.

Using this book

This handbook shows projects ranging from beginner level to advanced. It also includes hundreds of photos of real-world

1.18: *Richard relaxes in his cord-seat folding chair.*

grid beam projects as well as grid beam charts and tables of measurements.

Part 1 introduces you to the grid beam way of building: its history and advantages in Chapters 2 and 3; and its components and how they work together in Chapter 4.

Part 2 describes projects ranging from simple furniture to complex electric vehicles. **It is up to you to build projects that are within your skill level, and to build them safely.** When trying a new type of project, proceed cautiously. Get help from experienced people if you need it.

Some of the projects shown in this book require notching panels, or cutting sticks and panels to size. We assume you have basic shop skills. If not, get someone to show you. Using power tools is like driving a car: dangerous until you know how to do it, safe once you've had some practice.

Part 3 gets down to the basics of working with grid beam. This is where you'll learn about:

Sticks: how to buy them, cut them and drill them for your projects;

Skins: what materials work best for different projects, where to buy them, how to work with skin materials ranging from plywood to sheet metal to glass;

Panels: how to cut, drill and mount all the different kinds of panels you can use in grid beam; and

All the hardware, accessories and adapters that go with grid beam.

Part 4 describes the basics of grid beam project assembly and design. It takes you

Common units of measure used in this book					
Unit	Measures	Abbreviation & Symbol	Equals	Metric (exact)	Metric approximates
inch	length	in. "	$\frac{1}{12}$ foot	25.4 millimeters	25 mm
foot	length	ft. ´	12 inches	305 millimeters	300 mm
mile	length	mi.	5,280 feet	1.609 kilometers	
pound	weight	lb.	16 ounces	453.6 grams	
gallon	volume	gal.	4 quarts	3.785 liters	
horsepower	power	hp		745.7 watts	

1.19

from building and bracing simple frames to designing and building electric vehicles.

The book ends with two chapters that list additional resources to help you build, including suppliers of everything from wood and metal sticks to motors and suspensions for your vehicles.

A glossary defines special terms we use. To order kits, components and books, and to find out the latest news in the world of grid beam, visit our websites at grid-beamers.com and grid-beam.com.

Measurements

We live and work in the US, where most construction materials are measured by the US system, not metric units. The grid beam we use is designed to work with the standard sizes of those materials. Since this book is based on our experience, we've used US measures throughout. We list metric conversions for common stick widths and bolt diameters in Figure 1.20. You'll find metric conversions for common panel sizes and stick lengths in Figure 4.1 (page 26).

The names of standard US lumber sizes usually *don't* match the actual sizes.

Common stick widths	
US sizes	Closest metric size
¾ inch	20 mm
1 inch	25 mm
1½ inch	40 mm
2 inches	50 mm
3½ inches	90 mm
Bolt sizes	
¼ inch	6 mm
$\frac{5}{16}$ inch	8 mm
$\frac{3}{8}$ inch	9.5 mm
$\frac{7}{16}$ inch	11 mm

1.20: *Standard stick lengths and panel sizes are listed in Figure 4.1. Common US lumber sizes are listed in Figure 16.9*

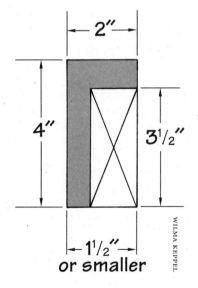

WILMA KEPPEL

1.21: *The incredible shrinking two-by-four. In 1955 it measures 2 x 4 inches. By 1990 it had shrunk to 1½ x 3½ inches. Tree farm lumber sometimes shrinks more — we have measured sticks as small as 1³⁄8 x 3¼ inches. Measure lumber before you buy.*

That's because most lumber is cut to its nominal (named) size while green, shrinks as it dries, and then smoothing it removes more wood. A modern "two-by-four" measures 2 x 4 inches when cut, but shrinks to 1½ x 3½ inches or less when dry. Lower-quality lumber shrinks more.

In this book, we **spell out the stated dimensions of lumber** (two-by-four, not 2 x 4 inches or 2 x 4½) and **write actual dimensions in numbers** (when we write 2 x 4 inches, we mean exactly 2 inches by 4 inches).

Ready to learn all about grid beam and what you can do with it? We'll start with a short history of the system.

History

Many of the very best inventions don't require a technological breakthrough. The inventor simply recognizes an idea that has been overlooked. Grid beam is such an invention.

Ken Isaacs developed grid beam in the late 1940s. To get more use out of a small apartment, he used space three dimensionally. A skeleton of square wooden struts that Ken called **matrix** supported tables, seating, storage and sleeping platforms at different levels. This frame had to be strong enough to hold lots of weight, rigid enough not to flop around, and inexpensive so Ken could afford it. And the whole system had to be simple so he could build it without a workshop, using ordinary materials such as wooden two-by-twos.

Ken called his 3-D creations "Living Structures." Today we call the bolted fabrication technique he developed **grid beam.**

Rather than try to patent or trademark grid beam, Ken went public in a series of

2.1: *Home in a Cube by Ken Isaacs supports a bed, closet, desk, couch and fireplace in an eight-foot frame. This photo appeared in* Life *magazine in 1954.*

articles that appeared in *Life, Popular Science* and other magazines. His *How to Build Your Own Living Structures* (1974) is probably the best book ever written about reusable building systems. Through his writing, Ken put grid beam in the public domain and made it available to everyone.

We learned about grid beam when Phil purchased Ken's book in 1974. Our friend

THREE-WAY CORNER LOCKED

NAILS

POPULAR MECHANICS

2.2: *The earliest reference we've found to a tri-joint is this nailed "crate joint" from the 1930s.*

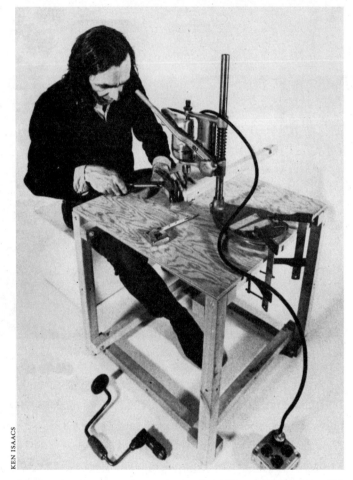

KEN ISAACS

2.3: *Ken demonstrates a low-cost setup for drilling grid beam. The drill table is a two-foot wooden cube assembled with flat-head machine bolts. Note the simple hole pattern.*

Reinhold (Peter) Ziegler immediately started drilling holes and assembling projects. "I wanted to be a builder, but wasn't even a decent carpenter," Reinhold remembers. Grid beam made it possible for him to start building right away. Richard was next, and soon a number of us were building with grid beam.

In 1976 a group of us moved to Earthlab I, a 25,000 square foot warehouse in Berkeley, California. Twelve of us — artists, designers and builders — lived and worked under one roof. This seminal group included Phil and Richard, Reinhold, and Tom Conlon. We all applied "the system" to our studios and offices, working together to improve Ken's invention. Phil did the most to standardize grid beam and make it fully modular.

By the early 1990s we called Ken's building method "box beam." In 1994 Phil and Richard self-published their first book about the system, *Box Beam Sourcebook*. They introduced Wilma to the system in 1995. Since "box beam" was already used in the construction industry as a term for something else, we decided to rename the system. We call it "grid beam" because the holes form a grid pattern.

A pictorial history of grid beam

Ken's 1949 Home in a Cube had a frame of two-by-two lumber, drilled at the corners and where frame members attached. He bolted it together using hex bolts with washers.

KEN ISAACS

2.4: *Each student in Ken's 1970 introductory architecture class at the University of Illinois built their own four-foot Study Cube, shown here without the privacy skin. These sticks had holes along their length to make seat and shelf adjustment easy. Although able to make tri-joints only at the corners, these sticks were more interchangeable than previous designs.*

REINHOLD ZIEGLER

2.5: *Earthlab I member Reinhold Ziegler pioneered repeating the tri-joint hole pattern in a series of sleeping lofts he designed, built and marketed beginning in 1978. To minimize drilling, the holes repeat on the vertical frame members only where needed to adjust desk and shelf height.*

PHIL AND RICHARD JERGENSON

2.6: *In 1976, Earthlab member Tom Conlon made grid beam from square steel tubes fastened with hex bolts. Tom was the first person to drill a repeating tri-joint hole pattern along the entire length of the sticks. These were the first "universal" sticks that could be used in any project, or cut to shorter lengths without requiring additional holes. Then Tom discovered two-inch Telespar, a commercial square steel tube with holes every inch on all four sides. This "double-hole" beam (it has twice as many holes as grid beam needs) can make a tri-joint anywhere. Phil used it to build his 1977 Portable House right inside the Earthlab warehouse. Once finished, he disassembled it, moved it to his land in the country, then reassembled it on-site.*

PHIL AND RICHARD JERGENSON

PHIL AND RICHARD JERGENSON

2.7: *Phil's 1978 Electric Vehicle Test Bed was the first grid beam vehicle we know of. It was also the first project built using sticks with the hole pattern we use today. "Building with double-hole sticks convinced me of the advantages of pre-drilling every hole so we could put a tri-joint anywhere," Phil remembers.*

2.8: *Phil's 1979 electric Scamp was the first grid beam vehicle framed with aluminum.*

REINHOLD ZIEGLER

REINHOLD ZIEGLER

2.9: *Reinhold Ziegler used grid beam in the wind and solar energy classes he taught in California colleges starting in 1979: "We never needed to weld one part in 7 years of classes." Here students install a steel-framed windmill and stand, which they designed and built, on a floating platform in San Francisco Bay.*

2.10: *Students assemble a solar cabin, framed with wooden four-by-fours measuring 3½ inches square, for a 1980 college fair in Oakland, California. Design by Reinhold Ziegler.*

2.11: *In the 1990s, students at several middle and high schools designed and built their own grid beam vehicles. A group of seventh and eighth graders built the Panther Electric, shown here and in Figure 11.20*

2.12: *By the early 1990s, we used carriage bolts to assemble wood frames. Panels attached right over the bolt heads, as shown on Richard's 1993 Corner Bench.*

In 1997, Richard discovered a nearly ideal fastening system for wood-framed projects. Joint connector bolts and weld nuts make a joint that is flat on both sides.

Today's grid beam is even better than the original. The parts are standardized and fully interchangeable. Improved fasteners and better hole placement make the system more versatile and easier to use. A wide variety of projects have been built, tested and used in the real world. And today, grid beam continues to evolve and improve.

Who we are and why we wrote this book

The three of us combined have built and used a wide variety of grid beam projects — everything from bookshelves to portable shelters to garden tractors and a solar-electric mini-van. We count as friends and colleagues several of the world's leading grid beam designers and builders, most of whom contributed generously to this book.

Phil and Richard's first book about grid beam, and J. Baldwin's 1994 reviews in *Whole Earth Review* and the *Millennium Whole Earth Catalog,* introduced grid beam to thousands of people. We have demonstrated grid beam at trade shows and alternative energy fairs, and taken it into the classroom to teach students building and design.

Grid beam has helped us build hundreds of projects, and saved us thousands of dollars and untold hours of construction time. We have proved that grid beam is a working, practical building system for the real world. Because it's benefited *us* so

A brief history of hole patterns

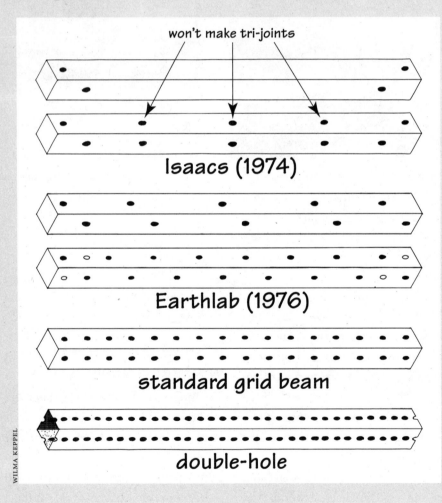

won't make tri-joints

Isaacs (1974)

Earthlab (1976)

standard grid beam

double-hole

WILMA KEPPEL

2.13: *We tried a bunch of hole patterns that had problems before settling on the patterns we use now — the bottom two.*

much, and because it's so Earth- and people-friendly, we want to share grid beam as widely as possible so that *you* can benefit also.

Richard's story

"I started building in childhood, and as a young man worked for two years as an apprentice carpenter. When I got my hands on Ken Isaacs's book, it was the eureka moment. The minimalism of his matrix idea spoke to my design and building sense. The simplicity and ease of using bolts and nuts rather than hammer and nails was liberating. It was also faster, cleaner and safer.

"In 1977 our design group had just moved into our giant warehouse in

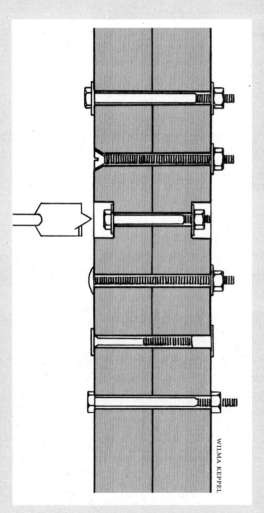

2.14: *Bolt and nut types*

Hex bolt and hex nut with washers are mostly used on metal frames.

Flat-head machine bolt is weak (because it doesn't spread the load), and may split wood.

Counterbored holes work great on big timbers, but weaken small sticks too much — and they're a lot of extra work. Drill with a counterbore bit or spade bit.

Carriage bolt's shoulder digs into wood and keeps it from turning. The head is fairly flat, but the nut end projects.

Joint-connector bolt and weld nut are flat on both sides.

Hex nuts and bolts without washers concentrate a lot of force on a small area, which can damage your sticks.

WILMA KEPPEL

WILMA KEPPEL

2.15: *Built in 1977, Richard's first grid beam project is still in daily use. He drilled the modern hole pattern later.*

"My desk was next. I'd salvaged some drafting tables from a school that was being demolished. We were minutes ahead of the bulldozers razing the building to rubble. I used one of the table tops, and added storage shelves underneath — a great combination.

"What to do with my clothes? Build a closet, of course. Many miles and moves later, I'm still using the same materials in various configurations that continue to adapt to my needs."

Phil's story

"In the early 1970s, the *Whole Earth Catalog* and *Domebook* filled my brain with alternative lifestyle ideas. I bought Ken's book in 1974 to study his microhouse designs. The book also included grid beam, which at that time was still pretty crude. Cross-members could only attach in certain places. Tri-joints only happened at the ends of sticks. With their custom dimensions and hole patterns, sticks and panels were not interchangeable between projects, and could not be cut into smaller standard pieces. Ken's grid beam was the beginning of a modular system, but hadn't quite arrived.

"As my friends built with grid beam, it improved. The hole pattern became regular. The distance between hole pairs decreased. The system was getting more usable. When Tom Conlon scaled it up to 2-inch steel tubes in 1976, I bought 600 feet of galvanized double-hole and used it to frame my Portable House.

Berkeley, California. We needed both furniture and shop benchwork. Several of us tried grid beam, exploring it together and sharing in the learning process. Life hasn't been the same since.

"My studio space needed furnishing, and I needed to get organized. I built a bookshelf that I'm still using 30 years later. Needing a bed, I built a combination sleeping loft/library/reading area that my friends dubbed "The Cave." The top was a plywood ping pong table top that I cut down to 5 x 7 feet, the mattress a piece of foam. This gave me an inexpensive bed/bookcase/reading nook/conversation area made from reusable pieces.

"My next project was a small electric vehicle. Built of salvaged 1-inch steel tubing, the EVTB started as an electric motorcycle, then morphed into a trike to give me more cargo space.

"A colleague and I used galvanized steel to improve and expand the assembly line used in our manufacturing business. Steel grid beam made tables, drill press and conveyor belt stands, even the frames for custom pieces of manufacturing machinery. We used grid beam scaffolds to repair and improve the buildings that housed our business.

"In 1979 a bunch of the Earthlab crew moved to Willits in northern California, and I finally got to assemble my Portable House on-site. The steep terrain soon convinced me that I needed a vehicle with a transmission. I built the Scamp that summer, and drove it up and down the hill on my property to get to my Portable House.

"Leaving the electrical power grid was a shock. In the following years I used grid beam in my daily life for solar trackers, small electric work vehicles, scaffolds and many other uses. In 1999 I started working with inventor Ed Burton, developing prototype machinery for harvesting smallwood — wood that is big enough to be a fire hazard, but too small to interest commercial timber companies. Grid beam has been tremendously useful for prototyping a wide variety of projects, including walk-behind carts, trailers and wood-processing equipment. I continue to use it for personal projects. Now my daughter Rona is old enough that we collaborate on projects, which is fun for both of us."

Wilma's story

"Like many girls in the 1960s I grew up thinking I wasn't mechanically talented, even though building and mechanical stuff fascinated me. Fortunately my mother took carpentry classes so she could remodel the kitchen, and taught me a bit. I bought a motorcycle, then had to learn basic mechanics to keep it running. Next I fixed up a wrecked bike and helped a friend remodel his house. Eventually I worked as a welder and metal fabricator.

I learned that conventional building methods are fun to build with, but frustrating when you need to change something. Once built, projects are difficult to disassemble for repairs or upgrades. When I saw grid beam in 1995, I could tell that it

2.16: Phil Jergenson test-driving the partially assembled Japanese Bear. Phil loves building with metal, and since 1978 has constructed more than 25 grid beam electric handcarts and vehicles. He and his brother Richard own QuikStix, a grid beam manufacturing company in Willits, California.

solved most of those problems. I had to try it.

"A friend salvaged some bent 2-inch (50-millimeter) galvanized double-hole sign posts for me, and I cut out the straight sections. It was hard to get the bent posts to lie flat on my chop saw table so I could make square cuts. As soon as I had enough straight pieces, I used them to build a saw table on which I cut the rest of the sticks. That was my first grid beam project.

"Wood came next, in the form of 600 feet of 1½-inch QuikStix™ purchased from the Jergensons in 1996. Soon I had a grid beam desk, then a closet organizer, shelves, and more. In the years since, I've built many other projects with those pieces. Most of this book was written on grid beam desks. The more I use grid beam, the better it gets!"

PHIL AND RICHARD JERGENSON

2.17: *Richard "RJ" Jergenson readies the electric Sol Train for a ride on the tracks. A railroad buff, Richard loves building with wood. Dozens of his projects aren't in this book because they never got photographed. Document your work!*

JEAN TANTRA

2.18: *Former welder and metal fabricator Wilma Keppel switched to grid beam in 1995. "With grid beam, I don't need to weld any more. It's faster, easier, and there's no waste."*

Advantages

Grid beam has a number of advantages over every other building system we've tried (and we've tried lots of them).

Most modern building methods require specialized tools and training. They are difficult to work with and inflexible. The materials require large amounts of energy and specialized tooling to manufacture. These materials are often expensive, and tend to have a short lifetime. When a project's useful life is over, recycling or reuse may be impossible or too costly to be feasible. The item is then demolished, abandoned, or junked.

Contrast that with grid beam:

Easy. Anyone who can count and turn a wrench can build with this system.

Simple. Standard components come in standard sizes. You can concentrate on what you're building, not how to build it.

Inexpensive. Metal beam costs less than hiring a welding shop to build the same project. With wood, you pay about the same as for conventional construction. Grid beam is much cheaper to fix or alter than other building methods. And you save money every time you re-use a component.

PHIL AND RICHARD JERGENSON

3.1: *Rona Jergenson, age four, assembles a play structure using joint connector bolts, weld nuts and a T-handle Allen wrench.*

Fast. We can sometimes build projects faster than we could plan them on paper. With conventional construction, planning and fabricating a complex project like a vehicle can take months. Phil often test-drives experimental vehicles within a week of starting them, sometimes within a day. He says, "Grid beam is the fastest way there is to get your idea from paper to reality!"

Strong. For even more strength, add a stiff skin such as plywood.

Versatile. We've personally built everything from beds to buildings to garden tractors.

Mistake-proof. If you goof or break something, simply unbolt the problem area and rebuild it.

Needs no shop. You can assemble most projects in your living room or yard, using simple hand tools. Grid beam makes square frames even on rough ground.

Adapts to your needs. You can reconfigure projects in minutes.

Modular. A few re-usable parts build many projects.

3.2: *Grid beam makes quick solutions to temporary problems. Wire reel by Tom Blinks.*

WILMA KEPPEL

Acts as its own blueprint. Once you've built something, just count the holes to build another one. It's easy to build from plans or photos. Projects on remote sites can be duplicated elsewhere for modification or repair.

Easy to store and move. Projects knock flat and store in a small space.

Minimizes waste. Common stick and panel sizes can be cut from standard materials, such as plywood panels, with only sawdust left over.

Environmentally friendly. Grid beam uses many of industrial construction's high-energy components, but because they get used over and over again, the environmental impact is minimized. We are still using sticks we drilled in 1976!

Low-tech. Grid beam can be locally manufactured, often from local materials, using widely available tools.

Ideal for project design. The average project takes two or three tries to get right. Grid beam gives you a refined design before your time, energy and money are exhausted. It is by far the best prototyping system we have ever used.

Well-tested. Grid beam is no pie-in-the-sky fantasy. We and our friends have lived with, on, and in this stuff for over three decades. It works!

With grid beam, you are never stuck with a bad design. You are never forced to "just live with it" because modifying a project will cost more than it's worth. You no longer have to endure "good enough." At last you can have what you *really* want!

Your own personal Industrial Revolution

Standardization made the Industrial Revolution possible and created great material abundance. Unfortunately, consumer products remain almost entirely nonstandard. Furniture wheels and handles, table heights, desk and dresser widths, even the wall-mounting slots on the back of electrical power strips, all differ from manufacturer to manufacturer and product to product. You can't easily take a part from one item to fix or modify another. Most of today's consumer products aren't designed to be modified or repaired. That gives you *less* choice.

Most mass-produced products, such as chairs, get designed to fit an "average" person. This leaves millions of not-so-average people unable to find products that fit.

With grid beam, you gain the advantages of your very own Industrial Revolution! Standardized, interchangeable parts. The ability to build a wide variety of objects from a few types of components. The option to customize anything, at any time, to fit *your* needs and desires. In a world of rapid change, grid beam allows you to adapt easily, quickly and inexpensively to today … and tomorrow … and to whatever comes after.

3.3a: *It usually takes about three tries to get a project the way you want it. The first version of Wilma's bed loft wasted floor space. The panel behind the file cabinet made the room seem cramped.*

3.3b: *Version 2: Better, but the file cabinet drawers bumped the dresser. Wilma put the 5 x 7 foot deck 5 feet above the floor so she could sit up in bed under the 8-foot ceiling.*

WILMA KEPPEL

3.3c: *Version 3: Decent use of space and plenty of room beneath for bookshelves and storage.*

WILMA KEPPEL

3.3e: *L-shaped space under Version 4 platform lined with 50 feet of bookshelves, with room to sit up comfortably. White bathroom paneling bounces light from the ceiling and end.*

3.3d: *Version 4: Lowering the deck height to 3 feet made the room seem much more spacious. A folding step stool provided access. After adding an end panel, Wilma put a conventional bookcase 5 feet tall at the head of the bed.*

WILMA KEPPEL

 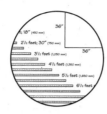 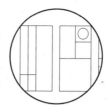 

The Grid Beam System

[Grid beam] amounts to an adult Erector Set that enables ordinary citizens to "wrench-build" a variety of machines and structures without expensive engineering and machine shop services. … Working prototypes can thus be constructed quickly right from crude sketches, without even a modest home shop. The principle seems obvious, but — as with all modular systems — there are tricky, subtle details that must dance compatibly for the system to work. Phil [Jergenson] has everything dancing very smoothly indeed.

— J. Baldwin, *Whole Earth Review*

If you build grid beam projects from a kit, you don't have to think much about the system — it's all been engineered for you. But if you're the adventurous type, you'll want to know a little more about how the pieces work together.

With any modular system, compatibility is everything. Each component should work with as many other parts of the system as possible. With grid beam, component size and hole placement determine which parts work together.

Grid beam stick and panel sizes are based on standard material sizes — in our case, the sizes used by the US construction industry. All stick widths we use are even divisions of our basic unit, the foot. This lets us use standard lumber, metal tubing, and panels with little or no waste. The hole spacing on our sticks permits components from many industries to bolt right on. If you live where material sizes are different, you may wish to create your own system to match.

Hole spacing

Hole spacing determines whether a stick will make tri-joints or not. If a stick won't make tri-joints it's not grid beam, no matter how many holes it has.

4.1: Standard-size components let you build the maximum number of projects with the minimum number of pieces. Stick widths are listed in Figure 1.20 on page 9.

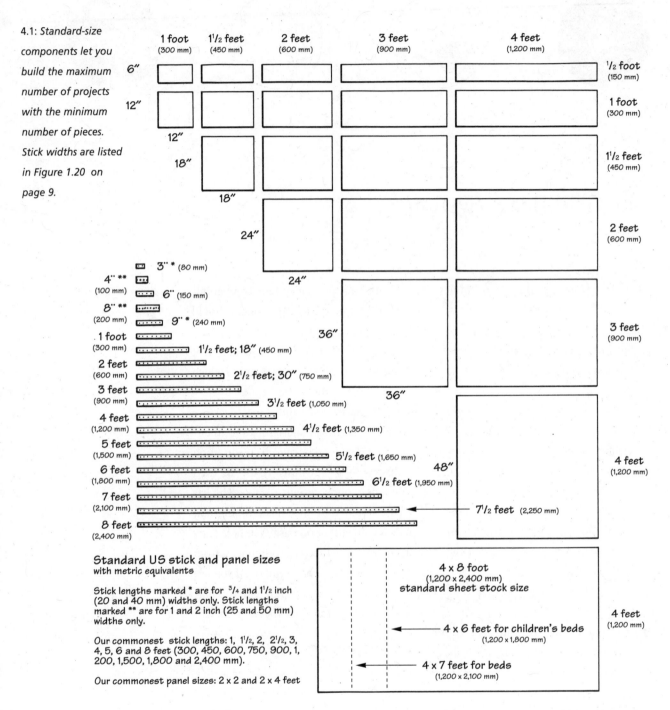

Standard US stick and panel sizes
with metric equivalents

Stick lengths marked * are for ³/₄ and 1¹/₂ inch (20 and 40 mm) widths only. Stick lengths marked ** are for 1 and 2 inch (25 and 50 mm) widths only.

Our commonest stick lengths: 1, 1¹/₂, 2, 2¹/₂, 3, 4, 5, 6 and 8 feet (300, 450, 600, 750, 900, 1, 200, 1,500, 1,800 and 2,400 mm).

Our commonest panel sizes: 2 x 2 and 2 x 4 feet

WILMA KEPPEL

Standard grid beam has a set of holes every one stick width. A stick 1 inch wide has holes every 1 inch, a stick 1½ inches wide has holes every 1½ inches, and so on. This hole spacing lets you build a tri-joint wherever you want one. When you cut a stick shorter, both pieces are fully functional.

Grid beam stick and hole sizes

We use three sizes of grid beam. Our main sizes are 2 inches and 1½ inches wide, with 1-inch sticks for light-weight projects and subassemblies. Sticks ¾-inch wide also work with the system. All of these sizes have holes every 3 inches, allowing the same parts to bolt to different size tubes. (Metric stick sizes work a bit differently — see Figure 4.3.)

1½" and ¾" sticks both have holes every 1½".   *1" and 2" sticks have holes every 1".*

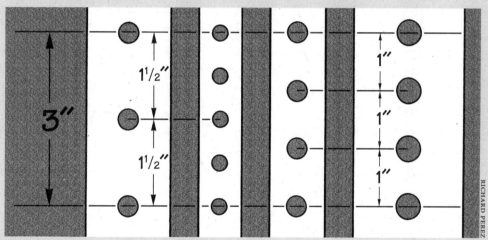

4.2

RICHARD PEREZ

Beam size	1½" (38.1 mm)	¾" (19.05 mm)	1" (25.4 mm)	2" (50.8 mm)
metal	$^{21}/_{64}$" hole (8.3 mm) $^{5}/_{16}$" bolt* (8 mm)	$^{9}/_{32}$" hole (7 mm) ¼" bolt (6 mm)	$^{11}/_{32}$" hole (9 mm) $^{5}/_{16}$" bolt (8 mm)	$^{7}/_{16}$" hole (11 mm) $^{3}/_{8}$" (9.5 mm) bolt or $^{7}/_{16}$" (11 mm)
wood	$^{5}/_{16}$" (8 mm) hole			
	¼" (6 mm) bolt			

* Phil's home-drilled 1½-inch (38.1 mm) aluminum tubes are aircraft alloy 6061-T6 with $^{13}/_{32}$-inch (10 mm) holes that fit $^{3}/_{8}$-inch (9.5 mm) bolts.

The extra holes in 2-inch steel grid beam mean that components with the right hole spacing bolt to all the stick sizes we use (see Figure 4.2). This minimizes the number of components you need to stock. Figure 4.4 shows metric stick sizes.

Standard stick and panel sizes

By standardizing stick lengths and panel sizes, you can build more with fewer parts. No more hacking off odd-sized pieces to fit the new project. No more waste when cutting panels. No more piles of odd-sized leftovers that can't be assembled into anything. Since the whole point of grid beam is convenience, it's dumb *not* to standardize!

When we first began building with grid beam in the 1970s, we cut sticks and panels in custom sizes to fit particular projects. We soon discovered that our odd-sized components were rarely reusable. You get

the most use of your components by stocking duplicates of just a few standard sizes. Here's our system:

- All stick lengths are even multiples of the beam width. This halves the number of sizes.

- Most of our sticks and panels are whole-foot sizes (multiples of 305 millimeter) — lengths such as 2, 3 or 4 feet, or panel dimensions such as 2 x 4 feet.

- If we need an intermediate size, we try for multiples of 6 inches (half a foot). We use a lot of sticks 18 and 30 inches (1½ and 2½ feet) long. Shelves 18 inches deep are good for heavy storage, and 30 inches is a good desk height.

- More than other projects, vehicles require building to exact sizes. Phil often has to use odd-sized pieces. These are still multiples of the beam width, such as 10½ inches and 15 inches for 1½-inch beam.

Most of the world now uses metric stick and panel sizes. Use the standard sizes for building materials in your area, and adapt the grid beam system to them (see Figure 4.3).

~

Now let's take a brief look at the different types of components that make up the grid beam system.

Stick materials

You can purchase sticks, or drill your own. Three stick materials adapt grid beam to almost any project:

4.3

Metric stick size options

Millimeters	Inches		Millimeters	Inches
20 mm	0.79″		25 mm	0.98″
30 mm	1.18″		50 mm	1.96″
40 mm	1.57″		75 mm	2.95″
60 mm	2.36″		100 mm	3.94″

All these sizes share 120 mm (4.7 inch) hole spacing, and work with panel sizes that are multiples of 120 mm.

All sizes share 300 mm (11.8 inch) hole spacing, and work with panel sizes that are multiples of 300 mm. The 25, 50 and 75 mm sizes also share 150 mm (5.9 inch) hole spacing.

1. **Wood.** Light-weight, inexpensive, beautiful and moderately strong, wood works well for indoor projects such as furniture, storage and light-duty shop benchwork. We use 1½-inch sticks. Timbers 3 inches square and larger can be used for building frames. Weather and dampness can damage wood. Oil-finished wood can last years outdoors if you renew the finish periodically.

2. **Steel.** Very strong, heavy and moderately priced, steel works well for shop benchwork and industrial uses. Several brands of pre-punched tubing work as grid beam. We mainly use 2-inch pre-punched galvanized tubes. Galvanized steel will last decades outdoors, making it ideal for scaffolds, windmill towers and building frames. Tubes 1 inch wide are good for furniture and children's go-karts. We would use 1½-inch steel if we could buy it with the correct hole spacing; it's not worth the hassle to drill our own.

3. **Aluminum.** Light, strong and impervious to weather, aluminum needs no finish. On a vehicle, it can reduce frame weight by hundreds of pounds (over 100 kilograms). Unfortunately aluminum is very expensive. We use 1½-inch sticks most often. Smaller sticks are useful for light-weight applications such as go-karts and bicycle trailers.

As you thumb through the projects chapters, you'll get an idea of which materials we find suitable for which types of projects. But don't limit yourself to what we do. If a wooden vehicle suits your fancy, build it!

Skin materials

We show our favorite panel sizes in Figure 4.1. Modular sizes make each piece usable for the maximum number of projects, minimizing the number of parts you need to stock.

A wide variety of skin materials work with grid beam, each suited to a particular range of projects. Here are our favorites.

Plywood is strong, easy to use, reasonably priced and available at any lumberyard. On projects where we need side panels with lots of bracing power, we use plywood ¼ inch or thicker. For loft decks and floors, use sheets at least ½ inch thick. Extra layers make "high-ply" hardwood panels extremely stiff and sag-resistant. We use them for desktops and shelves.

Signboard (also called Medium Density Overlay, or MDO) is very stiff, weatherproof plywood with a smooth, paintable

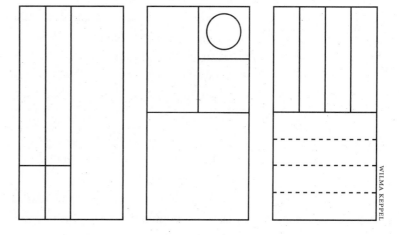

4.4: *You can cut 4 x 8 foot materials into standard grid beam panels with no scrap left over. Cut wood and plywood so the grain runs lengthwise, not crosswise.*

WILMA KEPPEL

4.5: *Vehicles are most likely to need panels in odd shapes and sizes. Vanda's Alucobond skin has safety glass windows.*

fiber surface. We use it for shelves and work surfaces that might get damp.

Hardboard (or masonite) is Jergensons' favorite inexpensive side panel for bracing light-duty projects such as furniture. It is not stiff enough for shelves or decks.

Pegboard is hardboard with holes every 1 inch. A wide variety of hooks, trays, shelves and other hardware plug into the holes. A pegboard workbench back makes a handy place to hang tools.

Alucobond is our favorite material for vehicle skins. Light-weight and vibration-resistant, it is impervious to weather. Made of two thin sheets of aluminum bonded to a hard plastic core, it can be cut with woodworking tools and bent to form rounded corners. Unfortunately, it's expensive and can't be recycled. **Dibond** is a thinner, less expensive version.

Sheet metal is easily formed. Phil bends aluminum diamond plate to make cargo decks and dump beds for vehicles. We also like galvanized sheet steel because we don't have to paint it.

Plastics. Fiberglass, ABS plastic and plexiglass (acrylic plastic) all make great vehicle body panels. We use plexiglass and Lexan for windows and view ports. These plastics scratch too easily for windshields, where we use **safety glass** instead.

Fabric can be used for roofs, awnings, mattress supports, shelves, curtains and a million other things. We have just begun to explore the possibilities of this versatile material.

Hardware

Virtually every grid beam connection is made by bolting. Bolts are strong, durable, quick to install, easy to remove, reusable and resistant to rust. The mind-boggling array of commercially available fasteners includes the right connection for virtually any job.

Our favorite fasteners for wood are joint connector bolts and weld nuts, because you can bolt panels right over both sides of the joint. These specialty fasteners are available by mail order. See the Suppliers chapter for sources. If you can't get them, substitute either carriage bolts (which aren't as flat) with hex nuts and washers, or hex bolts and nuts with washers.

For building-size wooden timbers 3½ inches and up, use hex bolts and nuts with washers. Counterbore (recess) the ends of the holes so the hardware doesn't stick up and you can bolt panels over it.

We build aluminum and steel projects using hex bolts and hex nuts, which are stronger than joint connector bolts and easier to tighten firmly. You can easily crush a steel tube by over-tightening the hex nut! Spreading the load with washers under the bolt head and nut makes a much stronger joint.

Vibration and pounding on a vehicle or trailer can loosen any ordinary fastener. **Always secure vehicle and trailer bolts with lock nuts, lock washers or liquid thread locker.**

Accessories

Accessories are parts that attach to or work with the rest of the grid beam system, and include practically anything you can think of. We've used wheels, lamps, sinks, cables, windmills, motors, transmissions, batteries, solar panels, winches, bearings, brakes, plastic tubs and dozens of other parts.

It's great fun walking into a hardware or hobby store, industrial supplier, go-kart shop or junkyard, and discovering components you can use with grid beam.

You can have even more fun figuring out how to adapt parts that don't quite work. And what about that $600 component you can duplicate at home using grid beam and a few $6 bearings? Grid beam isn't just a building system; it's an adventure!

Adapters

Adapters are what you use when the component you wish to attach won't bolt directly to grid beam because it:

- has no holes
- has holes that don't match grid beam
- is an odd shape or size, or
- requires special mounting.

You can make most adapters in a simple home shop. We usually fabricate ours from drilled or slotted plate steel, angle iron or aluminum. You can also have a welding or metal fabrication shop make the parts you need. A few are available by mail order (see the Suppliers chapter).

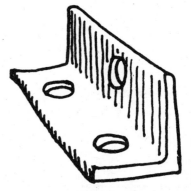

PHIL AND RICHARD JERGENSON

4.6: *Simple angle iron or aluminum brackets mate many items to grid beam.*

Part 2

Grid Beam Projects

5

Furniture

This chapter begins a tour of grid beam projects that will help you visualize what's possible. As you study the photos you'll discover that many projects can be copied by counting holes.

Ken Isaacs invented Living Structures in a quest to get away from conventional furniture. Ironically, grid beam builds great furniture — durable, customizable, adaptable.

Grid beam furniture can always meet your changing needs. It disassembles to make moving easy, and stores in a tiny space. Projects morph again and again, each time saving you the cost of buying more materials or another piece of furniture. Grid beam can squeeze into a dorm room, expand into an apartment or house, adapt to growing children. It

5.1: *Double posts keep this "stem frame" desk square. Panels are apple plywood, with a 2 x 4 foot desk surface 30 inches high.*

WILMA KEPPEL

33

changes with the times, and never goes out of style.

Tables

Need a temporary table for extra dinner guests, dealing with paperwork, or a special

5.2: *Phil's daughter Rona, age four, hosts a tea party. Phil built the chair when she was a toddler.*

PHIL AND RICHARD JERGENSON

5.3: *Richard guides a 2 x 3 foot mini-desk through the door of his home office. Panels are laminate- covered particle board.*

WILMA KEPPEL

project such as model railroading? What about a play table that grows as your child does? Grid beam can do it! It also makes nifty end tables, TV trays and the like.

Wilma's sewing table was a hollow-core door on a wooden frame. "It was sturdy, easy to move, weighed very little, and the table height adjusted. It gave me lots of room for quilting, and disassembled for storage in just a couple of minutes." Richard puts temporary tables on wheels.

Desks and workstations

For office use, a 30-inch desk height is convenient. A work surface 2 feet deep is adequate for most purposes; 30 inches is nice if you want to put computer peripherals or books on the back portion.

Computer workstations and desks are one of the best uses of grid beam because your workspace can adapt as your needs and equipment change. Wilma says, "Whenever I move, I reconfigure my desk to fit the new space and lighting. It works great every time!"

Mini-desks

Mini-desks are small enough to fit through doorways and wheel around the house. Ours use casters that plug directly into the frame holes.

Computer workstations

Richard's 1995 Corner Desk placed desk space and shelves to one side of the computer. Measuring 4 x 4 feet, the unit featured a work surface 30 inches off the

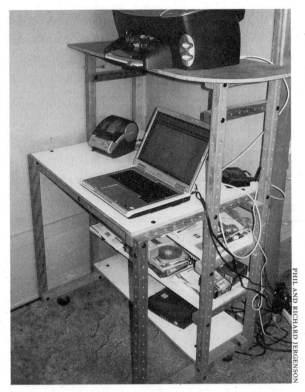

5.5: *Phil's computer desk uses shelf and side panels of ¼-inch plywood. It stands 5 feet high, with a 2 x 4 foot work surface. He later added a back.*

5.4: *Richard built this 2 x 3 foot mini-desk for Barbara Willens's home office. The printer sits on top; hard drives and office supplies store on lower shelves.*

5.6: *Richard's Corner Desk has plenty of space for computer, papers and supplies.*

5.7: *Iowa Desk holds Wilma's computer, stereo and books, with a two-drawer filing cabinet underneath.*

floor and 2 feet deep, with 2 x 4 foot shelves beneath and a curved top shelf. All panels were signboard. A mini-desk next to shelves creates a similar effect (Figure 2.18).

You can also put shelves above the desk — either wall-mounting them, or building them in as Wilma did on her 1997 Iowa Desk. To maximize usable desk space, even the monitor sat on a shelf. A shelf at knee height held seldom-used items, leaving plenty of room for Wilma to stretch her legs. A two-drawer filing cabinet sat under one end.

To avoid notching the panels, Wilma offset the frame uprights from the corners. (This is called an **offset frame**.) The desk had a 30 x 60 inch top, and a frame 31½ inches deep and 63 inches wide. All components were standard lengths.

A later L-shaped desk copied commercial cubicle desks that have a deep corner for the monitor. A 3 x 3 foot signboard panel with one corner cut off on a diagonal held Wilma's monitor and keyboard. Panels 2 feet wide on either side provided more desk space, with shelves above for peripherals, books and a stereo.

Need a big work surface? Richard's 1993 Corner Bench (Figure 2.12) provided 32 square feet of desktop in a 4 x 6 foot area. It stood 4 feet tall, with a work surface 2 feet deep and 30 inches off the floor. Back panels of ¼-inch pegboard measuring 2 x 4 and 2 x 6 feet provided plenty of space to hang tools, cables, bins and shelves. Hardboard end panels measuring 2 x 2 feet added extra cross-bracing. Adding a keyboard tray turned it into a computer workstation.

Desks, workstations and complete offices can also be combined with Living Structures (page 40), sleeping lofts (page 44), and even closets (page 54).

Chairs

Grid beam builds a variety of comfortable and stylish chairs that knock flat for storage or moving.

Superchair

The granddaddy of grid beam chair design, Ken Isaacs's 1962 Superchair (Figure C.1) featured a padded leather seat that lay flat to create an extra bed, and included a built in reading lamp, book holder and shelves. Diagonal cables under the arms cross-braced the frame to keep it square.

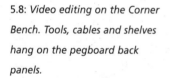

5.8: *Video editing on the Corner Bench. Tools, cables and shelves hang on the pegboard back panels.*

PHIL AND RICHARD JERGENSON

Thirteen-Two Chair

This 1977 design by Reinhold Ziegler uses 13 sticks 2 feet long to frame a comfortable and stylish chair. The seat is two pieces of plywood joined with piano hinge. The hinge keeps the seat pieces from sliding; they fold flat for storage. You can move the seat supports to adjust the seat height and angle. With a couple of seat cushions, it is very comfortable.

Designed to fit average-sized adults, this chair can be scaled down for children by using sticks 18 inches long, or scaled up for large adults. Very heavy people can add panels to the back and sides to help the chair stay square, or even build the frame from 2-inch steel.

Rietveld Chair

With cushions, Richard's grid beam reproduction of Gerrit Rietveld's famous "Red Blue Chair" from 1918 (Figure C.14) is extremely comfortable. Richard's favorite version of this chair was unpainted and had seat cushions, casters and a swing-away desk surface that pivoted on a bolt. He extended the uprights at the back of each arm to suspend a tilting grid beam frame overhead, then stretched white fabric across it. "When we opened the outside doors at our manufacturing plant, I'd roll my chair outside to eat lunch. The awning let me sit in the sun without a hat, and write or read comfortably without squinting. The swiveling desk surface pivoted out of the way when I wasn't using it."

X-Chair

Phil's X-Chair uses a minimum of materials to create a comfortable place to sit. He modeled it after the Barcelona Chair by Mies van der Rohe. The panels are 2 feet wide, the back 5 feet tall, and the seat poles 3 feet long.

REINHOLD ZIEGLER

5.9: *Thirteen-Two Chair. Reinhold's scale model uses sticks of ¼-inch fir fastened with ½-inch brads.*

PHIL AND RICHARD JERGENSON

5.10: *Kent Jergenson with Phil's X-Chair.*

WILMA KEPPEL

5.11: *Folding chair by Chris Koveleski.*

WILMA KEPPEL

5.12: *The Kiddie Chair has a seat of ¼-inch plywood.*

Folding chairs

Grid beam's bolted joints make folding chairs a natural idea. Cord run through the holes in the wooden frame makes a seat that's comfortable in hot weather. Chris Koveleski's design uses synthetic cord, with the seat woven in a grid pattern. Richard's version (Figure 1.18) uses soft hemp cord; inexpensive pipe insulation pads the frame.

Kiddie Chair

As every parent knows, children quickly outgrow everything, including their furniture. Grid beam keeps up with the needs of growing children without costing a fortune. Phil built the chair in Figure 5.12 for his daughter Rona when she was about a year old. It fit her beautifully, and she used it until she outgrew it around age three.

Beds

Most beds take up huge amounts of floor space while providing a minimum of usable storage. Enter the grid beam alternative! Grid beam beds are great for children's rooms, college dorms, small apartments and bedrooms, and any place where you can use more storage, more versatility, or both.

Platform beds can be built in any size. Add drawers or shelves beneath, or leave the space open for storing boxes, trunks, bags or rolling bins on wheels. The design in Figure 5.13 stands 2 feet off the floor. The 4 x 7 foot platform has 56 cubic feet of storage space beneath.

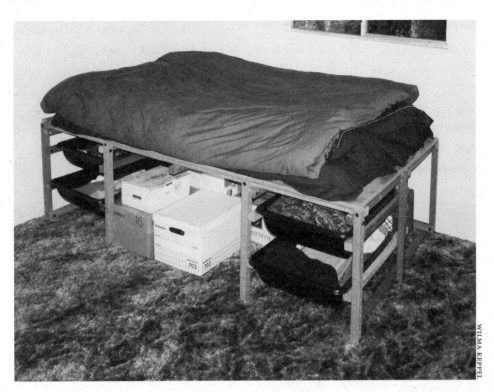

5.13: *Platform bed by Wilma uses the same plastic tub drawers as the Drawer Carts in Figure 6.9.*

WILMA KEPPEL

Some years ago we read a newspaper article about a California couple whose lives were saved when their four-poster bed kept their house from crushing them during an earthquake. In earthquake country, a grid beam four-poster could save your life, especially if you use a steel frame. Brace the frame using stiff panels, cables or threaded rod to keep the frame square no matter what happens.

A grid beam bunk bed provides a sturdy nest for young kids, and can be reconfigured into a bed/desk unit as they grow. Bunk beds also work well for dorm rooms and vacation cabins.

Dr. Jack Martin built a bunk bed for his six-year-old son Robert, who slept in it until he was 13. "Every time he would have a friend over, they would rebuild the bed into a stage coach, slide or fort." Phil and Rona built a similar bed for her bedroom when she was about 10. As friends with different preferences visited, she constantly altered it — changing it from two levels to one and back, and even adding a plastic slide from an outdoor swing set.

Including the railing, the improved version in figure C.12 of the color section measures 6 feet high and 6 feet square. A bottom deck 2 feet off the floor has room for storage beneath. Top deck height is 5 feet. Both decks measure 4 x 6 feet, leaving a bit of room at the sides of the 39 x 75 inch twin size mattresses. Extra space is handy when you make the bed, especially the top bunk.

Phil braced the frame with crossed pairs of ¼-inch threaded rod 6 feet long, bending the ends to fit through the frame holes. They make the frame very stiff, yet add little weight. You could also brace using cables or panels. (White-coated hardboard bathroom paneling makes a great dry-erase whiteboard.) A triple post strengthens the corner that has the least side support. Three-hole spacer blocks between the uprights create an attractive truss, an idea borrowed from Craftsman furniture.

Minor modifications reposition one bunk above the other. For an older child, remove the bottom bunk and replace it with a desk and bookcase.

Living Structures

Not content to give the world grid beam, Ken Isaacs also invented Living Structures. A Living Structure takes the function of separate pieces of furniture (and even separate rooms), and integrates them into a three-dimensional frame that uses space more efficiently. Living Structures have been called the first significant change in the idea of furniture in 1,000 years.

Utilizing space from floor to ceiling can double or triple the usable area of a room. In most cases you can do this without attaching anything to the building — a plus for renters.

Home in a Cube

Ken's first grid beam structure was his 1949 Home in a Cube. Built when he was a penniless, newly married design student, it converted a one-room apartment into a kind of two-story house. The area around the cube functioned as additional living space.

The frame of wooden two-by-twos made an 8-foot cube that supported a bed, closet/storage space, couch, desk and even a metal fireplace that vented through a roof or out a window. Ken stiffened the horizontal plywood decks with wooden rails underneath.

Ken and his wife Jo lived in their cube for about a year. The improved version shown here was featured in *Life* magazine

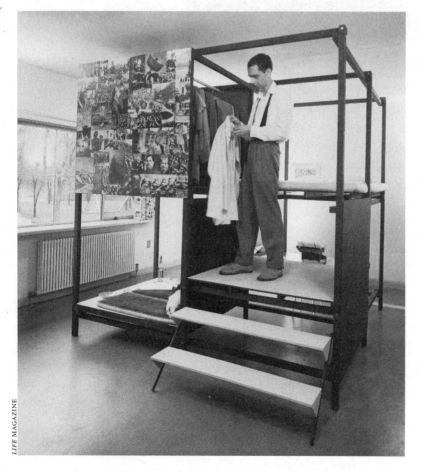

5.14: *Ken Isaacs in his Home in a Cube. Bed is behind him, office below the bed, living area at bottom left.*

in 1954. Using only wrench, pliers and screwdriver, Ken and Jo could set it up in less than two hours.

Six-by-Six Chicago Living Structure

Ken Isaacs built this Living Structure in 1961 for his Chicago apartment. Made from two-by-twos, the 6 x 6 foot frame fastened with hex bolts at the corners. Ken drilled the vertical sticks at intervals; these holes could not make tri-joints. The crossbars supported stiffened panels called **pallets.** Not bolted on, pallets could be added, subtracted or moved to make desk, shelf or sleeping surfaces. Ken's bookshelves were pairs of two-by-twos bolted to each side of the frame posts. The light-weight structure fit in a 1 x 1 x 6 foot crate for moving.

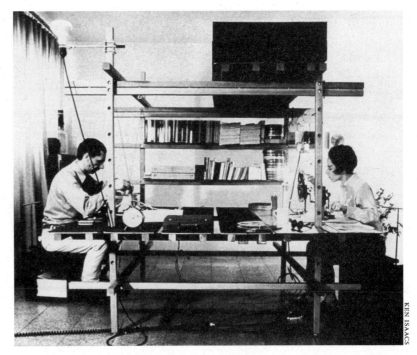

5.15: *Living Structure in Ken Isaacs's Chicago apartment. Movable hardboard pallets make a table, seats and an overhead storage platform.*

Study Cube

In 1970, each student in Ken's introductory architecture class at the University of Illinois at Chicago built his own 4-foot Study Cube. Frames were wooden two-by-twos connected with flat-head machine bolts. Adapting an idea from machine shop technology of the 1920s, Ken put a pair of intersecting holes every 3 inches along the length of each stick. This allowed students to adjust the height of the side rails that supported seat and work surfaces within the cube. Seat, desk surface and shelves were all made of pallets constructed of ¼ inch hardboard bolted to 1½-inch support rails. The pallets were

5.16: *Student can study inside or atop his Study Cube, here shown without plywood privacy walls.*

5.17: *Study Cube's top, main and side hatches. Two of Ken's students converted this unit into an outdoor toilet. A clear tarp overhead keeps out rain.*

5.18: *Four cubes 4 feet square provide sleeping, office and storage space for Ken and Carole Isaacs.*

not bolted down, and could be moved easily from one level to another.

For privacy, each cube had a top and sides made of exterior plywood, which resists delamination when exposed to dampness. This skin had a large entry hatch, a small side hatch for ventilation (it doubled as a foot support if the student decided to nap in his cube), and a top hatch so the student could use the cube top as a desk if he wanted a view or to work with others. Pushing two cubes together made a sleeping deck big enough for a mattress.

Loft Cubes

Ken and his former wife Carole built a workspace and loft for their apartment, using four 4 foot cubes. Hardboard pallets provided movable seating, desk and shelf space. Two cubes were face-to-face offices that converted to extra seating or sleeping space by rearranging pallets. A third cube stored clothes in the fiber containers used for bulk ice cream. The fourth cube held books, paper, and other media.

By concentrating so much function in their loft structure, Ken and Carole freed up most of the space in the surrounding room. Ken points out that this arrangement is a lot easier to clean than a room cluttered with separate pieces of furniture.

Kiddie Cubes

This ingenious cube system designed by Carole and built by Ken in 1972 provided a crib, changing table and play area for their son Josh Henry in two cubes 3 feet square. The cubes were not bolted together and could be moved in relation to each other. Holes spaced every 6 inches on the cube frames let the mattress, bench and table height adjust as Josh Henry grew. Corner joints had counterbored (recessed) holes so the hardware wouldn't project.

The top of the play cube/changing table was ¼-inch hardboard protected by glued-on Naugahyde. The tabletop and seat were ¼-inch hardboard supported on 1½-inch rails. A coat of wax protected them from spills.

The crib cube had painted hardboard panels on three sides, one with blackboard paint on the outside surface. The fourth side had a little door so Josh Henry could climb in and out. A square foam mat covered the hardboard bottom. Ken reports that the crib's top rails made great handles for exercise and teething.

Conversation Lounge

The idea for this project came from a photo of an unusual floor-level couch in *Domus*, an Italian design magazine from the 1960s. Phil sketched a grid beam version, and his 12-year-old daughter Rona built it.

A base 2 feet high and 4 feet square raised the lounging area to a comfortable height above drafts, and provided storage underneath. Diagonals 4 feet long supported the backrests, which were signboard panels measuring 2 x 4 feet. Two more panels made the main deck. A piece of

5.19: *Two cubes 3 feet square make a crib, play area and changing table. A closable side door on the crib lets Josh Henry Isaacs get in and out on his own.*

5.20: *Rona Jergenson relaxes in her Conversation Lounge.*

carpet with carpet padding beneath made a comfortable lounging surface. (For an even softer lounge, use double or triple padding.) Corner posts 5 feet (1,500 millimeters) high supported shelves for books, drinks and lamps.

The Conversation Lounge proved both comfortable and versatile. You can sit or snooze in it, or lounge with your feet supported by swiveling Button Shelves (round shelves attached with one bolt). The face-to-face seating is great for conversations. A lounge this size is comfortable for three adults or four kids. To accommodate more people, make the lounge longer.

Sleeping lofts

Lofts elevate a bed to free up the floor space beneath. The extra space can be used for a desk, office, couch, freestanding closet, storage or whatever you like.

Most homemade loft designs require attaching the loft to the frame of the building. This displeases landlords, and makes the loft difficult to modify, reposition or move. Grid beam lofts can be entirely free-standing. Or you can fasten an otherwise free-standing loft to the building in just one or two places, using lag screws.

Microdorm

Ken Isaacs's Microdorm went into commercial production in 1967. Designed for single people, it fit a bed, storage drawers and a mini-office with shelves into the same footprint as a single bed. Crossed cables braced the two-by-two (40 millimeter) wood frame.

MATRIX Habitat & Loft

Reinhold Ziegler built his first grid beam sleeping loft in 1977. By 1978 he started manufacturing and selling the MATRIX Habitat & Loft Kit (Figure C.11), which he sold through a knock-down furniture store in San Francisco. "These lofts allowed apartment dwellers to raise a bed off the floor and put an office, bookshelves and lounge area underneath. I remember many nights lying in my personal loft and thinking how much this building system had helped me to get *my* act off the ground. This was the building system I had been looking for all my life."

Designed for Victorian houses and apartments that had ceilings 9½ feet high,

5.21: *Ken Isaacs lounges on the Microdorm. Rails for the plywood drawers double as a ladder.*

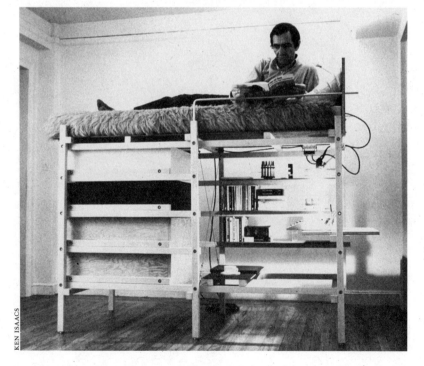

KEN ISAACS

MATRIX lofts measured 7 feet high, with the bed platform 6 feet above the floor. Bolted-on panels and panel art of tempered hardboard added cross-bracing and shear strength. The frames were sized slightly larger than 4 x 8 feet so that customers could slide in a standard plywood panel to support their mattress, with no cutting required. A larger version used a 5 x 8 foot deck to support a queen-size mattress. "The five foot width below made a perfect love seat for couples," Reinhold recalls.

By 1979 Reinhold began to call this type of loft structure "furnitecture," a cross between furniture and architecture.

The Cave

Built in 1977, Richard's Earthlab I sleeping loft was known as the Cave because of the cave-like living space beneath it. "I didn't like the flat-head machine bolts Ken recommended in his book," Richard recalls. "They required counterboring the holes, which was a lot of extra work, and the tapered bolt heads could split the wood if over-tightened. Instead I assembled my loft frame with hex bolts. To avoid snagging my clothes, I used stove bolts (slot-head machine screws) to attach panels."

The Cave's top deck was a 5 x 8 foot plywood ping-pong table top cut down to 5 x 7 feet. It supported a foam mattress 5 feet off the floor. The living space below had plywood slant-board backrests along the two sides of the loft that stood against walls. A single piece of carpet covered the loft's floor, the backrests and the walls up to the loft deck. The long room side of the loft was a bookcase, and the open end of the loft provided egress. "People loved crawling in there," Richard grins.

Loft Habitat

Richard's 1994 Loft Habitat featured pegboard sides for hanging tools or office supplies, plus decorative hardboard panels. The loft deck and desk surface were signboard, with drawers made from plastic tubs. Hang clothes from the crossbar beneath the overhanging end, or put shelves there.

5.22: *Jergensons' Loft Habitat fits a bed and work area into a 4 x 7 foot area. Ladder not shown.*

WILMA KEPPEL

5.23: *Wire shelves keep the inside of Wilma's Office Loft well-lit. A built-in ladder saves space.*

Office Loft

Wilma built the Office Loft in 1999. Measuring 5 x 7 feet, it housed her computer, scanner, printer and stereo, and provided a whopping 26 square feet of work surface. "This was the only time in my life I had too much desk space," she recalls. "It demonstrates how much office you can fit into a small floor area."

To give herself room to sit up in bed under her room's 8 foot ceiling, Wilma put the 5 x 7 foot loft deck 5 feet off the floor. To reflect more light into the office, the bottom layer of the platform was white-coated $1/8$-inch hardboard bathroom paneling. Above that, $1/2$-inch signboard supported the mattress.

Thanks to its U shape, the work space was very efficient. Rolling her chair out of the office gave Wilma instant access to file cabinets a few feet away.

Without the top deck, this design would make a good freestanding desk/office space. Add panels to the outside for privacy. Translucent materials such as sheet fiberglass let in light and keep distractions out — ideal for a home office.

File Loft

The Office Loft wasted a lot of space under the desk, and its placement prevented Wilma from looking out the window while she worked. To solve these problems, she moved her office to a separate desk, and rebuilt the bottom of the loft to accommodate her three 4-drawer filing cabinets. "This worked even better than the Office Loft. I liked the extra light and view at my

WILMA KEPPEL

5.24: *The File Loft holds three 4-drawer file cabinets, with a reading nook under the end.*

desk, the room felt more spacious, and the file cabinets were easy to access but out of my way."

One end of the File Loft contained a cozy reading nook with a bookshelf and hanging plant. A white hardboard brace panel behind the bookcase bounced light back into the room. The space between the panel and file cabinets stored a folding drafting table. A lamp clamped to the bed railing could light the reading nook, or be repositioned for reading in bed. Christmas tree lights wound around the frame provided diffuse lighting under the platform.

"Without grid beam, having my bed and office in one room would have been very cramped. With grid beam, I had plenty of space. I slept in these lofts for two and a half years. They were comfortable, sturdy and gave me a secure feeling."

Storage

Strong and versatile, grid beam is great for storage. When your needs change, so can your storage system. Since the pieces are interchangeable, you can combine shelf units, add drawers or a table top, and fit your shelves into odd spaces or around existing furniture.

Shelves

Shelves are one of our favorite grid beam projects. Wood frames are plenty strong enough for bookcases and other medium-duty storage. For really heavy loads such as boxes of bolts or shipping pallets, use steel frames. You can build shelves into virtually any stationary project, including desks, workbenches, beds, sleeping lofts, closet organizers, buildings and whatever else you like.

Standard shelves

We love grid beam shelves. They are super-sturdy, and you can put them virtually

6.1: *Phil's book-shelf uses panels of ¼-inch ply-wood supported lengthwise.*

WILMA KEPPEL

49

anywhere (over a piano, behind a door) with no holes in the walls. All of us use them in our homes, workshops and storage spaces.

6.2: *Wilma's ½-inch signboard kitchen shelves. Middle shelves are supported only at the ends.*

WILMA KEPPEL

Richard's wood-framed bookcase (Figure 2.15) was the first grid beam project any of us built. He used hex bolts for the frame, and carriage bolts to attach the painted plywood shelves. "When I built this bookcase in 1977, we were drilling only every other hole in the sticks. I could only adjust my shelves in 3-inch increments. Eventually I disassembled the bookcase, drilled the rest of the holes, and reassembled it. This project has now been in continuous use for 30 years — a fantastic investment."

The shelf supports on most of Richard and Phil's shelves run the long way. This lets them use sag-prone shelf materials such as particle board or plywood, even under books. Wilma prefers thicker board or signboard shelves supported at the ends. Both materials will support books

PHIL AND RICHARD JERGENSON

6.3: *Richard's home entertainment center.*

WILMA KEPPEL

6.4: *Steel-framed pallet racks at Earthlab Energy Systems in Willits hold crated wood stoves.*

for years without sagging. If a shelf does begin to sag, simply flip it over.

Richard's 1993 home entertainment center was simply a shelf unit with panels added to the sides and back. Leave space behind the shelves to route power cords, and cut a hole for them in the back panel. We recommend mounting a surge protector or power strip on the unit so you can turn off everything with one switch. Add casters, and you can roll even a large unit around your home.

Pallet racks are basically giant heavy-duty shelves. Frames of 2-inch steel can support thousands of pounds.

Slide-out shelves

What if you already own shelves in whole-foot lengths, and don't want to notch the corners? Wilma's solution: a way of framing projects that uses all standard components to build a frame *around* the shelves, with no notching. (We discuss the details of these **offset frames** on page 186.) The shelves slide out the front for easy height adjustment.

One of Wilma's favorite versions fit behind a door. Signboard shelves 30 inches long and 6 inches deep held paperbacks. "It was easier to build the frame around the shelves than to notch so many — and nine years later, I'm still using them unnotched."

Video shelves

To store Richard's videocassette collection, Michael Hackleman built a grid of wooden sticks, jamming the uprights between the carpeted floor and the ceiling. The horizontal sticks served as shelves 3 inches deep. Richard later added more shelves and filled the whole wall.

6.5: *Shelves for paperback books fit behind door. Bookcases brace each other and support the end of an overhead storage rack holding 400 feet (120 meters) of wooden grid beam.*

6.6: *Horizontal frame rails function as video shelves. Design by Michael Hackleman.*

WILMA KEPPEL

6.7: *Wood-frame shelves organize Richard's storage box outside the Jergensons' Willits shop. Wheeled wood-framed carts in the center aisle store additional items.*

Storage Grid

Ken Isaacs designed the Storage Grid (Figure C.15) to combine the functions of a shelf, stereo cabinet, TV table and desk — without cluttering the floor of your living room. Screw feet (Figure 15.9) clamped it between floor and ceiling. Since a design like this doesn't depend on wall support, you can use it as a room divider. Position it so it presses upward on ceiling joists, not unsupported plaster or drywall.

Ken used pairs of horizontal rails bolted to each side of the uprights to make "shelves" that could support CDs, DVDs, and most books. The desk and support platforms for a TV, stereo and larger books were plywood panels surfaced with plastic laminate. The desk and TV platforms clamped onto the horizontal rails using a bolt and crosspiece underneath. Hang plants from eye bolts or hooks.

Ken's 1968 *Popular Science* design used screw-adjust feet top and bottom to accommodate uneven floors and ceilings. Uprights were sized for the room's ceiling height minus 11 inches. Since we like to keep our sticks standard lengths, our version has tri-joints at the bottom, and the feet attach to adjustable sections at the top.

Storage locker shelves

Millions of people in the US (including us) own too much stuff. Rental storage facilities multiply faster than kudzu vines, and virtually every home supply center sells prefabricated storage sheds. But even after you've got that extra space, how do you arrange it?

Grid beam is fantastic for organizing your basement, attic, garage, garden shed or storage locker. You can fit shelves to odd-sized spaces, build them over or around plumbing and other obstacles, and easily connect them to each other or the building for greater stability.

Use wood frames for dry areas and light- to medium-weight loads, such as boxes of books or canned goods. Galvanized steel can withstand dampness, weather and flooded floors, and will support extremely heavy loads.

Bike Rack

Screw-adjust feet clamp Richard's bike rack between floor and ceiling. Add a second arm above to support more bikes, or position the rack in the middle of the room and make it two-sided. With shelves, it can support a TV, stereo or desk.

Drawer Carts

Richard uses drawer stacks on wheels for recycling bins, sorting mail, storage and organizing complex projects. The drawers are heavy-duty plastic tubs, which have to be stiff to stay on the rails. Furniture casters plug into the frame holes. To make a handy kitchen island on wheels, add a butcher block top.

Built in 1995, Richard's first Drawer Cart is still in use. A taller cart stores his clothes. It's more convenient than a dresser (you can see what's in the drawer without opening it), requires less floor space, and wheels easily wherever he wants it.

Pegboard

Add hanging storage to almost any furniture or workshop project by bolting pegboard panels to the sides or back. Pegboard panels ¼ inch thick provide more bracing power than thinner versions. Use pegboard on workbenches, desks and the ends of free-standing tool and workshop shelves.

Pegboard is widely used for store displays. An incredible variety of commercial hooks, boxes, bottles, shelves, racks, etc. plug right into the holes. If sturdily

mounted, it can support a lot of weight. The fasteners sometimes come loose when you remove an item, especially after the

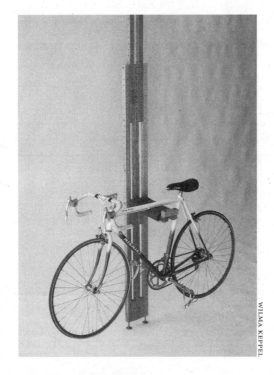

WILMA KEPPEL

6.8: *Richard's bike rack clamps between floor and ceiling. This version can hold two bikes.*

PHIL AND RICHARD JERGENSON

6.9: *Richard's Drawer Carts roll on casters. You can access drawers from either end.*

6.10: *Model of a closet organizer Wilma built in the 1990s. Use grid beam or a stiff material such as conduit for the clothes rods.*

WILMA KEPPEL

6.11: *Richard's clothes rack uses commercial round clothes rods 5 feet long, spaced 2 feet apart.*

WILMA KEPPEL

holes get worn from repeated use. We have not yet tried metal versions that claim to avoid these problems.

Closets and closet organizers

You can pay big bucks for a closet organizer that will provide shelves, drawers, clothes rods and more. Or you can do the same job with grid beam and have a system that can adjust to fit your next closet when you move. Hanging clothes need a space 2 feet deep.

Need extra closet space? Build a free-standing closet (Figure 17.1). You can easily integrate a computer workstation (Figure 17.15), stereo rack, desk, shelves or whatever you like. You can even put a sleeping loft on top. What a great system for dorm rooms!

More storage projects

- Storing your grid beam, page 59.
- Platform beds with storage underneath, page 38.
- Living Structures incorporate storage and furniture functions in one unit, page 40.
- Storage sheds and platforms, page 67.

Workshop and Industry

Quality shop benches, storage and machine stands cost many hundreds or thousands of dollars, and are usually heavy, bulky and hard to move. We guarantee that none of it is as versatile as grid beam. Using galvanized steel double-hole, you can create the ultimate working environment, with simple table tops and shelves cut from plywood or metal.

As you design your shop, think compatibility. If all the work surfaces are at the same height, you can easily slide work pieces from one machine to the next. Holding up large items is easy when you can rest each corner on a same-height table or workbench.

Workbenches and shop equipment on wheels let you easily reconfigure your shop for the next project. Use heavy-duty industrial wheels and casters that can hold the weight without jamming or breaking. In a large shop, wheels at one end of workbenches and casters everywhere else

7.1: *Soldering bench with vented hood for fumes. Part of a complete industrial assembly line Phil and a colleague built with galvanized steel grid beam in 1980, it's still in use.*

PHIL AND RICHARD

are easiest for one person to steer. In a small shop, use casters everywhere. On projects that need to stay in place once positioned, use locking wheels or casters on two corners.

7.2: *The lathe on this steel-topped, steel-framed workbench weighs over 300 pounds (140 kilograms). Movable workbenches and equipment stands make shop work much easier.*

WILMA KEPPEL

7.3: *Broom rack of 1-inch tube built by middle school students in Brad Booth's industrial technology classes.*

WILMA KEPPEL

We find galvanized steel ideal for assembly lines and industrial applications, where it quickly adapts to special jobs and new equipment. Before the engineers finish drawing plans for welded equipment and benchwork, you can have grid beam versions built and in use.

Grid beam does a fantastic job of solving those temporary shop problems that would otherwise require expensive equipment or hassles. It is also ideal when you need portability. Even building-size projects can be disassembled for easy moving. The modular components fit through doorways, and go up stairs and elevators. Phil and Richard have moved their manufacturing business's assembly line several times.

Workbenches

Grid beam makes great workbenches. For electronics, hobbies and most woodworking, wood frames are light-weight and easy to move. For metalworking and industrial applications, use steel.

A work surface 3 feet from the floor can be used while standing, or with a drafting chair with a footrest. A 30-inch height fits a standard office chair and makes a nice desk. Many desk designs also make good workbenches.

Shop tables

Steel double-hole makes great heavy-duty table-style workbenches. For additional storage, put shelves underneath. Hooks or bolts in the frame can hang tools — just position everything so it won't catch on your clothes. A crossbar of narrow angle iron or steel rod a few inches under the end of the table top makes a great place to hang C-clamps, locking pliers and welding clamps.

Exterior plywood at least ½ inch thick makes a good workbench top — ¾ inch is stronger. A solid-core door is even better. For metalworking, use ¼-inch or thicker plate steel. Aluminum bench tops are great for welding because melted steel won't stick to them. They're also expensive. Try scrap yards and industrial auctions.

We keep our Maximat lathe/milling machine, which weighs over 300 pounds (140 kilograms), on a steel-framed workbench topped with ¼-inch plate steel. A

bottom deck of thick plywood holds other heavy items. Heavy-duty industrial wheels and locking casters bolted to the frame let

PHIL AND RICHARD JERGENSON

7.4: *Kent Jergenson's outdoor workbench has a galvanized steel frame and a plate steel top. As you can see, Kent has many vises.*

WILMA KEPPEL

7.5: *Wood-framed workbenches are light and easy to move. Phil rolled this one outside to cut sticks using a battery-powered miter saw.*

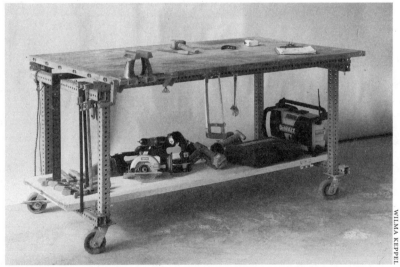

WILMA KEPPEL

7.6: *Steel-framed workbench in the Jergensons' workshop has a top made from a salvaged drafting table, and a shelf made from an old door.*

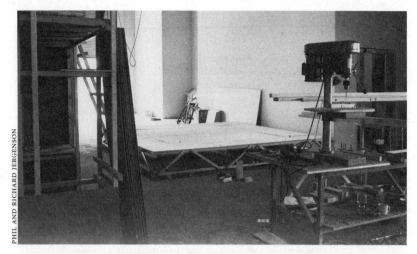

PHIL AND RICHARD JERGENSON

7.7: *Reinhold Ziegler's original wood-framed drill press stand. Diagonal braces add strength (this table holds a lot of weight). These sticks have holes every 3 inches.*

one person roll it around the shop. Wheels plus 30-inch legs put the tabletop height at a comfortable 37 inches.

Equipment stands

In 1976, Reinhold Ziegler was the first of us to build a grid beam project. "I drilled my first batch of sticks on the floor. That was lousy, so the first thing I built was a stand for my drill press."

Wood frames work well for supporting light- and medium-weight equipment. For heavy machinery, use 2-inch (50-millimeter) steel.

Work supports

We use grid beam for all kinds of temporary supports in the shop. Wood makes a strong, light-weight sawhorse you can

WILMA KEPPEL

7.8: *Honer stand of 1-inch steel grid beam built by sixth grader Philippe Napaa for Brad Booth's industrial technology shop has foot pedal control and attached power strip.*

WILMA KEPPEL

7.9: *Wilma's wood-framed sawhorse easily holds 250 pounds (110 kilograms). For heavier loads, use a steel frame.*

assemble in minutes. The one shown here measures 3 feet square, with legs 2 feet wide. This double post design is extremely strong. We don't recommend single-post designs, which are prone to racking (going out of square) unless cross-braced with diagonal sticks or wires.

Wilma's steel frame for air drying wooden sticks measured 6 feet high and 8 feet long, with a 4-foot crossbar. Sticks sprayed with a linseed oil finish hung from 6½-inch carriage bolts pushed through the frame holes from alternate sides. The 2-inch bolt spacing left air spaces between the 1½-inch sticks, and the bolt threads kept the sticks from sliding off.

Storage

Steel grid beam is ideal for heavy-duty shop storage. We use it to make racks for storing lumber, steel, pipe, panels and grid beam. When you use grid beam to support extremely heavy loads, cross-brace it with diagonal braces, cables, perforated metal strap or panels.

A panel rack 4 feet long is adequate for storing 4 x 8 foot sheet stock. A rack 6 feet long is easier to move around the shop, because you can reach past the panels to push the frame from the end. Put a deck on the bottom so short panels can't fall through. To protect the panels from scratches, use wood for the top rails, and attach them with joint connector or carriage bolts.

Use a trash can to store small amounts of wooden grid beam — just stand the sticks on end. Or use some of your sticks to build a rack for the rest.

You can store aluminum and galvanized steel outdoors. Steel lasts longer if stored off the ground and under a roof or tarp.

7.10: *Loaded rack dries 600 feet (180 meters) of wooden grid beam sprayed with a linseed oil finish. Frame is 2-inch steel.*

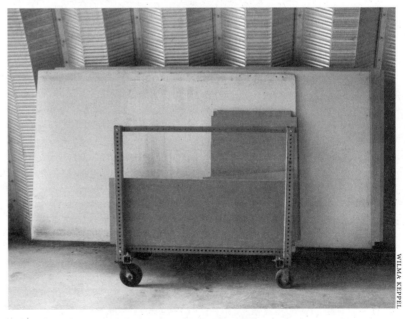

7.11: *Steel-framed panel rack in the Jergenson's Willits workshop.*

WILMA KEPPEL

7.12: *Grid beam stored overhead between joists, on a rack above a window, and in spaces between wall studs.*

WILMA KEPPEL

7.13: *Wilma's materials rack. There's no such thing as too much grid beam, cut to length and ready to build. It's like money in the bank!*

Grid beam stores well in odd places — behind a couch, on the floor of a closet, under a bed. Wilma once stored over 400 feet of wooden grid beam on an overhead rack in her bedroom. If you have a basement or workshop with exposed joists overhead, you can store grid beam (and boards and pipes) between them. Simply lag screw scrap lumber or grid beam across the gaps, then slide your materials in on top.

Wilma now stores all her grid beam and panels in a rack of 2-inch steel. A 3 x 8 foot space 6½ feet high stores over 1,000 feet of sticks and shelves organized for quick access. Sheet materials stack vertically behind the rack; sticks 30 inches and shorter stack crosswise on the top shelf, with short pieces in boxes. Access is from one side and one end. Pulling long sticks off the end of the rack takes a lot of room, so that end faces the doorway.

The rack frame is 6 feet long and 6 feet high. The bottom crossbars are 3 feet deep; the top sets 30 inches. Shelves are one-by-twelve pine boards 8 feet long. Tri-joints keep the frame stiff with no cross-bracing.

A rack on wheels lets you roll materials to projects as you work on them. Use heavy-duty industrial wheels that can withstand the weight. Put locking wheels or casters on one end, and use plain casters everywhere else.

In 2006 Wilma built a wood-framed portable rack to organize the wooden grid beam in the Jergensons' high-ceilinged

Storing grid beam — the critter problem

"I built my first steel-framed rack for grid beam in an outdoor shed," Wilma recalls. "A tarp kept dust off the sticks. The only problem was wasps! The holes in my wooden grid beam were the perfect size for mud daubers to nest in. I waited until freezing weather, then used a bolt to knock the nests out. My current rack is in a garage, where wasps can't find it."

Paper wasps sometimes nest in metal grid beam if the tubes stay dry. If you store your sticks outside, handle them cautiously until you make sure they're not inhabited. We're not into killing wasps — they destroy garden caterpillars and other pests — but if you must remove them, a spray of anhydrous (water-free) isopropyl alcohol kills them on contact, and leaves no toxic residue.

Store wooden grid beam away from the family cat. She may think you've installed a giant scratching post just for her.

shop (Figure 18.6). Measuring 2 x 4 feet, the rack holds sticks from 30 inches to 8 feet long. The top frame height is 30 inches, with 3 foot uprights to keep sticks laid across the top of the rack from falling off when we move it. Crossbars divide top and bottom into eight sections about 1 foot square. Four heavy-duty casters mount directly to the ¾-inch plywood bottom; ¼-inch threaded rods cross-brace all four sides.

Industrial machinery and assembly lines

One of the first uses of steel grid beam was by machinist/designer Tom Conlon, who used 2-inch tubes to build several large pieces of manufacturing equipment for making wind turbine blades.

One of our most successful projects was part of Richard and Phil's T-shirt printing business. An electric conveyor system with a bank of 220 volt spot heaters cured the ink on screen-printed T-shirts. The steel grid beam frame on this project

7.14: *Tom Conlon's clamp for making wind turbine blades. Frame is 2-inch steel tubes that Tom drilled every 1 inch.*

PHIL AND RICHARD JERGENSON

WILMA KEPPEL

7.15: *Drill press table, part of a steel-framed industrial assembly line that Phil and a colleague built for a manufacturing business. The table top is an L-shaped steel plate salvaged from a loading dock.*

saved us thousands of dollars over a commercial stand for the same equipment.

Phil has built several industrial assembly lines using grid beam. It began with a drill bench built for our manufacturing business inside the Earthlab I warehouse in 1977. A frame of 2-inch galvanized steel held five drill presses and a milling machine. Inexpensive chairs designed for floor mounting bolted to the frame. A second grid beam stand held a chop saw. A grid beam frame overhead supported hanging fluorescent work lights and carried electrical power to the machines with no cords on the floor. Richard later built wood-framed product-assembly workbenches nearby.

We expanded and improved this setup many times, and moved it twice. Three

decades later, much of our grid beam production line is still used for manufacturing.

Building our own equipment stands saved us thousands of dollars over welded stands, and allowed us to innovate. Usually manufacturers contract with off-site jobbers to build and test new equipment. With grid beam, we were able to do our own in-house testing. For instance, we built an experimental buffing machine to smooth batches of 30 parts. We learned right away that it didn't work well enough to go on the production line, with minimum time and money invested.

Another experiment was a soldering bench with a seat on rollers that ran on grid beam rails. This allowed workers to line up 8 feet of parts, then solder continuously while moving the chair. It worked so well that we incorporated it into our production line.

We found that grid beam easily adapts to expansions, changes in production sequence, and new equipment. When it's time to move, photograph your setup, disassemble it, and use your photos to guide you as you reassemble the system in its new home.

More workshop projects

- 12-Minute Workbench, page 4.
- Richard's wood-framed router stand, Figure 16.11.
- Many desks also work as workbenches; see page 34.

Structures

Grid beam is an ideal way to build temporary projects such as trade show booths, platforms, stage sets and scaffolds. It has many advantages:

- Sets up and knocks down in a hurry.
- Stores and transports in a small space. The pieces fit through narrow doors and stairways, and in trucks, cars and elevators too small for a conventionally built structure or its components.
- Telescoping legs adjust to uneven terrain. We have built steel-framed temporary structures on slopes of over 30 degrees!
- Weatherproof. Galvanized steel tubes last decades outdoors.
- Strong. Phil's steel-framed Portable House withstood winds of over 80 mph (130 km/h).

Buildings and scaffolds are *not* projects for amateurs. Get experience building smaller items before you try this type of project. Once you have a good understanding of how grid beam projects work, scale up projects gradually. We recommend having an experienced builder check large-scale projects for safety issues.

Booths

We use grid beam to build booths for trade shows, fairs and festivals. Grid beam lets us adapt each booth to suit the environment, the weather, and what we brought to sell.

8.1: *Students assemble a solar cabin with a frame of wooden four-by-fours at the 1980 Laney College S.I.T.E. fair in Oakland, California. Design by Reinhold Ziegler.*

REINHOLD ZIEGLER

The steel-framed pavilion we built for SEER 1990 (the Solar Energy Expo and Rally in Willits, California) stood 16 feet high (Figure C.5). Its bright yellow canvas awning attracted lots of attention. For indoor trade shows we use wooden frames because they are lighter, easier to move, and less likely to scuff floors.

Railings

Grid beam makes sturdy railings for stairways, balconies and porches. They are easy to assemble and attach to the building. We usually lag screw the railing to the building or stair frame.

Baby and pet gates

To keep his infant daughter off the stairs, Phil built a baby gate from 1½-inch wooden grid beam. "It took about five

8.2: *The Jergensons' wood-framed trade show booth at an alternative energy fair.*

PHIL AND RICHARD JERGENSON

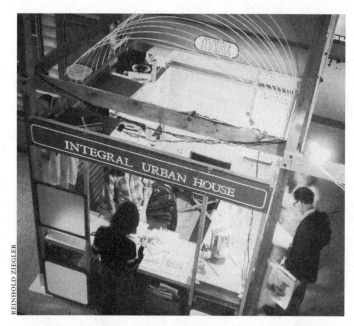

8.3: *Integral Urban House trade show booth by Reinhold Ziegler, 1980.*

REINHOLD ZIEGLER

8.4: *Phil put up this wooden stair railing in about an hour. It lag screws to the stairway. The balcony railing screws to the floor through the carpet.*

WILMA KEPPEL

minutes to build, worked great, and was used for a couple of years." Puppies and babies like to chew, so use nontoxic finish (or no finish) on your sticks.

Temporary kitchen

Phil installed a wood-framed temporary kitchen (Figure 20.2) so he and his family could move into the house he was building before he finished it. Temporary fixtures can help you plan how to arrange a kitchen or bathroom before you do the final installation.

Partitions and walls

We find grid beam very useful for partitions and temporary walls — especially in business, where a building must adapt to each tenant's needs. A solid or partial wall that clamps between floor and ceiling (Figure C.15) can go virtually anywhere.

While photographing projects for this book in Richard's odd-shaped living room, we put up a temporary wall to get a right angle corner. It took about forty minutes to build the frame, using wooden sticks that we drywall-screwed to the ceiling beams and right through the carpet into the floor. We C-clamped drywall panels in place, drilled them, and attached them to the frame using carriage bolts. Two hours from starting, we had the wall's seams taped and mudded. We painted it the next morning.

A series of open-fronted bays along the inside walls of an industrial building we owned created extra wall space for housing

8.5: *Gate keeps Phil's daughter Rona and her puppy safe from the stairs.*

8.6: *We built the wall behind this Drawer Cart in about two hours. Grid beam stick above window holds photo paper.*

equipment. Framed in 2-inch steel, the bays also provided overhead storage.

Earthlab Energy Systems in Willits uses partitions and product display walls framed in 2-inch galvanized steel. Trim at top and bottom hides any unevenness of the plywood wall panels. "The building department considers these walls 'temporary partitions' because they are not load-bearing and merely bolt to the building's frame," the owner explains, "so we didn't need permits to install them." When he moved the business to another

8.7: *Fireplace display wall in Earthlab Energy Systems' Willits showroom. Built of plywood on a frame of 2-inch galvanized steel, the wall lag screws to the building frame.*

WILMA KEPPEL

8.8: *Michael Hackleman built these wood-framed drywall picture display walls.*

PHIL AND RICHARD JERGENSON

building, he simply disassembled the walls and reinstalled modified versions in the new location.

Store displays

Grid beam is great for store displays. You can quickly build walls, platforms and whatever else you need.

A Willits business displayed children's art in its front window. Taped to the glass, the pieces displayed poorly and got wet from condensation. The Willits Rotary Club donated $200 for materials, and Michael Hackleman put up wood-framed drywall display walls in a couple of days.

Stage sets

Wooden grid beam makes fantastic stage sets — strong, durable, and easy to reconfigure. For years, Dr. Jack Martin's industrial technology classes have donated their less-good wooden sticks to the college theater department. "We don't have any pictures," Jack explains, "because once they paint the sticks black, you don't see them on-stage — just whatever painted panels they bolt to them." The actors see the unpainted insides of the holes, but the audience doesn't. An object attached to a black stick held by a stage hand seems to float through the air.

Jack's church needed sets that were extremely light-weight and could be moved from the church to the performance area. "We used wooden grid beam frames, then wrapped them with cardboard tubes from the local textile industry. By painting them we could make them look like trees and scenery. When we broke or bent props or scenery, we could quickly fix them and reattach them to the grid beam."

Jack later discovered that grid beam sticks left behind after a production at a local theater were still being used for stage scenery — but people were drilling holes in them and screwing them together. "They completely missed the point."

Scaffolding and platforms

Grid beam makes sturdy scaffolds that are quick to assemble and remove (Figure C.6). Telescoping legs let them stand firmly even on steep terrain. To make a safety rail, install a crossbeam with two bolts.

Our tallest scaffold to date was a three-story galvanized steel unit Phil built to paint his old house. He sets scaffold feet on scraps of sturdy plywood. Lag bolt the scaffold to the building every 8 vertical feet to ensure that it can't fall over.

In 1990, Phil helped organized the first Solar Energy Expo and Rally (SEER) here in Willits. For various SEERs we built steel-framed race observation and flagger's towers. One year we set up an aluminum-framed tower at San Francisco's Exploratorium to start an electrical vehicle rally to Willits.

In 1979, Reinhold Ziegler built a 12 x 12 foot elevated platform as a sleeping loft for a San Francisco preschool. Ladder trusses made from two-by-twos supported a plywood deck and grid beam railing. Reinhold rounded the ends of the

diagonal braces to keep them flush with the deck. The finished platform proved remarkably light, somewhat springy, and very stable.

8.9: *Steel-framed observation tower at SEER 1992.*

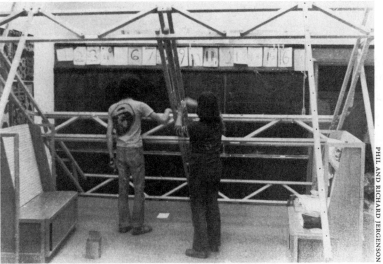

8.10: *Installing a sleeping loft designed and built by Reinhold Ziegler in a preschool classroom. Truss construction keeps it strong and light.*

Buildings

With grid beam, you can quickly put together children's play houses, small sheds and storage buildings. We mostly build with galvanized steel because it is so weather-resistant. Protect wooden frames from the weather with exterior panels.

What about housing? Buying a home is an investment — but only if you can afford it. Renting is a bottomless pit that will eat cash forever. What to do?

That was our situation in the 1970s when Phil, Richard and their brother Kent all decided they wanted to move to the country. It seemed impossible on our limited budget. Purchasing land with a house

8.11: *Grid beam outhouse built by Richard in 2006. The frame is damaged 1½-inch wooden sticks, with sides of reused plywood and a roof of scrap Alucobond. The panel with the round hole was recycled from Phil's Portable House.*

WILMA KEPPEL

would create high mortgage payments that required a city job. Buying land without a house would leave us with no place to live while we built, and no money to build with. We couldn't build our houses until we owned land … or could we?

Portable House

In 1977 Phil began constructing a portable house inside our Berkeley warehouse. He used 2-inch galvanized steel for the main frame, with 1½-inch galvanized steel diagonals to reduce weight. Body panels were plywood covered with sheet aluminum, with Filon fiberglass panels for windows. As you can see, as long as you keep spans under 8 feet you can make pretty wild shapes and still cut a project's skin from standard 4 x 8 foot panels.

In 1979 Phil dismantled the house and hauled it to his land outside Willits. He transported the pieces up a hand-built trail using an electric golf cart converted into a micro–pickup truck, then reassembled it at the top of the mountain. He lived at that site for a year, then dismantled the house and moved it to a second site. He lived in the Portable House on and off for about two years total.

The Portable House proved its strength through many storms with high winds, and an accident. While learning to fell trees, Phil dropped a tree with a base 1 foot in diameter on the house. "It was pretty scary looking up at the tree through the clear Filon roof," Phil says. "But to my surprise, the house was undamaged."

8.12a

8.12b

Tent House

In 1978 Phil and Richard's brother Kent and his wife needed a place to live while they built a house in the country. Kent bought a military surplus mess tent measuring 12 x 24 feet. Inside our Berkeley warehouse, he built a frame for the tent from 2-inch galvanized steel, installing a plywood floor and sleeping loft. After moving the Tent House to their homesite, he and his wife Jennifer lived in it for 15 months while they built their house, had their first child, and weathered the worst winter in many years.

Ziegler House

While Phil and Kent built micro-houses using galvanized steel, Reinhold Ziegler used models to design full-scale grid beam houses. In 1980 he and his students built a demo cabin framed with wooden four-by-fours about 3½ inches square (Figure C.7). The two-story, 16 x 20 foot cabin used

8.12c

8.12a-c: (a) *Phil's Portable House under construction inside Earthlab I (b), and being reassembled on site. A grid beam crane (top right of photo c) lifts the panels. Diagonal braces keep the frame from racking during assembly.*

8.13: *Inside Phil's Portable House.*

structural elements such as box beams (large, hollow beams built like a box) and plywood web trusses (wooden I-beams).

8.14: *Kent built the frame of his Tent House inside the Earthlab I warehouse in Berkeley. The recessed kitchen floor at left fits under the sleeping loft.*

Prefabricated wall, floor and Filon window panels bolted in place, making on-site assembly very rapid.

The timbers for this building were as long as 24 feet, drilled with three drill presses spaced 8 feet apart on a table framed in steel grid beam. Counterbored (recessed) holes let the house skin sit flat on the beams, and washers on each end of the bolts spread the load.

"The frame beams were the same width as a two-by-four," Reinhold recalls, "which made constructing wall panels really easy. Wall panels with two-by-fours inside were the right depth to bolt between the four-by-four uprights. We pre-drilled the studs inside the panels for electrical and plumbing, dropped them onto a grid beam table, and an air cylinder pressed everything

8.15: *Tent House in use on site. With no insulation, it was difficult to keep warm in winter.*

8.16: *Model house by Reinhold Ziegler. Sticks are ¼-inch fir, with cardboard panels.*

together tight and square for gluing and nailing." He used the spaces inside the walls for heating and cooling ducts.

The cabin's floor panels were two-by-fours sandwiched between two sheets of plywood. These floors were as stiff as a standard floor made with two-by-sixes because the plywood skin turned the two-by-fours into I-beams. In other words, the floor was a box beam. Panels used like this are called *stressed skin* because the skin is a structural element that carries part of the load. It's a very strong and light-weight way to build.

Our experience with grid beam houses has proved that grid beam is a real building system. By prefabricating your house before you acquire land, you can build and pay for a house or cabin without owning real estate. In some areas, renting an abandoned

Weather-tight portable buildings — a cautionary tale

Portable shelters create difficult design challenges. They need to be easy to assemble, disassemble and move. This requires avoiding conventional caulks and sealants, the usual cure for leaks.

In 1972, Phil built a bolt-together portable micro-shelter with a welded steel frame and corrugated fiberglass roof. The wall panels were aluminum-skinned polystyrene foam with two-by-two frames. Phil moved directly from Los Angeles to northern California, and his shelter worked fine … until the winter rains arrived. "My poor job of installing the fiberglass roof created a very drafty shelter," Phil recalls. "When the rain came straight down, everything stayed dry, but when a big storm hit, the wind drove water through every seam. I didn't want to gum up my panels with caulk or sealant, because that would make the shelter too difficult to disassemble and move. And some of the gaps were too big to seal. At times almost all of my possessions became wet, and my homemade wood stove only kept me dry if I stayed right next to it. One storm lasted two weeks, and my books and drawings were destroyed by mold. My back-to-the-land move had been ruined by my own bad design."

Phil's next design — the grid beam Portable House — was a big improvement. "My land partners at that time built a similar structure and experimented with insulated exterior panels. We used 3M Tedlar tape to seal our panels at the seams, but found when the wet season arrived that our taped seams weren't perfect, and our buildings leaked some. My Portable House was still drafty and cold, but it was much better than my first attempt."

Phil never perfected a weather seal between the Portable House's joints. This isn't because of the grid beam. Portability and waterproofness are a difficult combination, and Phil likes to put buildings atop mountains where they get hammered by rain blowing in horizontally at 80 to 100 miles per hour (130 to 160 kilometers per hour). The Portable House also lacked overhanging eaves. Eaves shed water before it can sneak in a building's joints. They also catch wind; the Portable House's streamlined shape helped it endure extreme winds without tipping.

Phil has built one weatherproof portable, which has eaves and uses conventional stud construction. The secret is that the building is on a trailer and does not disassemble. Instead, the roof lowers 3 feet for moving. This would be easy to duplicate with grid beam.

home site in the country is very inexpensive. Or find a friend with a spare half-acre where you can park your house while you look for property in the area where you want to live. The possibilities are unlimited!

Supporting a building without a foundation

8.17: *We have built platforms and small buildings on slopes of over 30 degrees.*

8.18: *Tent House feet bolt to the steel legs of a building or platform. This foot can swivel to match the terrain. Non-swiveling feet have a short double-hole post that fits inside the building leg.*

One of the biggest advantages of grid beam buildings is that they require no foundation. Set the building on pads, then adjust the legs to compensate for sinking or frost heaves.

Kent Jergenson's Tent House was firmly supported by welded feet he cut from steel channel. These feet bolted to the steel legs of the building.

The Ziegler House used screw-adjust feet (Figure C.7) that slid into holes drilled in the ends of the vertical frame members. To keep the timbers from splitting under side loads, Reinhold lined the holes with 1-inch diameter stainless steel inserts. A piece of $7/8$-inch threaded rod slid inside, with a nut and washer to adjust the rod height. Another nut welded to the center of each round foot screwed onto the bottom end of the rod.

Phil first set up his Portable House on a site sheltered by trees, which reduce wind a lot. The steel legs rested directly on the ground. When he moved the house to a steep, windy site, he set the legs on pieces of wood, then attached the legs on the windward side to earth augers (mobile home anchors) screwed into the ground.

Ken Isaacs set small portable buildings on cast concrete pads 2 feet square and 6 inches thick. Each weighed about 250 pounds (110 kilograms) and screwed to one of the building legs. If your site is exposed to wind or subject to tornados, also use earth augers.

Recently someone we know installed a 20-foot steel shipping container in his back yard to use for storage. Wanting to preserve the level part of his yard, he put it on a slope by propping up the downhill end. "I tried a welded support, but that didn't work, so I built a frame of 2-inch galvanized grid beam instead." The bottoms of the posts are set in concrete.

PHIL AND RICHARD JERGENSON

Renewable Energy

We learned about grid beam in 1974, the year the OPEC oil embargo sent fuel prices sky-high. It has become even more obvious since then that alternatives to industrial civilization's expensive, wasteful, and damaging patterns of energy use must be found.

Alternative energy is a great field for grid beam innovation because:

- The technology is changing fast.
- The number of products on the market is still quite limited. The item you want may be unavailable or ridiculously expensive. In many cases homemade can provide a cheap and simple alternative to commercial products.
- By building a project yourself, you can make sure it suits your needs and situation, and that it really works.
- You can easily build from other people's plans, and improve the design as you build or after you've tested it.

- A finished grid beam product is easy to mass produce, and can be modified by the end user.
- Modular construction simplifies maintenance and repair.

REINHOLD ZIEGLER

9.1: *Tensioned cables brace a wind turbine tower made of 2-inch galvanized steel, built by students in Reinhold Ziegler's 1980 alternative energy classes. The grid beam turbine generates electricity.*

73

The whole alternative energy field is wide open for development. Grid beam makes it easy to build projects and test ideas in a short time. Instead of getting frustrated by the slowness, difficulty and expense of building one-of-a-kind projects using conventional methods, you can use and enjoy your creations right away.

Solar panel mounts and trackers

Metal grid beam makes terrific solar panel mounts and trackers that adapt to nearly any situation. Use aluminum where you need light weight or portability, steel where low cost or strength are more important. Steel base frames are useful where a roof is very uneven, or making holes in a flat roof would cause problems. Support one or more sides of the base on the roof parapet, then use screw-adjust feet on the roof itself. A solar panel mount made from grid beam or conventional materials bolts to the base.

Photovoltaic panels are usually mounted to allow seasonal adjustments as the sun's path changes. The higher the latitude, the more power you gain. Keeping your panels aimed at the sun as it travels from east to west can generate even more power — around 15 percent over a year's time, and up to 40 percent more on a clear summer day in temperate latitudes. If you power your home with solar, that's a lot of panels you don't have to buy.

You can spend thousands of dollars for a fancy automatic tracker, or follow Phil's lead and power your home using a grid beam tracker. Inexpensive tracker controllers can be purchased online.

REINHOLD ZIEGLER

9.2: *Photovoltaic panel mount with a base of 2-inch galvanized steel uses screw-adjust feet to accommodate a dished roof. Design by Reinhold Ziegler.*

PHIL AND RICHARD JERGENSON

9.3: *Phil built this manually adjusted tracker in 1994 to power his home. The light-weight frame of 1½-inch aluminum makes it easy to move.*

You can also mount ground-level PV panels on wheels. Using bolt-on wheel mounts, Phil has built solar panel carts in as little as ten minutes. Steel clips hold the undrilled panels to the frame.

In some locations, getting enough sun requires lifting solar panels above surrounding buildings or trees. In 1995, Michael Hackleman built a tower on the Jergensons' land. Solar panels at the top powered a water pump in a shady location that gets no ground-level sun during Willits's winter rainy season. It worked for about 8 years, until the surrounding trees grew tall enough to shade the panels in winter.

The tower mast was two sections of 2-inch galvanized steel joined with a 6-foot section of 1¾- inch tube. The mast was braced with two sets of four guy wires, which attached to thimbles (metal fittings that protect the looped ends of the cables) slipped through eye bolts. Instead of a foundation, the bottom of the tower was a large tri-joint. The center of it sat on a scrap of exterior plywood about 2 feet square. The weight of the tower plus the tension in the guy wires kept the base securely anchored. This arrangement isn't ideal, but it's cheap and easy to move, and worked on this tree-sheltered site. A lever at the bottom of the tower adjusted the panel angle.

Wind turbines and towers

Reinhold Ziegler used grid beam in the wind and solar energy classes he taught at various California colleges from 1979 to

9.4: Phil built this aluminum-framed solar panel rack in about 10 minutes, using bolt-on wheel mounts. Note the steel-framed grid beam fence in the background.

PHIL AND RICHARD JERGENSON

9.5: Solar panels atop a 34-foot (10-meter) steel tower built by Michael Hackleman. Bolts sleeved with plastic pipe provide a built-in ladder. Washers at outside ends keep feet from slipping off.

WILMA KEPPEL

9.6a: *Reinhold Ziegler with a student-built wind turbine and tower of 2-inch galvanized steel. Rotor diameter is 7 feet (2,100 mm).*

1987. His students built a variety of steel-framed wind turbines and towers. Some turbines generated electricity. Others compressed air that could be used to run tools (Figure 1.1).

High winds can damage propeller-type wind turbines by causing them to spin too fast, so most designs include some way to limit the turbine speed. In 1983, Ziegler's Wind-Energy Systems class built a gimballed wind turbine designed to tilt sideways to the wind if its speed became too high (Figure 2.9). Both the turbine and its mount were galvanized steel grid beam. The blade and generator shafts mounted on pillow blocks (metal blocks that support bearings) bolted to the grid beam frame. The fork holding the turbine was bolted together using L- and T-brackets that Allied Tube makes for their double-hole tubes.

9.6b: *Raising the 40-foot (12-meter) tower using the gin pole.*

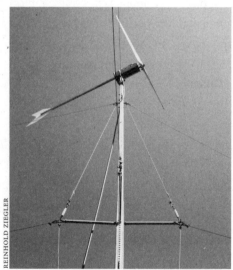

9.6c: *Tower installed. Cables stiffen the mast and keep it vertical.*

The production version of this turbine did not tilt, but changed the tail vane angle to turn the rotor sideways in strong winds. Reinhold and his students mounted it on a grid beam tower. Towers increase wind turbine output because wind blows faster away from ground-level drag.

The support cables on Reinhold's grid beam towers attached to crossbars up to 4 feet long. Made of threaded rod, they fit through the holes in the mast, with a nut on each side to keep them centered. Rod ends (screw-on tips with loops) served as attachment points for cables.

A gin pole, which sticks out like the bottom of an L, provided leverage for lifting and lowering the tower when it was close to the ground. Use a bottom hinge and gin pole to lower towers to the ground for servicing.

While working at Turbostar in 1984, Reinhold built a test platform to elevate wind turbines above the fence surrounding the property. The frame of wooden four-by-fours was cross-braced by cables on three sides. The deck detached for mounting on a pickup truck. A plywood wind tunnel was later added beneath the platform.

Savonius and helical rotors

Vertical axis wind turbines spin in winds from any direction with no need to point the machine at the wind. This makes them ideal for gusty locations.

In the 1970s Savonius rotors became popular among home builders. These turbines boast high torque and decent

WILMA KEPPEL

9.7: *Phil added this galvanized steel gin pole to a commercially welded windmill tower. A gin pole lets you drop a tower to the ground for servicing.*

REINHOLD ZIEGLER

9.8: *Wood-framed platform by Reinhold Ziegler elevates wind turbine above fence for testing.*

efficiency at low speeds, a good combination for pumping water. The simple design adapts easily to grid beam. Reinhold Ziegler and his students built their first Savonius turbine in 1980. The rotors were 55 gallon (210 liter) oil drums split in half vertically. A crankshaft at the bottom attached to a diaphragm-style water pump. Diagonal wires bracing the 2-inch galvanized steel

9.9a-b: *Savonius rotor made of split 55-gallon oil drums powers a diaphragm water pump. Design by Reinhold Ziegler.*

frame proved unnecessary. Reinhold eventually removed them because students kept tripping over them.

With every revolution a Savonius rotor delivers two pulses of power. If you know where the prevailing wind comes from, you can position the rotor to use that pulse for a water pump's power stroke. But a Savonius rotor that stops with its edge facing the wind won't start again until wind direction shifts. To overcome this problem, the rotors are often installed in sets of three, rotated 120 degrees from each other. This ensures that at least one rotor is always well-positioned for starting.

A more elegant solution is to use a helical (spiral-shaped) rotor. These rotors always have a section facing the wind, so they start from any direction. They deliver power much more evenly than standard Savonius rotors. This makes them less effective for pumping water, but better for generating electricity. Reinhold's first helical rotor design dates from 1980 (Figure C.32). Unlike propeller-type turbines, helical rotors are virtually silent and vibration-free, making them suitable for roof and city use.

Hydro power

Galvanized steel will withstand decades of weather and splashing, making grid beam a good choice for small hydroelectric power installations. Or you can prototype in grid beam and build the final installation using conventional methods. (See color section).

Solar concentrators

Solar concentrators produce intense heat that can be used for cooking, distillation, making charcoal and methanol, or generating steam to run turbines. The reflector requires sunny conditions, and must point directly at the sun.

Reinhold Ziegler's 1977 single-axis solar furnace (Figure C.33) was built to research renewable sources of concentrated heat for the developing world. Built from salvaged materials for under $40, it had a frame of painted 1½-inch wooden grid beam. Strips of scrap mirror lining the 4 x 4 foot parabolic reflector concentrated about 20 suns on a variety of targets. Target temperature could reach 350 degrees Fahrenheit (175 degrees Celsius). The furnace was used to boil water, steam vegetables, toast bagels, and bake bread. The two-axis design shown in Figure 9.10 is better suited to automatic tracker controllers.

Portable power

A portable source of power is incredibly handy when you work at a remote site, especially if it can recharge itself without trips to town for batteries or fuel. The ideal portable power station features a charging source (usually a solar panel), storage (usually batteries), and an inverter so you can run AC equipment. It is easy to move, so you can charge it in the sun and then work at a shady site.

Living off the grid since 1978, Phil has developed a wide variety of portable power sources. Most of his electric vehicles can run tools, either directly from the battery or through an inverter. His Bear series garden tractors (page 95) feature rooftop solar panels. His Vanda micro-van (page

9.10: *Scale model of a two-axis 4 x 8 foot solar furnace designed by Reinhold Ziegler. It concentrates about 50 suns.*

REINHOLD ZIEGLER

PHIL AND RICHARD JERGENSON

9.11: *Aluminum portable tracker by George Buono.*

9.12: *Personal Power Cart supplies 12 volt DC and 120 volt AC power.*

100) could generate up to 400 watts of power from solar panels mounted on its roof and sides.

Personal Power Cart™

In 1999, Phil, Richard and Reinhold Ziegler collaborated to create a power cart for urban users. Originally intended as Y2K protection, the cart could also be used to run computers, radios, lights and other equipment during storms or extended power outages. It could be charged from a solar array or wall socket.

Solar Power Trailers

Phil's Solar Power Trailer provides power on remote sites — such as the Jergensons'

workshop and guest RV. The frame is galvanized steel, with a welded frame supporting the box and a rear cargo shelf of aluminum diamond plate. The four-bolt trailer wheels have 8-inch rims.

Designed to pull behind a car or truck, this trailer is used on gravel roads on the Jergensons' land. Because it doesn't have shock absorbers, it is not suitable for highway use. A smaller version pulls behind an ATV.

Firewood harvesting

Willits is a lumber town. Most of the forests in the area have been cut at least once. The original trees were large, fire-resistant redwoods and firs. Once clear-cut, these forests regrow as dense stands of small, easy-to-burn madrone, tan oaks, and brush. This creates an extreme fire hazard, especially around rural homes. Most of this "small-wood" is too small to harvest for lumber,

9.13a-b: *Four 75 watt solar panels charge Phil's Solar Power Trailer. Aluminum diamond plate box carries tools, batteries and a compressor.*

and consists of species that lumber companies don't want. Fortunately, these small hardwood logs and branches are ideally suited for firewood and biogas use. The problem is how to harvest them quickly and easily, without burning large amounts of fossil fuel.

Since 1999, Phil has worked with Willits inventor Ed Burton, developing technology for harvesting smallwood. "I want to make cutting firewood as much fun as playing golf," Ed explains. EBC (Ed Burton Company) has developed a variety of small, hand- and electric-powered wood-harvesting equipment, much of it built from or prototyped in grid beam.

Smallwood Bundler

Sticks and branches are good firewood, and require no splitting. In the US they usually get left in the woods or burned in piles because they are such a hassle to move and store. Ed's Smallwood Bundlers help turn loose branches into handy packages just the right size to stack and carry. Various versions mount on Yard Trucks, vehicles and trailers. Each features a branch clamp for chain sawing, a bundle

9.14: *Phil's electric Yard Truck garden carts can power an electric chain saw, then haul logs out of the woods.*

9.15: *Welded Yard Truck built for Ed Burton is fitted with (left to right) shear, smallwood bundler and branch clamp. Phil says, "I didn't like the welded frame. It wasn't nearly as stiff as grid beam, so I had to reinforce it with diagonal braces under the bed."*

9.16: *Inventor Ed Burton, age 83, demonstrates a Smallwood Bundler mounted to the front hitch of his Toro electric mini-pickup.*

holder, and attached branch shears that give you far more leverage to cut than hand-held shears.

Solar Band Saw Trailer

Some of California's native woods are not commercially harvested because they will split if not sawn into boards within days of felling the tree. The portable band saw developed for Ed Burton's smallwood research program sawed boards in the woods. Batteries plus additional charge from two solar panels mounted above the saw gave three to four hours sawing time. The frame was spray painted 2-inch galvanized steel. A branch clamp at the rear held tree limbs for chain sawing. Boards can be piled in the trailer's open center

section to haul them out of the woods at the end of the day.

For a suspension, Phil mounted 8-inch trailer wheels on commercial torsion axles with four-bolt spindles. Purchased from Northern Tool, these axles come with a weld flange. Phil drilled six holes in each flange and bolted them to the frame. A heavy-duty industrial caster under the front end made the trailer easy to hand-wheel around a parking lot or garage.

Solar Wood Dryer

EBC develops fuelwood technology. Since wood dries eight times faster through its ends than through its sides, EBC has developed equipment for chopping branches into short lengths that can be used as fuel pellets. Heat helps them dry even faster.

EBC's solar wood dryer has a frame of 2-inch galvanized steel, plywood sides and windows made from inexpensive tempered sliding glass door panes. Painted black for better heat absorption, the inside sometimes reaches 170 degrees Fahrenheit (75 degrees Celsius).

More energy projects

- Energy Cycle, page 91.
- Solar-Assisted Mountain Bike and trailer, page 91.
- Bear series garden tractors, page 95.
- X-Wing, page 98.
- Vanda, page 100.
- Sol Train, page 106.

9.17: *Phil examines branches drying in a solar wood dryer he built for Ed Burton. Front access drawers and a rear door double as air vents.*

WILMA KEPPEL

Trailers, Racks and Carts

In this chapter you'll learn about a variety of mobile projects. Some, such as truck racks, attach to a vehicle. Others, such as garden carts and trailers, have their own wheels.

Projects like these are subject to vibration and extreme loads from road shocks and shifting cargo. **Spread loads on mobile projects by using washers under every nut and bolt head.** To resist shock loads, use $7/16$-inch bolts on steel double-hole trailer frames.

Vibration tends to loosen nuts and bolts. **Use a lock nut, lock washer, or liquid thread locker on *every* nut.** Mount lock washers on top of plain washers. On the safety-critical parts of projects subject to maximum impact loads and vibration, such as trailer axles and suspensions, drill through the bolt

shaft where it projects past the nut, and insert a cotter pin.

Truck racks

Galvanized steel makes marvelous truck racks — strong, versatile and easy to modify. Bungee cords and load binders hook right into the holes. Add eye bolts, cleats,

10.1: *The galvanized steel rack on Richard's flat-bed Datsun pickup was in daily use from 1980 until 1994 — one of our best projects ever!*

PHIL AND RICHARD JERGENSON

hooks or cable reel holders anywhere on the frame. Attach sideboards or racks for pipe, glass, lumber or ladders, then unbolt them when the job is over. Wilma's

WILMA KEPPEL

10.2a: *Wilma and Tom Blinks built this plywood box around a rack similar to Richard's. Cargo rails on roof, here carrying a 600-pound (270-kilogram) steel tank, were originally supports for a 4 x 7 foot sleeping deck inside.*

WILMA KEPPEL

10.2b: *Rack rebuilt for transporting salvaged windows. Wilma then rebuilt it into a stand for washing the windows.*

"mutant truck rack" began as a rack for her Toyota pickup, which she bolted to the sides of the truck bed. It then morphed into various forms over a 2-year period (see photos).

Trailers

Automotive trailers are a natural application for galvanized steel. A grid beam trailer can be modified to haul various kinds of loads. The same basic trailer could be used as a flat-bed or with sideboards, be fully enclosed, or haul a boat or livestock.

Phil's Solar Power Trailer (page 80) used a galvanized steel frame with a coupler bolted to the tongue. Phil sometimes bolts a grid beam tongue to a welded frame.

Tom Blinks used 2-inch galvanized steel to adapt a commercially welded flatbed trailer for loading and carrying logs. Grid beam ramps deployed to one side. A steel cable looped around the log and attached to an onboard electric winch rolled it on board. To unload, two hand-powered farm jacks tipped the log cradle to the side. Tom found that the weight of a green (undried) log 18 inches in diameter and 20 feet long bent ramps made of single pieces of 2 inch steel. To make a stronger ramp, bolt two or three pieces of sticks together into a beam 4 or 6 inches tall.

Electric Mower

Gasoline-powered string trimmers make a racket, and their 2-stroke motors pour out air pollution. Phil designed his

Electric Mower to cut grass and weeds quietly, using power from the sun. "Using grid beam allowed me to adjust the battery, motor and handle position until the mower balanced perfectly on two wheels," Phil says. Simple steel adapters attached the angled handle, a battery tray bent from aluminum diamond plate, and plastic garden cart wheels. Two batteries powered a 1 horsepower (750 watt) 24 V motor spinning either a string trimmer, or three homemade aluminum blades. (Steel will spark if it hits a rock, and Willits is very fire-prone in, summer.) This direct-drive design proved too hard on the trimmer (even commercial-grade heads broke) and the motor bearings. But when it worked, it would cut through any weeds. Phil plans to move the motor near the batteries and connect it to the trimmer head using a V-belt that will act as a shock absorber. This design will let him put the mower head farther ahead of the wheels, where it can cut a wider swath.

Garden carts

Garden carts center the cargo weight near the axle, minimizing weight on the handle. This allows an average-sized person to move several hundred pounds without straining. Phil and Richard used a wood-framed cart (Figure C.34) for transporting batches of young trees weighing 50 pounds (23 kilograms) each over rough, steep terrain. To protect the cart frame from wear, they mounted the wheels on short sections of aluminum grid beam bolted to the wood. Plywood panels and stiff plastic tubs configured it for various uses.

Yard Truck

A Yard Truck is basically a motorized garden cart with a tilting dump bed. You may

10.3: *Phil's Electric Mower has a frame of 1½-inch aluminum.*

10.4: *Early Yard Truck with crossbar handle and rear caster. The dump bed is aluminum diamond plate.*

PHIL AND RICHARD JERGENSON

have seen gasoline-powered versions in TV ads with bouncy musical soundtracks. In reality, those machines produce an ear-shattering roar and the operator gets to breathe exhaust fumes all day. Phil's electric Yard Trucks are quiet and fun to use.

Phil got the idea for the Yard Truck while riding electric work vehicles on slopes as steep as 22.5 degrees (41 percent grade). When hauling heavy loads uphill, his vehicles only went 3 miles per hour (under 5 kilometers per hour). "I can *walk* that fast!" he thought. "Why should my vehicle carry me?" The Yard Truck was born.

In hilly terrain, walk-behind vehicles are more versatile and safer than ridden vehicles. Rolling a vehicle is always a risk on steep slopes. With a Yard Truck, your feet are on the ground. A shift of your weight is often enough to prevent tipping. If a roll is unavoidable, simply step out of the way.

A Yard Truck has many uses on the ranch or farm. Phil has built several for Ed Burton that are fitted for brush cutting and firewood harvesting (page 81). They can power tools and lights directly from the batteries or through an inverter. Tilt the dump bed to unload cargo or gain access to the drive train and batteries.

10.5: 1988 Yard Truck with a deeper dump bed recharging from a Solman portable power cart. This model can haul 450 pounds (200 kilograms) of cargo. An inverter under the bed supplies AC power.

PHIL AND RICHARD JERGENSON

PHIL AND RICHARD JERGENSON

10.6: Wheelbarrow-style handles are much more user-friendly than a crossbar. Two rear wheels make this 2003 Yard Truck more stable and maneuverable than versions with one rear wheel.

PHIL AND RICHARD JERGENSON

10.7: Economy Yard Truck built for Ed Burton in 2004 has rear legs, 3½ x 4 foot dump bed, and a simpler, lighter frame. Instead of a transmission, this one-speed model uses a reduction gear and chain drive.

When carrying loads uphill, the weight is right over the wheels for positive traction.

Although the five-speed garden tractor transmission used in most models has a built-in brake, Phil found he rarely needed it. "In high gear, you can push the Yard Truck on flat ground. In low gear, which I use on steep terrain, it stops as soon as I take my finger off the power switch. This keeps it from rolling, even on hills." In low gear these Yard Trucks move about ½ miles per hour (0.8 kilometers per hour), and can haul 450 to 500 pounds (200 to 230 kilograms) up a steep grade.

More carts and trailers

- Solar Power Trailer, page 80.
- Yard Trucks fitted for firewood harvesting, page 81.
- Solar-Assisted Mountain Bike trailer, page 92.

Yard Truck tech

Phil's Yard Trucks feature all-aluminum construction (including the transmission) to reduce weight and maximize cargo capacity. Most have rear casters so that you don't have to lift the load, only guide it. The main advantage of legs is that when you let go of the handles, the vehicle stops.

The drive train is extremely simple. Most Yard Trucks use a 1 horsepower (750 watt), 24 volt electric motor and V-belt to drive a 5-speed aluminum garden tractor transmission with a built-in disk brake. This setup yields five speeds in either forward or reverse. Changing gears requires stopping the vehicle.

A built-in differential facilitates maneuvering in tight quarters. The transaxle (a combination transmission, differential and axle) delivers up to 450 foot-pounds of torque through a 1-inch hardened steel axle.

A simpler one-speed drive train (Figure 11.2) uses a low-speed ¾ horsepower (560 watt) 24 V floor polisher motor. A six-to-one gear head reduces output shaft speed to just 165 rpm. A chain drive delivers power to the 1-inch axle. Cargo capacity is around 500 pounds (220 kilograms) on flat ground, about 200 pounds (90 kilograms) up a steep hill. Universal four-bolt spindles on all models allow the mounting of many different types of wheels with various tread patterns and tire sizes.

Vehicles

People shouldn't be afraid to try building an electric car. A lot of people might think it's daunting, especially if you're talking to a sixth or seventh or eighth grader. They don't think they can *do it. But you really can do it, and it's a lot of fun.*

— Constance Wu, whose all-girl eighth-grade team designed and built an electric go-kart in 2006

In 1976 Phil and Richard's design group rented the 25,000 square foot Earthlab I warehouse in Berkeley, California. Our manufacturing business fit in a back corner of the huge main room, which also held Tom Conlon's windmill business. The 1,000-watt wind turbine Tom mounted on the roof was great advertising, and the breeze off San Francisco Bay generated power virtually 24 hours per day. Several of us determined to tap into this source of free electricity.

When Michael Hackleman came to visit Tom in 1977, he gave Phil a copy of his new book, *Electric Vehicles: Design and Build Your Own.* Within two months Phil had built his first electric vehicle (EV), using grid beam.

At first, Phil's objective was simply to build a light-weight EV. A virtual explosion of electric vehicles resulted. None weighs over 550 pounds (250 kilograms),

11.1: *George Buono in his SPUV (Solar Powered Utility Vehicle), an electric pickup truck.*

PHIL AND RICHARD JERGENSON

and each took only about one month to design and build. Nothing is built to automotive scale. Instead, Phil uses industrial, go-kart, and alternative energy hardware.

Grid beam is ideal for prototyping vehicles because you can easily change your design hundreds of times during the building process. Try that with a welded frame! A completed prototype can be tested and modified as needed, used as a template to build a welded version, or become the final version. As a result, grid beam is becoming popular for middle school, high school and college design classes.

Why electric vehicles?

Virtually all grid beam vehicles to date have been electric. That's because:

11.2: *Simple drive train on a one-speed Yard Truck.*

PHIL AND RICHARD JERGENSON

- Compared to combustion-powered vehicles, EVs are much simpler to build — no starters, fuel pumps, water pumps, radiators, carburetors, mufflers, exhaust pipes or fuel tanks. On many projects, you can also eliminate the transmission. Fewer parts means less to buy and maintain.
- EV drive trains are flexible. You can use different motors with the same transmission, or different transmissions with the same motor. This makes projects easy to modify, plus you can re-use parts on other projects. Combustion-powered vehicles mostly require a specific transmission to go with a specific engine.
- EV batteries can provide portable power. With an inverter, your vehicle can provide AC power.
- You can refuel an EV using photovoltaic panels or wind. This is a huge advantage on remote sites.
- Even if you buy your power, an EV is cheaper to run and produces less pollution than an internal combustion engine.
- EVs are quiet and a lot less stressful to use than noisy gasoline engines.
- EVs are much more environmentally, economically and politically friendly than internal combustion motors. As we write this, the US is involved in an overseas war for oil. No one goes to war over sunlight, which won't run out.

The biggest disadvantage of EVs is the weight of the batteries. Lighter batteries are currently being developed.

Vehicles are more complicated to build and duplicate than other types of grid beam projects, so we've provided additional technical details. You'll find each vehicle's main description in the text, with technical notes in sidebars.

Solar-Assisted Mountain Bike

Because of its low rolling resistance, a bicycle will give you a pretty good idea of how much usable power an electric motor can provide. Phil's 1988 experiment used a mountain bike fitted with a 15-inch ring pulley attached to the spokes of the rear wheel. This gave a large gear reduction with very low weight. Phil concluded that a ¹⁄₅ horsepower (150 watt) electric motor is the minimum size practical for EVs that carry adults. A vehicle using a smaller motor must either be very small or very slow.

It takes ¼ horsepower (190 watts) to carry an adult rider at around 15 miles per hour (24 kilometers per hour) on flat ground. A much lower gear ratio is needed in steep terrain. Even with a ½ horsepower (375 watt) motor, Phil's steep home site

(about 20 percent grade) still required pedaling to get him up the hill. It's important to know the terrain where your vehicle will be operating so you can design accordingly.

This prototype was crude. When overcharged by the solar panel, the wet cell batteries dripped battery fluid, corroding the bike's aluminum bottom bracket and chain ring. The motor mounted at the back of the bike sent a severe shock through the frame every time the rider hit a bump. A suspension system would have

11.3: *Solar Assisted Mountain Bike.*

PHIL AND RICHARD JERGENSON

Solar-Assisted Mountain Bike tech

Phil used 1-inch aluminum sticks to attach the motor and solar panel to the bike frame. A hinged motor mount took up slack in the V-belt drive. Ten used nickel-cadmium batteries from an army surplus store hung from the top tube of the bicycle in a homemade box. These batteries are very durable but weigh a lot more than equivalent lead-acid batteries. The 30-watt solar panel didn't produce enough power to run the motor, but could recharge the batteries in around 10 hours.

helped (suspensions were very expensive then), but a better solution is to move the motor.

These issues inspired Phil to start a new frame made of 1-inch aluminum grid beam. The motor will go right behind the seat tube. A battery will go just ahead of the bottom bracket, with a charge controller to prevent overcharging.

11.4: *Prototype bicycle frame of 1-inch aircraft aluminum. Sections of round aluminum tube make light-weight frame spacers.*

Phil also built a solar trailer so the bike could pull its own power source. Made of 40 feet of 1-inch aluminum, the frame weighed just 10 pounds (4.5 kilograms). Total trailer weight was only 40 pounds (18 kilograms) including four 30-watt Solarex Lite photovoltaic panels, which generated 120 watts. Phil tried a wider version that tipped up to make a portable tracker, but found it was too hard for cars to pass in traffic.

Electric Vehicle Test Bed

A test bed is a reusable chassis that can be used to try out various components. Built in 1978, the Electric Vehicle Test Bed (EVTB) was Phil's first driveable grid beam vehicle. Originally an electric motorcycle, it became a tricycle when Phil wanted more cargo capacity.

The EVTB's frame was 1-inch steel tubing, obtained from store dumpsters and old projects. Phil drilled the holes 1 inch apart — the first use of the hole pattern

11.5: *Solar Bicycle Trailer.*

11.6: *EVTB trike with wooden battery box.*

we use today — then cut the tubes to standard lengths.

A welded adapter attached the front end, a BMX bicycle fork with a motorcycle-type suspension and 20-inch wheel. (BMX was cross-country racing that predated mountain bikes.) Tiller steering allowed Phil to sit back on the frame with plenty of leg room. The cast BMX rear wheels were modified to accept a ⁵⁄₈-inch axle strong enough to support them from one side. A 12 volt, ¼ horsepower (185 watt) electric motor gave the EVTB a top speed of 10 to 15 miles per hour (16 to 24 kilometers per hour) on level ground, but was too small to climb hills. With a ⁵⁄₈ horsepower (560 watt) 1,200 rpm motor, the EVTB had a top speed of 18 to 20 miles per hour (29 to 32 kilometers per hour), and went up 5 or 10 percent inclines very nicely.

Scamp

Built in 1979, the Scamp was the first vehicle Phil built from 1½-inch square aluminum tubing. It was lots of fun and got driven more than any of his other vehicles. Top speed was only 20 miles per hour (30 kilometers per hour), but Scamp could wheelie a 120 pound (54 kilogram) battery pack. On pavement it could lay two feet of rubber in second gear!

Phil built Scamp the summer he moved to Willits. The steep terrain on his home site required an EV with more power than the EVTB — one with wider tires, a transmission and the ability to

11.7: *Early version of Scamp with a plywood seat and cargo deck. The front end came from a Honda 50 motorcycle.*

PHIL AND RICHARD JERGENSON

11.8: *Phil wheelies the Scamp. Grid beam vehicles are lots of fun, but wear a helmet!*

RICHARD JERGENSON

Scamp tech

The EVTB's 1-inch steel frame flexed under torque from the vehicle's ¾ horsepower (560 watt) motor. To increase motor power, Phil needed to build a stronger frame. By switching to 1½-inch aircraft aluminum, he got much stiffer tubes that weighed the same per foot. The bigger tubes more than doubled the contact area within each tri-joint, making much stiffer frame joints.

Scamp's frame used 23 feet of grid beam, later expanded to 29½ feet. A 1-horsepower (745-watt) 24-volt DC electric motor was side-mounted with a spider shaft coupler and attached directly to the 3-speed transmission, creating a clean drive train with a surprising amount of power. Wide 18-inch diameter turf-tread tires delivered plenty of traction without tearing up the trails.

11.9: *Phil's Electric Tote Goat demonstrates the simplicity possible with a grid beam frame and drive train. The ¾-horsepower (560-watt) motor is geared directly to the rear wheel.*

carry modest amounts of cargo. George Buono later rebuilt Scamp, adding a much-needed seat and cargo bed, both shock-mounted. He also raised the handlebars and installed a two-speed foot switch.

Three-wheel ATVs similar to Scamp got taken off the market a few years ago because of roll-over problems. The weight of Scamp's battery pack, mounted between the three wheels and only 5 inches off the ground, gave the vehicle good stability. We have been asked many times if this vehicle is for sale as a kit, but due to liability and changes in the law we sadly must say no.

Electric Tote Goat

The Electric Tote Goat was Phil's second electric motorcycle. He was inspired by Tim Hunt, the neighborhood mechanic where the Jergensons grew up. Starting in 1962, Tim built two complete gasoline "tote goats" for fishing and deer hunting. Fabricating the frames was painfully slow because of all the gas-welded joints and bends in the tubing. The day Tim finished the power train, his tote goat effortlessly climbed six concrete steps.

Where we live today the terrain is very steep and hilly, and a narrow, maneuverable way to haul cargo can be very useful. Instead of a suspension, Phil's Tote Goat used soft 12 inch wide all-terrain knobby tires, 22 inches in diameter. A 24-volt, ¾-horsepower (560 watt) motor drove a chain connected to the rear wheel, making a very simple drive train that could push the vehicle about 6 miles per hour (10 kilometers per hour) on level ground.

Phil's first version had grid beam forks, with pillow blocks bolted on to hold the front axle (Figure 21.7). He later fabricated a welded front end. Steering still takes more effort than we like. Although this project is not finished, we include it to show how simple a grid beam vehicle can be.

Bear garden tractors

After moving to Willits, Phil built a house on a remote site using solar power to run tools. The Bear vehicles came out of his need for something that could move materials easily and provide a portable source of power.

If you look at the garden tractors on the market, you'll notice that you sit over the rear tires and look down a long hood housing the engine. Phil got rid of the nose and put the operator there, on a seat wide enough to carry a passenger.

The Bears are designed to move bulky items and loose materials. A dump bed allows quick and easy unloading, and provides easy access to the drive train. Tilt the bed as needed to get the best charging angle for the solar panels on the vehicle's roof.

A Bear can provide DC power direct from its batteries, or AC power through an inverter. In some cases, a Bear can replace a gasoline generator. On a shady site, drive this power station into the sun-

shine, then drive your charged batteries right where you want them!

Welded Bear

Built in 1984, the Welded Bear was Phil's last welded vehicle. It required lots of sheet-metal forming. Two of the four batteries sat behind the rear axle. Phil discovered that when driving up a steep grade with a load, the front end would get too light to steer. "Because of the welded frame, I was stuck with the bad geometry," he says. "I decided to build only with grid beam from then on."

Solar Bear

Built in 1988, the grid beam Solar Bear was a big improvement over the welded version. Only three feet wide, with a short wheelbase and responsive handling, it could U-turn in a space 13 feet wide.

11.10: *Phil and Nolan Jergenson in the Welded Bear garden tractor. Roof of the dump bed is two 50 watt solar panels.*

PHIL AND RICHARD JERGENSON

The Solar Bear is more useful for gardening than its commercial counterparts. It can also carry a passenger. Thanks to its light-weight frame of 1½-inch aluminum,

PHIL AND RICHARD JERGENSON

11.11: *Tilting the Solar Bear's dump bed aims its solar panels.*

PHIL AND RICHARD JERGENSON

11.12: *Lifting the dump bed gives access to the Solar Bear's battery boxes and drive train.*

Phil's Bear weighed just 450 pounds (200 kilograms), with a 600 pound (270 kilogram) payload — less on steep hills. A tractor needs weight on the drive wheels, so that's where Phil put four deep-cycle batteries weighing 200 pounds (90 kilograms). Two 20-inch rear tires provided traction. A small disk brake on the four-speed transmission stopped the rear wheels. "I don't put front brakes on my rear-bed work vehicles," Phil explains. "The main weight is over the rear wheels, and loads are generally carried uphill, putting even more weight on the rear."

Three 50-watt photovoltaic panels on the roof generated enough power for about one hour of driving per day, and kept the batteries charged when the vehicle was not in use. For longer running times, the Solar Bear charged through a plug.

At SEER '91, the Solar Bear competed in a pulling contest with a commercial electric tractor manufactured by General Electric. The GE machine had knobby tires and was probably 200 pounds (90 kilograms) heavier. Phil had trouble with his front wheel coming off the ground, which probably wouldn't have happened if he had loaded the Bear to match the weight of the other machine. In spite of this, the Solar Bear equaled the GE tractor's performance — amazing when you consider that this was a big-budget, commercially produced vehicle competing against a lone inventor's shoestring home-built.

Solar Bear tech

Phil's Solar Bear featured a 2 horsepower (1,500 watt) DC motor, comparable to a 6 or 8 horsepower (4.5 to 6 kilowatt) gasoline engine. Phil reused the Welded Bear's heavy-duty cast iron transaxle, which had four forward speeds and a reverse gear. Its compound low gear ratio of 172 x 1 gave the Bear plenty of power. With no clutch, Phil stopped the vehicle to shift gears. A V-belt and pulley between the motor and transmission allowed the operator to adjust the vehicle's speed range to suit the terrain it usually worked in: a low ratio for hills, or a high ratio for flat ground. The Bear wasn't fast, but once it got traction it was unstoppable.

An early version of the Solar Bear used a two-speed parallel-series motor controller. With four gears, that gave eight speeds total. This type of controller is low-cost, and the parallel circuit allows a softer start on takeoff than a series circuit. It also allows simple regenerative braking (regen), which charges the vehicle by braking with the motor. Regen can extend the vehicle's work day by up to one hour on steep sites.

Two side-by-side switches controlled motor speed. Pressing one switched on 12-volt power for low speed; pressing both switched on 24 volts. By mounting a piece of rubber over them, Phil created a button where a light touch would activate low speed and a firmer touch turned on high speed.

Later Phil added a 175-amp Curtis electronic controller. An older model, it did not allow regen. A motorcycle-style twist throttle allowed the driver to vary vehicle speed while staying in one gear, and drive the vehicle as slow as ¼ mile per hour (0.4 kilometers per hour).

Japanese Bear

Phil built this small-scale version of the Solar Bear in Willits in 1991 for a demonstration project at an international school in Japan. He then took it apart and rebuilt it into three crates. The wheels and other specialty components went inside, padded with his clothes. The three packages traveled on the airplane with him as luggage. Only the larger panels and batteries got replaced in Japan. At the school, children and teenagers from 20 countries, speaking many different languages, reassembled the vehicle. "I assembled one side, and they copied what I did on the other side," Phil recalls. "My biggest problem was making the class last a week. A few of us could have reassembled the vehicle in a few hours."

The original disk brake was too weak for the school's hilly terrain. Back in Willits, Phil used a photo to re-create part of the vehicle's rear end, then built an

Japanese Bear tech

To attain a top speed of about 15 miles per hour (24 kilometers per hour), the Japanese Bear used a 1 horsepower (750 watt), 24 volt motor, and a chain drive with a 5-to-1 gear reduction. Two 80-pound batteries provided power through a 175-ampere Curtis controller. A forward-reverse switch allowed the vehicle to back up. A Peerless live split axle acted as a differential that kept the rear tires from scrubbing when going around corners.

11.13: *Students in Japan reassemble and drive Phil's Japanese Bear.*

11.14: *Phil in the X-Wing, his most fun grid beam vehicle ever. Its low profile — less than 45 inches (1,150 millimeter) including roll bar — kept it stable in high-speed turns.*

adapter to attach a new drum brake to the frame. The new brake assembly had to be accurate to within $^1/_{32}$ inch to work. Back in Japan for a second year of classes, Phil and the students replaced the old brake in a few hours. Only a bit of hand filing was necessary to perfect the alignment. This demonstrates one of the main advantages of grid beam over other building systems we've tried: modular construction is easy to replicate, and parts are truly interchangeable.

X-Wing

Phil spent the summer of 1988 building and testing a low-slung solar-electric tricycle. "The X-Wing was probably the most fun of all the grid beam vehicles I've built and driven," Phil says. "With a top speed around 25 miles per hour (40 kilometers per hour), it stuck to the road like glue, and had great handling and lightning-fast responsiveness in turns. Turning on pavement, you could feel the side G-forces

X-Wing tech

A vehicle going faster than about 10 miles per hour (16 kilometers per hour) needs a suspension to protect it from road shocks. For the X-Wing's MacPherson strut rear suspension, Phil fabricated welded A-arms. Hydraulic brakes on the A-arms stopped brake disks on the axles. The motor for each wheel mounted on the base of the A-arm, so drive chain tension remained constant as the vehicle bounced. The top ends of the shock absorbers bolted directly to the vehicle frame.

For the front wheel, Phil built a leading link suspension with about 4 inches of travel, which really softened the bumps. Leading links are fairly easy to fabricate, but to make them stable the geometry must be right. Phil's leading link put the contact patch (where the tire touches the road) too far forward, so the steering felt skittish at speeds over 10 miles per hour (16 kilometers per hour). Once Phil installed an adjustable damper, the X-Wing handled beautifully.

The driver sat leaning back with feet extended. Handlebars wouldn't fit inside the streamlined body, and a tiller would have bumped during sharp turns. Instead, Phil created a push rod steering system. To turn, the driver pulled one steering lever while pushing the other. This felt comfortable and natural. Brackets at the front of the cab held the push rods in place. A spherical rod end bearing (hime joint) at the front end of each push rod kept it from binding.

A thumb button atop each steering handle controlled X-Wing's speed. Holding down one button activated low speed; holding down both buttons switched to high speed. These buttons were momentary switches, which shut off if the driver let go. Vehicle throttles must always have some kind of automatic shutoff so the vehicle can't drive off by itself.

11.15: *X-Wing's push rod steering system and home-built leading link front suspension.*

The thumb buttons controlled a 100 amp double-throw, double-pole solenoid. This supplied the motors with 12 volt current for low speed, and 24 volt current for high speed. One electric motor powered each rear wheel. The motors were 1¼ and ¾ horsepower (930 and 560 watts), running at different speeds, with chain gearing to compensate. Ideally you want to use matching motors, but Phil had these handy. Even when only one motor was powered, the X-Wing drove in a straight line.

Series-parallel wiring for the motors allowed regenerative braking. Regen quickly slowed the vehicle to about 12 miles per hour (19 kilometers per hour), after which the driver could use the conventional brakes. A 200-amp electric meter that measured positive, negative and zero showed whether the vehicle was using or producing power.

A foot pedal controlled hydraulic disk brakes on the rear wheels. These brakes had double-acting cylinders, which squeeze both pads against the brake disk. They are less prone to drag than brakes that squeeze only one pad.

slam you into the side of the seat. Turned sharply on gravel at 15 miles per hour (24 kilometers per hour), it would slide predictably and with an amazing amount of control. Unfortunately, it's not safe to drive a vehicle this small on city streets, which is why I never licensed it."

Trikes with a single front wheel have a tendency to overturn when cornering, especially when going downhill. To compensate, Phil built the X-Wing low and wide. The main chassis stood only about 20 inches high. The floor pan was just 6 inches off the ground, putting driver's butt just 9 inches above the pavement. Combined with rear wheels spaced 6 feet apart and batteries placed over and between the rear axles, this gave the X-Wing an incredibly low center of gravity and fantastic cornering abilities.

The X-Wing's 250-pound (110-kilogram) batteries weighed more than the 180-pound (80-kilogram) vehicle. Phil attributes the low weight to the vehicle's aluminum grid beam frame.

When Phil brought the X-Wing out on the road, he discovered that it was quite intimidating to drive in traffic: "When I pulled up to a regular passenger car, the top of my head didn't even come up to its door handles! This gives you a very vulnerable feeling, especially when you pull up beside someone in the next lane who cannot see you at all." And with a top speed of around 25 miles per hour (40 kilometers per hour), the X-Wing was too slow to keep up with auto traffic.

Light weight is great for getting good mileage, but in a two-vehicle crash, the lighter vehicle almost always loses. At 430 pounds (195 kilograms), the X-Wing weighed less than most mid-sized motorcycles! In an accident with even the smallest car, the X-Wing would lose. Because of its super-low profile, it could even get wedged underneath the other vehicle. This shows how a design that's good from an engineering standpoint may be less than ideal for real-world use.

Vanda

Convinced that the X-Wing needed a larger profile for safety on the streets, Phil decided to alter the upper half. He scaled the existing undercarriage onto graph paper, and after just a few designs came up with the Vanda (Figure C.28).

Phil raised the seat to put the driver's eye level about 30 inches above the road, and moved it 2 feet forward. Almost 6 feet wide, the Vanda had an interior deck 4 feet wide and 5 feet long. With a deck extension over the front of the cab, it could sleep two adults. Total interior volume was around 90 cubic feet (2.5 cubic meters) — not bad for a vehicle under 9 feet (3 meters) long!

"The futuristic shape of the Vanda is something I'm rather proud of," Phil says. "Previous experiments had shown how hard it was to get streamlined bodies without spending a small fortune on molds. The conventional way to produce these shapes is with fiberglass. I spent about two weeks making the fiberglass front end for

Vanda tech

Because the seat position had changed so much, Phil replaced the push rod steering system with a tiller, which had a less precise feel he didn't like. A friend installed a speed controller with a foot pedal. The foot brake remained the same.

Made of four 55-watt solar panels, Vanda's roof could tilt to follow the sun. Larger panels on the fold-up sides brought total capacity over 400 watts, making Vanda an effective portable power station. A 220-amp-hour battery pack sat between the axles, with two solar panels connected to each battery.

11.16: *Tilt Vanda's solar roof and side wings to follow the sun. Open the nose to step in or out.*

the X-Wing. I formed the Vanda body from Alucobond panels, bending the lower ones a bit at the front end, and installed a rain channel where the body joined the roof. For $150 a glass shop installed safety glass in the body panels, using black rubber gaskets. Fabricating this body took about two days"

The more Phil played with the design, the more possibilities became apparent. With its large solar array, the vehicle could be lived in for short periods. He toyed with making it unfold into a tent. There was room under the deck for a small refrigerator as well as lots of storage. What if the vehicle manufactured ice while it sat idle? Or ran an air compressor, or power tools? Once you have power, many types of conversions are possible.

Like the X-Wing, the Vanda had a top speed of about 25 miles per hour (40 kilometers per hour), and was too wide for cars to pass easily. Before Phil could upgrade the motors and finish Vanda's interior, he moved to a mountain top. Because batteries are so heavy, long drives uphill are one of the most difficult applications for EVs. The steep 12-mile drive from town was too much for the Vanda's small battery pack. Rather than completely redesign the vehicle, Phil dismantled it and used the components to power his home and create other vehicles. Vanda has such terrific possibilities that we hope someone will fully develop a similar project.

Go-karts

Go-karts are scaled-down miniature race cars used for recreation and racing. Most have welded steel frames and use gasoline motors. Using grid beam for the frame makes recreational go-karts easier to build and modify.

Dozens of grid beam go-karts have been built, many by children. We even heard of one father-son team who bought a grid beam go-kart on eBay from another father-son team who built it!

Dave Beard vehicle

It took master mechanic Dave Beard about 12 weeks of part-time work to build this frame in 1989. Made of 1-inch aluminum grid beam, it weighed only 65 pounds (30 kilograms) when finished. It featured rack and pinion steering and an adjustable rate double-wishbone suspension. Dave's main tool was a drill press. He used hand saws and files to shape the many custom parts. He later added a gasoline engine and a styrofoam body with fiberglass outer shell.

Electrathon racers

An environmentally friendly variation of go-kart racing, Electrathon racing is one of the most exciting motor sports today. Competing vehicles attempt to outdistance each other in one hour, running on a 67-pound (30 kilogram) battery pack, the equivalent of less than half a cup (0.1 liter) of gasoline. Electrathon drivers are required to wear helmets and use five-point safety harnesses, and the light-weight vehicles have built-in roll bars. The result is an exciting sport that is also one of the safest racing events around. Races can be run on racetracks, blocked-off surface streets, or even parking lots. With parts for a race vehicle costing as little as $500, this sport is accessible to almost anyone. Even junior high schools have built vehicles and competed.

11.17: Dave Beard tests the fit of his go-kart frame.

11.18: Electrathon racing at SEER '92. Built by students at Willits High School, the nearer vehicle has a grid beam frame.

We got involved in Electrathon when Phil helped organize a race for SEER '91 (Solar Energy Expo and Rally). At that time winning vehicles averaged around 35 miles per hour (55 kilometers per hour). By 2006 winning vehicles averaged almost 50 miles per hour (80 kilometers per hour), which requires top speeds of up to 70 miles per hour (110 kilometers per hour). Try that with your seat just a few inches above the road!

The keys to winning are driver skill, good battery management, and engineering a car with good streamlining and an efficient drive train. The Electrathon format rewards strategy and conservation rather than power or sheer speed. Winning vehicles tend to be small, sleek and light-weight.

Willits High School Electrathon Racer

The Electrathon race Phil organized for SEER '91 inspired Willits High School auto shop instructor Alan Kearney and a group of his advanced students to build an Electrathon vehicle that competed in SEER '92. Phil donated 30 feet of 1½- inch aluminum tubing for the frame, which students drilled into grid beam. The resulting frame allowed for easy design changes. "Our first vehicle had a trike layout (one wheel up front and two in the rear)," Alan writes. "While this simplified the steering and brakes, the vehicle would tip over in fast, tight turns. We quickly rejected this for a motorcar layout." Costs

ALAN KEARNEY

were kept to a minimum: $500 cash, about $800 worth of materials donated by local businesses, and an estimated 400 hours of construction time. The group's goal was to race safely in as many different events as possible in each school year. They beat every high school vehicle they competed against.

Panther Electric

During the 1994–1995 school year a group of 30 seventh- and eighth-grade students in Felton, California, designed and constructed an Electrathon-qualified street-legal vehicle. They were supervised by Carter Milhous, instructor for the Gifted and Talented Education (GATE) program at the San Lorenzo Valley Junior High School, and experienced electrical vehicle designer Michael Hackleman.

11.19: *Willits High School students figure out where to position the dashboard gauges on their vehicle.*

The Panther Electric's body was a purchased blown-ABS Murphy Aerocoupe shell. Wheels were modified moped rims and tires. The frame was 1½-inch aluminum grid beam, donated by Phil. This allowed the students to change the frame as much as they liked. In the end, only one component was welded.

"We welded some aluminum to the grid beam in order to do the rear suspension pieces," Michael Hackleman told us. "We ended up abandoning the welded version for the bolted version because once it didn't work a little bit, it didn't work at all."

MICHAEL HACKLEMAN

11.20: *Panther Electric's control circuitry is mounted on the plywood side plate for easy access. Even the steering tiller is grid beam.*

Two steered wheels in front and a powered rear wheel gave a very stable motorcar configuration. Knowing the vehicle would eventually be licensed for the street, the students positioned the top frame rails at 18 inches, the same height as most car bumpers, so that in a collision the vehicle would bounce away. The finished vehicle got driven in the home town parade. It was so quiet that many people thought it was human-powered.

Panther Electric tech

Borrowing a technique used on solar race cars, the students used skis for the front suspension. They sawed the tips and tails off two laminated micarta/aluminum/steel skis, then spaced and stacked them to support hime joints at the tops and bottoms of the kingpins, approximating traditional double wishbone suspensions. Caster (rake) angle was built in; camber was adjustable.

A 1-horsepower (750 watt) motor drove the rear wheel. The motor shaft was at the same center as the suspension pivot, keeping the V-belt tension steady regardless of suspension travel. A simple series-parallel (12 or 24 volts) control circuit provided low and high speed, with a relay added to provide reverse gear.

Electric Moose Club

In 1994, industrial technology teacher Brad Booth started an electric car club for his seventh- and eighth-grade students at Jane Lathrop Stanford Middle School in Palo Alto, California. Brad wanted to use a modular, reusable building system. The first cars were built from metal conduit and compression fittings. The next year he saw our first book, and switched to grid beam.

"As simple as this material is, it takes kids this young all year to build a car," Brad reports. "They have limited experience with tools. Even teaching them to cut a piece of beam and deburr it is a big deal."

Each year begins with students test-driving the previous year's cars, and evaluating them for braking, turning radius, comfort, acceleration and speed. "Most kids have never thought about these factors before," Brad says. Next, students tear apart the vehicles. For many, it's the first time they have held a wrench. Student teams then design and build their own vehicles. At the end of the year, they drive their cars in Palo Alto's May Fair parade, then race against competing grid beam cars from Terman Middle School.

All cars are 1-inch grid beam — either purchased pre-punched steel, or aircraft aluminum drilled by the students. Motors, wheels, seats and about 80 percent of the grid beam get re-used. (Very short pieces get thrown away.)

Brad's job is to keep the students and their cars safe. Padded bumpers are mandatory. Plywood decks prevent students from using their feet as brakes. Brad keeps vehicle batteries in a locked battery safe (Figure 14.5). Teams get their batteries only after their car passes an extensive safety checklist.

Inspired by the Electric Moose Club, industrial technology teacher Eileen Chang took grid beam cars into the San Jose school system in 1995, as described in the "Electric vehicles" section of Chapter 12. She now heads the electric car club at Terman Middle School in Palo Alto.

Competition to get into the car clubs is fierce. By encouraging girls to join, both teachers keep their programs about 50 percent female. They tried coed teams, but found that all-girl and all-boy teams get along better.

11.21: *Eileen Chang's simple go-kart design. The control lever activates throttle and brakes; the driver's feet pivot the bogie-steered front wheels.*

Electric car club tech

Both electric car club teachers have standardized on similar parts: 1-inch grid beam, plastic seats from Atari arcade games, plastic wheel guards, and pairs of 12-volt, 17-amp-hour batteries. Chang's club uses spoked wheels with solid tires that can't go flat; Booth's club uses cast wheels with pneumatic tires. With no cooperative supplier for new motors, the schools use a mix of EV Warrior motors, ZAP bicycle motors, and surplus computer tape drive motors. Fuses limit motor output to comparable levels.

Chang's simple car uses easy-to-construct bogie (single-pivot) steering. A spring-loaded grid beam rectangle controlled by a tiller holds brakes in front of the rear wheels, and motors behind them. Pushing the control lever forward disengages the brakes and presses the motor drive wheels against the rear wheels. Pushing the control lever backward disengages the motors and applies the brakes.

11.22: The first automotive-scale grid beam vehicle we know of, built around 1980 by a former Earthlab I member. Frame is 2-inch steel with components from two models of Volkswagen cars. An electric car conversion kit mates a military surplus aircraft starter motor/generator to the transmission.

Solar Powered Utility Vehicle (SPUV)

Our friend George Buono wanted an electric vehicle that would have the utility of a flat-bed pickup truck, carry passengers, and run on a modest amount of power supplied by photovoltaic solar panels. The result was the SPUV. It weighs roughly 600 pounds (270 kilograms), plus 600 pounds of batteries, and will travel rough terrain for hours carrying substantial loads without recharging. This is possible because George took great care to conserve power whenever possible.

Built with 1-inch grid beam frames, the bucket seats weigh just 7½ pounds (3.4 kilograms) apiece — one-third the weight of the lightest bucket seats on the market. The vehicle's curved corners are trusses fabricated from short sections of round aluminum tube sandwiched between parallel aluminum strips. One bolt through the center of each tube clamps it in place.

Double wishbone suspensions on all four wheels give the SPUV fantastic handling and a very tight turning radius. Modified cast aluminum motorcycle wheels and motorcycle brakes are much lighter than car wheels.

An 8-horsepower (6-kilowatt) permanent magnet motor drives each rear wheel through a rubber gear belt. SPUV uses MOSFET motor controllers and has regenerative braking.

Sol Train

Trains are one of the best applications for battery power because of their low rolling resistance. Steel wheels on steel rails are up to ten times more efficient than rubber tires on a road. With a maximum four percent grade on hills, rails make an ideal environment for electric vehicles.

Our first Sol Train was a solar-powered model railroad that Richard built with Scott Bowers for SEER '90. We introduced the full-sized version one year later at SEER '91.

PHIL AND RICHARD JERGENSON

PHIL AND RICHARD JERGENSON

11.23: SPUV's curved aluminum trusses are light and strong.

The Sol Train began life as a speeder (a railroad work vehicle) donated by California Western Railroad. With help from the Mendocino County Railway Society, Richard and Phil stripped it down to the main frame, transmission and wheels, then added battery boxes and a sloped Alucobond nose. We reinstalled the cast-aluminum control panel in its original location so we could use the existing control handles. Made of 160 feet of aluminum grid beam, the frame supporting the seats and body weighed just 120 pounds (54 kilograms).

Phil mounted nine 30-watt Solarex Lite photovoltaic panels on the roof, providing 270 watts charging capacity — about 1/3 horsepower. They extend the vehicle's range 5 to 10 miles (8 to 16 kilometers) if it is in the sun all day. They also shade the riders, a big plus in sunny California.

The crowds loved the Sol Train when we unveiled it at SEER '91. A 2-horsepower (1,500-watt), 24 volt DC motor borrowed from Phil's electric bulldozer ran the train nicely at about 15 miles per hour (24 kilometers per hour). We couldn't use the

11.24: *Giving rides in the Sol Train, a hit with the crowds at SEER 91. Phil and Richard chat with Howard Letovsky (standing), who helped with construction.*

REINHOLD ZIEGLER

PHIL AND RICHARD JERGENSON

11.25: *The pre-1940 speeder that became the Sol Train.*

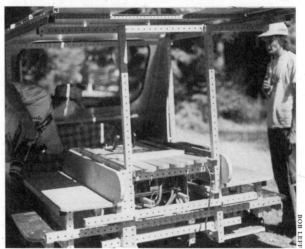

BOB LEFF

11.26: *Richard with the Sol Train on the Fort Bragg to Willits run in 1992. Crossed and stacked frame members create trusses; 1-inch sticks support the solar panel roof.*

upper gear in our two-speed transmission because of our short 300-foot test track.

For SEER '92, Howard Letovsky got General Electric to donate a 27-horsepower (20-kilowatt) motor, roughly equivalent to a 70-horsepower (50-kilowatt) gasoline engine. This motor would probably push the Sol Train over 70 miles per hour (110 kilometers per hour) — we doubt we've ever used more than 5 horsepower (4 kilowatts). Our new Trojan batteries didn't get installed until the evening before the test run, so we didn't have time to cycle them the recommended 12 to 15 times. We planned a 40-mile (64 kilometer) trip from Fort Bragg (elevation 80 feet, or 24 meters) to Willits (elevation 1,364 feet, or 415 meters) over the Summit Pass (elevation 1,740 feet, or 543 meters). This is the famous Skunk Railroad, so-called because the track is so curvy you can smell the train before you see it.

With properly cycled batteries we would have made it. Instead, we ran out of power 28.7 miles (46 kilometers) from Fort Bragg at an elevation of 808 feet (246 meters). A California Western speeder pushed us to Summit Pass. Using regenerative braking to recharge the batteries, we had plenty of power by the time we rolled into Willits. We vowed to return for more testing.

For SEER '94 we ran the Sol Train from Willits (elevation 1,364 feet, or 415 meters) to Ukiah, a distance of about 30 miles (48 kilometers), over the Ridgewood Summit at 1,953 feet (595 meters). This time the new batteries, donated by Amp King of San Francisco, had been cycled and we made it into Ukiah with no problems. The station there lies at 675 feet (206 meters), so our batteries were nicely recharged by the time we arrived. Our calculations indicate the Sol Train could travel 200 miles (320 kilometers) or more with the right battery pack.

Everyone who has ridden the Sol Train has been amazed at how quiet it is. Although the ringing of the wheels can get pretty loud, it doesn't compare with the unbelievable racket of gasoline-powered railroad speeders.

We estimate the Sol Train's weight at between 1,000 and 1,200 pounds (450–540 kilograms), with room for four times more batteries than we've used. With more batteries, the Sol Train could pull lightweight cars behind it, perhaps with solar roofs. Imagine the tourism potential!

Rail Rocket

The Rail Rocket was intended to improve on the Sol Train. We wanted a vehicle light enough that two people could lift it onto and off the tracks (the Sol Train requires a fork lift). We also wanted something as quiet as a bicycle so we could see and hear more wildlife.

To achieve these goals, in 2003 we scratch-built a speeder powered with a combination of pedals and an electric motor. Since the aluminum frame weighed so little, its motor and batteries could also be small and light-weight. To minimize noise, we used plastic wheels.

Our design team of Phil, Richard and Michael Hackleman started by building a wooden grid beam frame to work out the basic proportions and component positions. Next came several aluminum versions. The one we chose for track testing had pedals on one seat, plus electric drive from a 2-horsepower (1,500-watt), 24-volt motor (Figure 21.3). A plastic control box between the front seats housed the electronics.

As planned, the vehicle was light enough that two of us easily positioned it on the tracks. Whether pedaled or electrically powered, it was virtually silent. Everything was fine until we hit the first curve, where the vehicle repeatedly derailed. During one derailment, the bicycle chain wrapped around the front axle, snapping off the 1½-inch aluminum post supporting the pedals. This is only the third time in 30 years we have broken a piece of grid beam. (The other times involved autos hitting projects.) We eventually discovered that our plastic wheels were flexing enough to pop off the rails. Once we replace them, this promises to be a great project.

FOCUS research submarine

The most unusual grid beam vehicle we know of was a remote-controlled deep-sea submarine built by researchers at the University of Hawaii in 1991. FOCUS (Fiber Optic Camera Under Sea) was designed to carry lights, cameras and instruments up to four miles deep in the ocean.

Deep-sea subs typically cost around $1 million. After talking to colleagues, the FOCUS team decided that about 80 percent of the underwater observations that researchers wanted could be done relatively inexpensively. The FOCUS sub was designed to reach 90 to 95 percent of the sea floor, and transmit real-time instrument readings and at least six simultaneous TV pictures to the surface via fiber-optic cable.

The sub's frame was built from 2-inch steel grid beam, powder-coated to protect it from seawater. Instruments could bolt anywhere on the frame. Built by the Institute of Geophysics for only $60,000, the sub was used for data collection where conventional subs would be too expensive to risk. Researcher Roy Wilkens said, "The whole idea is to get a little risky with it and get data we wouldn't get otherwise."

Originally built as one unit, FOCUS was later reconfigured into two. A power and optical conversion unit was attached directly to the bottom of the power/data cable. A "fish" containing lights, camera and other sensors was towed about 30 feet below the power pod on a coaxial cable. The sub's grid beam frame allowed it to be reconfigured to accept different sensors for different missions.

Project possibilities

We think grid beam will prove ideal for building light-duty agricultural equipment. This could include solar-electric tractors as well as specialized planting and

harvesting equipment for organic farm-
ing. Widely available in Europe, this kind
of equipment remains expensive and difficult to find in the US.

12

Learning and Innovation

Grid beam is the inventor's best friend.

— inventor Ed Burton,
who holds 23 patents

With grid beam there are no permanent mistakes. If you find a problem, or think of a better way to build something, just unbolt and reconfigure your project. This makes grid beam ideal for:

• **Learning.** People with no building experience can successfully assemble projects right away.

• **Teaching.** Fast grid beam assembly lets students quickly build multiple projects or project versions. Reusable materials keep costs to a minimum.

• **Innovation.** Designers, inventors and hobbyists can test and refine a design very rapidly, and at minimal cost, before building a finished version.

WILMA KEPPEL

Teaching and learning

Grid beam is ideal for teaching because:

• It's simple to use.

• Projects happen fast, so students stay interested.

• Students can test and improve projects much faster than with other building systems.

12.1: *Satoru Hasegawa driving an Electric Moose car designed and built by his team of five eighth-grade boys. It has foot-operated bogie steering, belt drive and a toolbox behind the driver.*

- There's no need to document projects with time-consuming measurements and drawings. Even complex projects can be reassembled from photos.
- Most projects require only simple tools. A workshop and advanced building skills are not required.
- People with limited building experience can successfully teach classes.
- Projects disassemble, and the components store in a small space.
- Standard parts can be re-used, and shared between programs.

"The most important thing about grid beam is that you can build without fear," says Eileen Chang, who teaches industrial technology to middle school students (sixth to eighth grade). "Many of my students have never built before. If something mechanical doesn't work the first time, they'll just put it down rather than risk failure trying to fix it. With grid beam, they can change it until it works."

As you'll see below, grid beam is particularly useful for teaching topics that involve innovation.

Architecture and design

Each student in Ken Isaacs's 1970 beginning architectural class at the University of Illinois at Chicago built a 4-foot Study Cube (see page 41). The idea was to create a private, distraction-free study area for each student that allowed them to interact when they wanted to.

Ken's design featured a plywood skin with access and ventilation hatches. Seating, shelves and desk space were all made from movable 1 x 4-foot hardboard pallets stiffened by a pair of two-by-twos underneath. The pallets rode on grid beam rails inside the frame.

Alternative energy

Reinhold Ziegler used grid beam in the hands-on wind and solar energy classes he taught in California colleges from 1979 to 1987. Using 2-inch galvanized steel, students fabricated wind turbines and towers. "The system was an excellent tool for hands-on learning," Reinhold says. "Student design teams could build machines and change the design at will. We never needed to weld one part in seven years of classes.

"It soon occurred to a number of us — teachers, students and users — that this was the finest appropriate technology kit we had ever encountered. By standardizing our components, we could use and reuse a building element a thousand times. Gone were the days when a structure had to be destroyed because it was too much trouble to pull all the nails out. Here was re-use and recycling at its best: a building system that could be passed on to future generations!"

Industrial technology

Dr. Jack Martin teaches industrial technology in North Carolina. His classes at North Carolina Agricultural and Technical State University (A&T) used grid beam to introduce students to measuring, marking, drilling and basic shop skills. "Most of my students had never turned on a power tool before they took my class. Many didn't even know how to measure correctly." Jack had each student drill a wooden stick, then combine it with two other students' sticks to make a tri-joint. This quickly demonstrated the importance of standardization for creating interchangeable parts. Next, Jack's students used the sticks they drilled, plus sticks drilled by previous classes, to build projects. The prospect of building with their sticks keeps students engaged during the rather tedious drilling process. "We used the aluminum to introduce the kids to the CNC (computer controlled) machine. They learned how to set it up and use it, and we got really nice sticks with clean, deburred holes."

Over the years, Jack's classes drilled about 750 feet of wooden grid beam, plus smaller amounts of 1½-inch and 1-inch aluminum. "My dream kit for classroom teaching is to have 250 feet each of 1½-inch wood, 1½-inch aluminum, 1-inch aluminum, and 2-inch galvanized steel. This is about the right amount of sticks for a class doing prototyping."

Electric vehicles

Grid beam vehicles are one of the most exciting ways to introduce kids to technology, science and math. "Building real stuff motivates the kids with no interest in academic subjects," Eileen Chang says. While building a vehicle, teams of students learn how to work with tools, materials and each other.

In 1992, Phil donated 30 feet of 1½-inch aluminum tubing to Willits High School. Students drilled it to make grid beam, then built an Electrathon racer (page 102). "Grid beam allowed us to easily vary the vehicle's configuration during the design process," writes instructor Alan Kearney.

During the 1994–1995 school year, a group of 30 seventh- and eighth-grade students at San Lorenzo Valley High School in California designed and constructed an Electrathon-qualified street-legal vehicle (page 103). Co-instructor and experienced electric vehicle designer Michael Hackleman writes, "From the beginning, it was clear that most of the students lacked even basic material-working and tool-handling skills. Yet in the end, a car was built by students, and it worked!

"Our smartest move was using aluminum grid beam for designing and fabricating the chassis. Like Lego pieces, this permitted the constant shifting of components, support and suspension elements throughout the project. The vehicle was reconfigured about fifty times! At the end, only one component was welded. I'm certain we could have found a non-welded alternative, but we chose expediency over purity to get it done."

About 500 Silicon Valley seventh- and eighth-grade students have built grid beam electric go-karts. Industrial technology teacher Brad Booth's Electric Moose

Club at Jane Lathrop Stanford Middle School in Palo Alto has built with grid beam since 1995. Teams design and build vehicles framed with 1-inch aircraft aluminum or steel. "I have never seen so many kids so eager to be in class," says Wilma, who visited the class in 2007.

Inspired by the Moose Club, Eileen Chang ran a similar program at Castro Middle School in San Jose from 1995 to 2000. Many kids in that district come from troubled homes. Few plan on college, and interest in academic subjects is low. "I brought the electric cars down as an enticement — something real and hands-on to give the kids incentive to learn science and math." And it worked! One student's math skills advanced four grade levels due to his interest in electric cars.

To accommodate her school's small budget and shop, short class periods, and her students' limited building skills, Eileen developed a simple car design that students can assemble quickly (Figure 11.21). Tubes are 1-inch pre-punched steel fastened with $5/16$ -inch bolts. In 2001, Eileen moved her program to Terman Middle School in Palo Alto, where some student teams now design their own cars. She says, "Grid beam is great for teaching girls because they can build right away, and see the payoffs for building, without having to learn to use tools first."

Many members of the prestigious Gunn Robotics Team at Gunn High School come from these middle school programs. "The students from the electric car clubs aren't afraid to build or make mistakes," says instructor Bill Dunbar. "Students who have completed projects approach design problems completely differently. They know that it's important to just make something that works. You may start with a simple idea and make it complicated later, but the first thing to concentrate on is getting something that works."

The Electric Moose Club has proved potent for generating grant funding for schools. The classes involve science, math and industrial technology, and the results can be shown in photographs. Students write Brad's grant applications, illustrate them, and include photos of their projects. "Our grant doesn't look like anybody else's grant, so it's more likely to get funded."

Hands-on experience also helps kids leverage college applications. "A ton of kids have straight A grades," Brad says. "What can you say you've done that's different?" A number of electric car club students have gotten into top colleges such as Stanford and M.I.T.

Fairs and demonstrations

Grid beam is great for demonstrations at fairs and trade shows. Industrial technology teacher Jack Martin likes it for technology fairs. "We post photos of projects we've built, and have grid beam pieces lying around. We have people build a tri-joint. As soon as they build one, the light bulb goes on. Then we tell them, 'You've just built the most complicated part.'"

C.1

C.2

C.3

C.1: Ken Isaacs's Superchair, the first commercial grid beam product, has built-in shelves and a book holder, snack tray and overhead reading light. The seat back lowers to make a bed.

C.2: Ken Isaac's 1967 Microdorm fits a micro-office, dresser and sleeping loft into the floor area of a single bed. It was commercially produced in the late 1960s.

C.3: Rona Jergenson, age four, in a playhouse she built.

C.4: Rona Jergenson, age 12, in the Conversation Lounge she built in 2005. Corner posts support shelves for drinks and books.

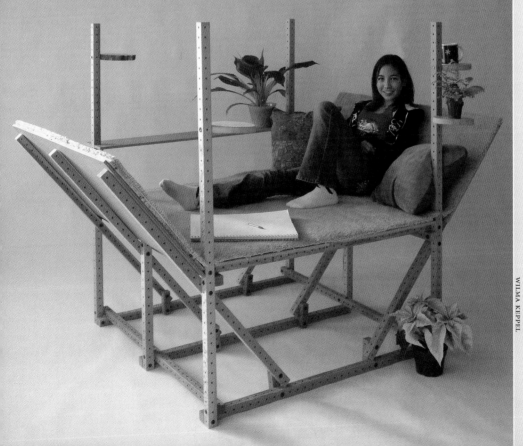

C.4

C.5: *The trade show booth we built with Michael Lightrain for SEER 1990 had canvas awnings on a galvanized steel frame 16 feet tall. Phil parked his grid beam Vanda solar micro-van in front.*

C.6: *Galvanized steel scaffold. Phil has built grid beam scaffolds as high as three stories.*

C.7 and C.8: *College students assemble a prefabricated solar cabin designed by Reinhold Ziegler. Framed of four-by-fours, it used stressed skin floor and wall panels. The building was trucked in for a college fair and assembled in one day.*

PHIL AND RICHARD JERGENSON

C.5

PHIL AND RICHARD JERGENSON

C.6

C.8

REINHOLD ZIEGLER

C.7

REINHOLD ZIEGLER

C.9

C.11

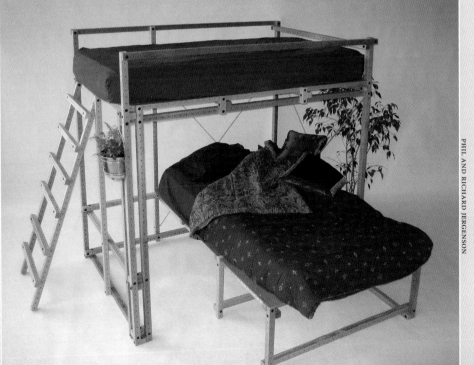

C.10

C.9: *Richard's mini-desk has a 2 x 2-foot desktop. Button Shelf (left) and half-moon shelf (top right) bolt on.*

C.10: *Slide-out shelf unit built around wooden boards 4 feet long. Wilma used these shelves for six years.*

C.11: *MATRIX loft by Reinhold Ziegler (seated, in blue).*

C.12: *Cross braces made of threaded rod plus a triple front post make a sturdy bunk bed. Space beneath bottom bunk fits commercial roll-out storage containers (not shown).*

C.12

C.13

C.14

C.15

C.13: *Wilma's 1997 free-standing closet also works as a closet organizer.*

C.14: *Richard's grid beam reproduction of Gerrit Rietveld's famous Red Blue Chair.*

C.15: *Screw-adjust feet at the top clamp Ken Isaacs's Storage Grid between floor and ceiling, so you can put it anywhere in the room. Our 6 x 8 foot version has tri-joint bottom feet.*

C.16: *Macintosh programmer Jean Tantra's Recliner Workstation got rid of most of his back problems by suspending a computer over a recliner chair. A wooden grid beam shelf at left holds Jean's track ball and external hard drives.*

C.16

WILMA KEPPEL

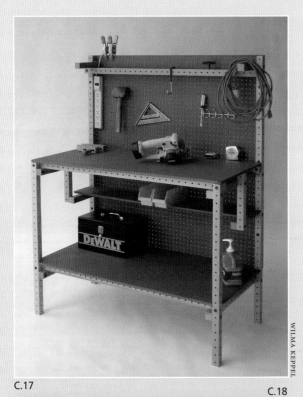

C.17

C.17: The wood-framed workbench that Phil assembled in Chapter 1. A power strip attached to the pegboard back runs tools.

C.18: Inventor Howard Letovsky testing the driving simulator prototype he built in a weekend

C.19: Richard built this wood-framed book booth for Bell Springs Publishers in 1996.

C.20: The commercial version of the driving simulator at a trade show. Patent rights and design owned by Howard Letovsky.

C.18

C.19

C.20

C.21: *Phil cuts firewood with an electric chain saw powered by the Solar Bear.*

C.22: *Phil's Solar Bear garden tractor is also a 24-volt portable power station, with solar panels on the dump bed roof.*

C.23: *George Buono drives his SPUV (Solar Powered Utility Vehicle) outside his off-grid workshop.*

C.24: *Alan Kearney (on bicycle) supervises a test drive of the Electrathon racer built by Willits High School students in 1992.*

C.25: *Phil's electric Scamp, used for trail riding on his steep rural property.*

PHIL AND RICHARD JERGENSON

C.21

PHIL AND RICHARD JERGENSON

C.22

PHIL AND RICHARD JERGENSON

C.23

C.24

C.25

PHIL AND RICHARD JERGENSON

ALAN KEARNEY

C.26

C.27

C.28

C.29

C.30

WILMA KEPPEL

JOHN JENSEN

PHIL AND RICHARD JERGENSON

WILMA KEPPEL

BOB LEFF

C.26: Travis Cottle racing a Moose car he and four other eighth-grade boys designed and built.

C.27: Phil in the X-Wing — his most fun-to-drive vehicle to date.

C.28: Built on the X-Wing chassis, the Vanda solar-electric micro-van is more visible in traffic.

C.29: Over 3,000 middle school children have driven this electric vehicle, built by seventh- and eighth-grade students in Brad Booth's Electric Moose Club. During parades and rallies, it charges Moose car batteries. Frame is 1½-inch aluminum. A tiller between the driver's legs (not shown) controls steering, power and brakes. Removing the tiller disables the motor.

C.30: Richard and the Sol Train arrive in Willits after coming over the mountains from Fort Bragg on the coast.

C.31: *Reinhold Ziegler with a portable aeroponics tower he designed as a demo. A solar panel powers the pump; tray at bottom collects the water for recirculation. Water trickles constantly through the tower, keeping plant roots moist.*

C.32: *HELIOS wind turbine by Reinhold Ziegler. Frame of four-by-four timbers stands 16 feet (5 meters) high, with rotors of clear Filon fiberglass. Screw-adjust feet level the six legs.*

C.33: *A student polishes the glass on Reinhold Ziegler's wood-framed solar concentrator.*

C.34: *Richard harvests fire-wood using wood-framed garden cart. Plastic tubs hold tools and cargo; plywood top provides a flat place to service the chain saw in the woods.*

PHIL AND RICHARD JERGENSON

C.31

PHIL AND RICHARD JERGENSON

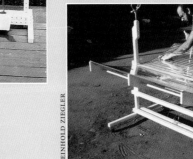

REINHOLD ZIEGLER

C.32

REINHOLD ZIEGLER

C.33

PHIL AND RICHARD JERGENSON

C.34

Jack recommends using students to staff booths. "People hesitate to ask me questions, because I'm an adult. But they'll ask our college kids *anything*."

In 1998, Phil built energy cycles for the Tehachapi Wind Fair in northern California with help from Michael Hackleman and John Schrader. Stationary bikes with grid beam frames powered banks of 25-watt lights. A set of switches let fairgoers control how many watts they powered, so they could feel the load.

Innovation and product development

Want to improve an existing idea? Test a new one? Figure out how something works?

12.2: *Energy cycle at the Tehachapi Wind Fair lets people feel how much power it takes to light one to eight 25-watt light bulbs.*

RICHARD JERGENSON

Fast prototyping

According to technology expert Michael Schrage, "Effective prototyping may be the most valuable 'core competence' an innovative organization can hope to have." He points to rapid-prototyping champions such as 3M, Hewlett-Packard and Sony. While competing companies take months to implement prototypes, Sony's average time from idea to prototype is five *days*.

Instead of trying to get the whole project right the first time, the trick is to use simple tests to gather real data about *aspects* of your project or design as quickly as possible, then improve from there. Business guru Tom Peters provides the following basic steps for successful fast prototyping in his book *The Circle of Innovation*:

• Define a small, practical test in a page or less of text — right now.

• Gather inexpensive "found" materials.

• Find a partner/customer who can provide a test site and act as a sounding board.

• Set a tight deadline of about five days for the next practical step.

• Conduct the test within your five-day deadline.

• Debrief and record the results in a (paper or electronic) notebook.

• Set the next test date, approximately five days ahead.

Using this method, "virtually anything ... can be tested in the real world, for an astonishingly small amount of money."

Check a design for problems, or determine how its elements will combine?

Prototyping is the process of creating a working model (a prototype) of part or all of a project in order to test it. Done well, you get answers fast for minimum cost.

When *not* to use grid beam

"Not every project is suitable for prototyping in grid beam," notes designer Michael Hackleman. "With grid beam you're dealing with right angles all the time, and that's not always what you need. Also, some prototypes are too complex, or require angles or continuous adjustment. It's better to prototype those in another system, and use grid beam for what it's good for." Due to the limited strength of the parts, grid beam is also unsuitable for extremely high-strength applications.

Grid beam is the best prototyping system we've ever seen, used or heard of. Since everything bolts together, you can reconfigure a project dozens or hundreds of times as you experiment. Standard-sized pieces can be recycled as many times as you want. Even if you build the final product with conventional materials, grid beam lets you quickly work out the basic dimensions and make sure the project will work before you cut, glue or weld.

Driving simulator

Professional inventor Howard Letovsky does much of his prototyping with $500 of aluminum grid beam that he bought from us in 1997. "I use grid beam to determine spatial relationships in a project.

12.3a: *Howard Letovsky built this driving simulator prototype in a weekend. The steering wheel rotates the drive wheel in the opposite direction to simulate G-forces.*

HOWARD LETOVSKY

12.3c: *This version adds a sturdy front bearing and belt drive, plus an auto seat, plywood rear panels and a plastic front body from a video game.*

12.3b: *Front end pivots on a steel lazy Susan. Socket wrench parts and hose clamps link the steering wheel to the gearbox.*

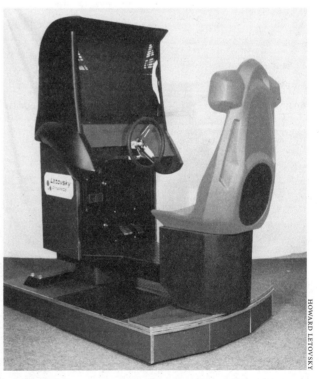

12.3d: *The first welded version.*

12.3e: *The finished product. Patent rights and design owned by Howard Letovsky.*

Then I bolt in wheels, gears, seats and so forth. I have a large stock of components I reuse for prototyping different projects." These include a variety of commercial driving and flight simulators.

"My grid beam versions never last more than about a day. Many are grid beam for only half an hour — just long enough to prove the concept and generate the shape relationships." He prefers to build final project versions out of welded aluminum or steel.

He built the basic prototype for his pivoting driving simulator in a weekend, using a grid beam frame and bolting on components from his collection. Turning the steering wheel on this patented system rotates the back wheel in the opposite direction, providing a realistic feeling of cornering.

The drive system on the prototype consisted of a go-kart steering wheel assembly,

a universal joint made of socket wrench extensions and joints, a gearbox, a drive shaft, and a go-kart wheel. The front end of the first version pivoted on an ordinary metal lazy Susan — not strong enough for commercial use, but adequate to test the design. Commercial versions use a welded frame with heavy-duty bearings, and a belt drive from the steering wheel to the axle.

Pelton water wheel prototype

Designer Michael Hackleman also uses grid beam to establish the spatial relationships of a project and its components.

12.4a-b: *Pelton water wheel prototype and underside of the final version.*

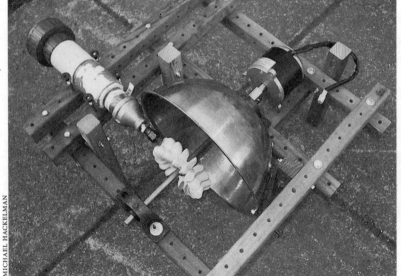

Pelton wheel tech

The installation site for this unit has a head (elevation drop) of 100 feet (30 meters), and can supply up to 20 gallons per minute when the stream flows during and after storms. The turbine eliminated the need to use a standby generator except during worst-case conditions.

With a 5/16-inch jet installed, the turbine produced 150 watts (10 amperes at 15 volts). With a 3/8-inch jet, it produced 200 watts, using about 20 gallons per minute of water. Using the smallest jet, which produced 45 watts, the unit worked in flows as small as 8 gallons per minute — a pleasant surprise.

"Drawings are very two-dimensional. A mock-up or test bed with grid beam lets you deal with the subject matter in three dimensions, and that's critical. You can detect interfering parts right away. Without any drilling or materials modification, you can very quickly get a pretty good idea of where things are in relationship to each other. Since you have numbers for those relations, you can quickly translate your design into other materials."

In the spring of 2006, Michael used grid beam to prototype a Pelton water wheel installation that generates winter electricity for a rural homestead outside Willits. One of the most efficient types of water turbines, Pelton wheels are driven by jets of pressurized water. This makes them suitable for streams with small flow and large changes in elevation. The stream where this unit was installed does not run season-long, but does flow for a week after rainstorms. It supplies power during cloudy weather when the owner's solar panels generate the least electricity.

Michael's design featured a housing fabricated from two stainless steel salad bowls. Fittings on the drive shaft flung off water before it could creep out of the housing. The generator sat close to the wheel yet stayed dry, making a compact installation.

Michael's wooden prototype allowed him to experiment with design variations, and make sure that the final version would be easy to assemble, adjust and maintain. It provided precise measurements for the final version's frame, fabricated from angle iron salvaged from old bed frames and bolted together. The grid beam frame was also used to position the final unit over the existing concrete and drill holes for anchor bolts.

"Once installed, the unit ran for 36 hours straight to fill a large, depleted battery pack," Michael reports. "Everything worked perfectly. The owner was ecstatic."

Prototyping your prototypes

We sometimes prototype aluminum grid beam projects in wood. Wood lets us establish the spatial relationships and most of the part sizes before we cut any expensive aluminum. We built several wooden versions of our Rail Rocket (Figure 21.3) before constructing an aluminum frame.

Related projects

As you've seen in other chapters, grid beam has been used to develop a wide variety of innovative projects, especially renewable energy (page 73), vehicles (page 89), and Living Structures (page 40).

Other Projects

Grid beam has been used to build a wide variety of projects that defy categorization. These range from very elaborate to quickly built "McProjects" that fill a temporary need or save a trip to the store.

Grid beam is handy for many uses around the home, workshop, yard, and garden. It is great when you need something temporarily, or need it right now, without a trip to the store. Sometimes when the tool or gadget you need is too expensive to buy or impossible to rent, you can use materials you have on hand (plus maybe a few parts from the hardware store) to build an adequate substitute.

Animal cages

Phil and his daughter Rona used wooden grid beam to frame a bottomless 4 x 8-foot rabbit cage covered with chicken wire so their rabbits could eat grass. It worked well, except that the rabbits kept digging

13.1: *Tom Blinks built this gadget to pry apart stuck 5-gallon buckets. The bolt heads at right fit between the bucket flanges.*

13.2: *Cable turntable by Tom Blinks unrolls wire, cable or hose without twists or damaging kinks.*

121

out. They didn't add wire to the bottom of the cage because it would have flattened the grass. (Commercial cages use large-mesh wire on the bottom.)

Chair arms

Our only available office chair lacked arms, so Chris Koveleski added grid beam arms in 1998. A pair of bolts dropped through the frame holes into the back support, plus a loop of string, anchored the rear support. A lag screw attached each arm to the chair's plastic bottom. The two-hole grid beam kept the arm support from pivoting forward. Although they had no tri-joints, these chair arms were rigid, sturdy and so comfortable we kept them in daily use in our business office for over three years.

Clotheslines and laundry drying racks

If it's too rainy to dry clothes outdoors, use a grid beam clothesline. Where you want a string, slide a bolt through the frame, then wind the string around the shaft just under the head.

13.4: *Wooden chair arms by Chris Koveleski.*

13.5: *It took Wilma about 15 minutes to assemble this folding laundry rack. The most important part is the diagonal brace, which keeps the frame square.*

13.6: *This indoor clothesline, which doesn't fold, can hang long dresses and trousers.*

13.7: *Sweater drying rack Wilma made from a bed sheet rolled around sticks. An outdoor version with legs has a sheet on top to protect sweaters from sun, dirt and cat footprints.*

Desk organizer

Wendi Fetzer used wooden grid beam to make an H-shaped organizer that holds books on her desk.

Disability aids

Need a bathroom railing until a friend's broken foot gets better? What about a wheelchair ramp for an aging relative? Grid beam adapts quickly and easily as people's needs change. It's also the most accessible building system we know. Blind builders can measure by counting holes.

Easel

Three sticks connected by a long bolt make a simple tripod that folds for moving. Bend the bolt into an arc so that the

13.8: *Easel legs flare thanks to a curved bolt at the top.*

WILMA KEPPEL

tripod's legs can flare. Add a crosspiece to make an instant easel. Design by Phil.

Exercise desks

An exercise desk combines a computer workstation with a treadmill or exercise bike so you can exercise while you work. The latest trend in exercise, these desks are helping thousands of desk workers get fit and lose weight. Even light exercise such as slow walking burns an extra 100 calories per hour. Sustained low-intensity exercise increases your metabolic rate so you burn more calories while you're not exercising. We've heard numerous reports of people shedding 10 to 16 pounds per month using exercise desks just 2 or 3 hours per day while they web surf, check e-mail or do computer gaming.

Wilma uses two exercise desks, one treadmill and one bike. "I can finally get plenty of exercise no matter how busy my work schedule — and exercise no longer cuts into my free time. I use my bike desk for phone calls and watching movies, and my treadmill desk for writing, web surfing and e-mail. I only notice that I'm exercising for the first few minutes, then I get completely absorbed in what I'm doing. Exercising two to four hours per day, I feel fantastic and sleep great. In the first month, my waist size decreased two inches with no dieting!"

Rather than buying a dedicated exercise desk, you can use grid beam to add a desk to a existing treadmill or exercise bike. Most exercise equipment doesn't get used, so quality models are often available used for $200 or less. Check craigslist.org online, and your local newspaper or bargain paper want ads.

To keep your joints healthy during workouts, keep your workout at low intensity. This makes it easy to type, dictate, mouse and use the phone, and keeps you feeling alert even if your workout goes on for a long time. Many people prefer to treadmill at 0.7 miles per hour (1 kilometer per hour); Wilma prefers double that speed.

Make sure the treadmill you get can run at low speed for long periods of time without overheating. At low speeds it should remain quiet and run smoothly, not get loud and jerky. Use a recumbent exercise bike, which has a seat like a chair. Get a model that has a low console, and make sure the seat is comfortable. The best type uses magnetic resistance rather than a friction belt. For photos and tips, visit exercise-desk.com.

Fences

Phil's house sits on a windy ridge. Built in 1998, his steel-framed yard fence has some fiberglass panels to give garden plants next to the fence more light. Two right-angle bends help brace the fence.

Float switch

Tom Blinks's homemade switch turned on a pump when the water tank supplying his house was almost empty, then turned the pump off when the tank got full. An inexpensive toilet-tank float assembly activated a heavy-duty wall switch that wouldn't burn out from the pump load. Tom had most of the materials on hand, and the rest cost just a few dollars. At the time, commercial level switches cost around $70.

13.9: *Phil's steel-framed yard fence has a mix of corrugated steel and fiberglass panels.*

13.10: *Homemade float switch by Tom Blinks.*

WILMA KEPPEL

13.11: *Potting bench by Tom Blinks.*

Growing equipment

Grid beam is very useful for the short-term needs common when growing plants. Built in under an hour when he needed to transplant a batch of seedlings, Tom Blinks's steel-framed potting bench was supported at one end by a metal porch railing. The top was a piece of plywood, an old sink, and a wire refrigerator shelf. The bench proved so handy for potting plants, feeding cats out of the dog's reach, holding bags of groceries while unlocking the door, drying buckets, and a host of other uses that it remained in place for over a year. A classic McProject: ugly, but functional.

Tom and Wilma's cats liked to sunbathe on their seed flats, crushing the seedlings. Wilma protected the plants with a tent of ½-inch hardware cloth (galvanized wire mesh) on a galvanized steel frame. Attached only at the top, the wire sides flipped up for removing the flats in case of heavy rain.

Aeroponics grow tower

Aeroponics is a way of growing plants with their roots in air, bathed in a trickle of nutrient solution. No growing medium is used. Roots find their ideal balance of oxygen and water, so plants grow faster than those grown hydroponically or in soil, and require far less water. The containers are light-weight, easy to move, and ideal for vertical growing.

Reinhold Ziegler developed a full-scale Vertical Aeroponics (VAP) growing system for commercial greenhouses. "Clients always said, 'Can I *see* one?', so I built a portable demo unit," shown in Figure C 31. A frame of painted wooden grid beam held fiberglass rods that suspended plastic growing containers. A small pump powered by a solar panel pumped water to the top. A hole in the bottom of each growing container trickled water into the container below.

Indoor grow rack

While living in Iowa in 1996, Tom Blinks built a wood-framed grow rack with five shelves, which held up to 1,250 seedlings in 2-inch soil blocks. The blocks sat on coated hardboard panels inside plastic seed flats with no drain holes.

Knowing that the frame would get wet, Tom built it from the cheapest fir he could find, using a grid beam stick as a drill guide. Rather than using standard stick lengths, he sized the sticks to fit his light fixtures and 10¾ x 21¼-inch seed flats. Two fluorescent light fixtures, each holding two bulbs, lit each shelf. One cool white plus one warm white tube in each fixture made an inexpensive substitute for grow lamps. The lights hung on chains for easy height adjustment as the plants grew. A heavy-duty timer turned all lights on and off.

To protect the lights from water, Tom and Wilma mist-watered the flats in an old sink held in a frame of galvanized double-hole. A bucket under the sink drain caught drips. During harvest season they used the sink outdoors with a hose.

Tom's design maximized air circulation to prevent plant diseases. Each flat sat on a separate scrap of wood, with air gaps between. (An even better solution is shelves of galvanized welded wire mesh.) An oscillating fan blew air over the seedlings 24 hours per day to prevent fungus and encourage sturdy stems. The center shelf was a solid plywood panel with greenhouse heating wire stapled to the top for starting seeds.

"I grew 1,800 seedlings in this rack one spring," Wilma says. "Because of the good air circulation we had no problems with damping off, and everything grew like crazy under the lights. Soil blocks and mist watering are a very easy-care combination, and Tom's grid beam rack made it happen."

Laboratory and scientific equipment

We think grid beam will prove ideal for building scientific equipment and laboratory setups. Use Quik-Punch tubes if

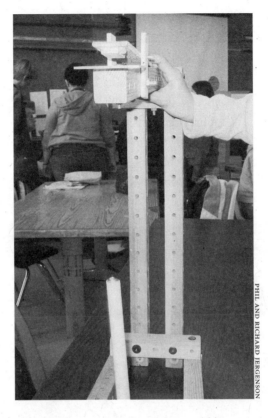

PHIL AND RICHARD JERGENSON

13.12: *Rona Jergenson's reflex tester measures how fast test subjects can grab a dropped dowel.*

getting debris inside the sticks would be a problem, and knock out only the holes you need to use. Powder coat all metal to protect it from moisture and corrosives.

Rona Jergenson's 2006 science fair project measured and compared reflex speed in 12- and 13-year-old girls and boys. To measure reflexes without high-speed equipment, you need a way to measure the *effects* of the reflex. Rona's tester dropped a wooden dowel marked every half inch. The subject's aim was to grab the dowel as quickly as possible once it started to move.

To get an identical drop every time, Rona and Phil built a wooden stand that suspended the dowel using a magnet. A steel washer screwed to the end of the dowel rested against the bottom of a piece of acrylic plastic. Depressing a lever moved the magnet away from the top of the plastic, dropping the dowel.

Rona's testing showed that boys respond significantly faster than girls. A winner at the school and county levels, her project went to the California state science fair finals.

13.13: Tom Blinks uses 2-inch steel grid beam and a pair of jacks to lift a propane tank.

WILMA KEPPEL

WILMA KEPPEL

13.14: Wilma's steel-framed lightning rod puller.

Lifting equipment

Grid beam is useful for a wide variety of lifting jobs. The owner of Earthlab Energy Systems in Willits used a vertical gin pole made of 2-inch galvanized steel to raise a metal fireplace chimney so he could lower it through the roof into a building. "It took two hours to set up and five minutes to use it."

While repairing a well, engineer Tom Blinks used a telescoping bar of steel grid beam to lift sections of concrete culvert. A short section of 1-inch pipe screwed into holes cast into each side of the culvert. Tom extended the lifting bar so its ends fit around both pipes, then locked it with a bolt.

Once he had installed the culvert sections as the new well casing, Tom used 2-inch steel grid beam to suspend a hand-cranked winch over the well so he could raise and lower its new pump assembly. Vertical legs on the winch mount fit on each side of the well casing, allowing Tom to position the winch anyplace on the rim.

In 1998, Tom built a lift frame to raise a large propane tank so he could replace a leaking gas line. All the grid beam was straight sections salvaged from bent road sign posts, except the bent top bar. Tom figured its arch would resist sagging, and if it bent he wouldn't have wrecked a good stick. Farm jacks hooked over the lift frame's top bar raised chains attached to the tank's lifting eyes.

Tom's first design was inadequately braced and racked when loaded. Once he diagonally braced *all* its corners, the frame easily lifted and lowered the 800-pound tank.

A friend of Wilma's needed a lightning rod pulled out of dry, hard ground next to his rural house. A big, strong man couldn't budge the rod by yanking on it. "I built this little jack from four pieces of steel grid beam, four bolts, and a piece of rope tied in half-hitches around the lightning rod. It took maybe 15 minutes to build, use and disassemble."

Moving

Wilma used to move frequently, and grid beam made it easy. "I disassembled my furniture, moved the pieces, then reassembled them or built new designs. I could move grid beam anywhere — up narrow stairs, around corners — and always knew my furniture would fit in my new home. I had great fun customizing my desk to fit each room and its natural lighting."

Grid beam is handy for a thousand and one moving tasks: ramps, racks, shelves, steps, hand trucks (dollies), etc. If you have sticks around, you'll find ways to use them.

Model railroad benchwork

Commercial model railroad benchwork is expensive. Home-built layouts are often hard to change. We like the flexibility of grid beam benchwork, such as the G-scale model of the Sol Train that Richard built for SEER '90. To keep wires under the layout tidy and out of the way, thread them through the frame holes or attach them to the frame using plastic wire ties.

Photographic equipment

A camera tripod or monopod makes it easier to get sharp pictures, especially in low light. Wilma took some of the photos

13.15: *Ramps of wooden two-by-sixes lock into a frame of 1-inch steel. Designed and built by middle school students in Palo Alto, this platform stores the double-ended electric vehicle shown in Figure C.29, with storage space beneath.*

13.16: *Wilma snaps a picture using her grid beam monopod.*

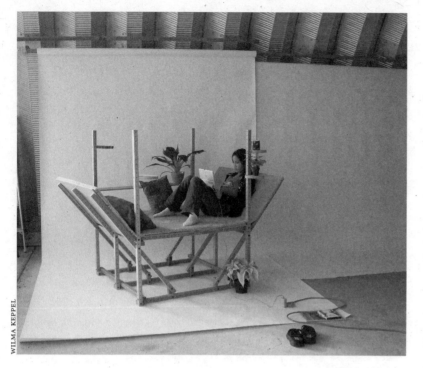

WILMA KEPPEL

13.17: Photo paper backdrop in our Willits workshop.

paper (Figure 8.6). Two more sticks lag bolted to the ceiling beams supported lights. We made diffusers and reflectors by stretching white Lycra over grid beam frames.

In 2006 we turned our Willits workshop into a temporary studio. It's a Quonset-style building with curved side walls made of bolted steel sections. We used coupling nuts to attach hex bolts to bolt ends projecting inside the building. We mounted 10-foot sticks on the hex bolts, then used wire to suspend the sticks that held the paper rolls.

Projection screen

Dr. Jack Martin wanted a slide projector screen that would be easy to store and transport, wouldn't look worth stealing, and would discourage theft of the projector. He prefers rear-projection screens because audience members can't bump the projector or cast shadows on the screen, and lights don't shine in the presenter's face.

Jack's setup used a 1 x 1 x 5-foot plywood box on the floor. The projector sat inside where the audience couldn't see it, facing the rear wall. The screen was an "opaque white" (actually semitransparent) plastic shower curtain from the grocery store, hung on a frame of 5-foot grid beams bolted to the box. A 10 x 12-inch eyebrow-plucking mirror held 5 feet behind the box by strings bounced the picture onto the back of the screen. For storage, everything except the projector fit inside the box.

in this book using a monopod built from a Button Shelf (a round wooden shelf held by one bolt) on a 6-foot stick. "I found that a Button Shelf works better than a fixed crossbar because you can rotate it as you point the camera."

To get clean backgrounds for some of the photos in this book, we used photo paper. The paper comes in rolls 9 feet wide. Hang one or more rolls high on a wall, unroll the paper to shoot, then re-roll to get it out of the way. When the paper gets dirty, cut it off and unroll some more.

In 1994 and 1995 we turned Richard's living room into a photo studio. To make a hard floor under the paper, we screwed plywood panels over his carpet. Grid beam brackets lag bolted to two walls supported 10-foot sticks holding our photo

Recliner Workstation™

By suspending a flat-screen computer over a recliner (Figure C.16), Macintosh programmer Jean Tantra eliminated most of his back problems and minimized repetitive stress. The C-shaped frame of 2-inch galvanized steel double-hole supported a post that held the computer on an arm designed for wall mounting. A locking pin in the two-part post allowed instant height adjustments at 1-inch increments. A round USB/FireWire hub with a hole in the middle bolted to the post. Hooks designed for ¼-inch pegboard plugged right into the frame holes to hang cables. The feet were bolts tipped with rubber ends.

Jean liked his creation so much that he added a second post and computer on the other side of the chair. See additional photos at recliner-workstation.com.

Signs

Dr. Martin devised a simple roadside sign for his church. The 4 x 4-foot plywood board was supported on 6-foot uprights, with feet 4 feet long. "The wooden sticks were very soft wood, so I diagonally braced them with string. The sign could be assembled and disassembled in minutes. It was also tough. A wind storm blew it over, but it stayed put and did not become airborne."

Content for the sign went on two 4 x 4-foot paper panels. Once joined at the top, they hung over the plywood to cover each side. A 4 x 8-foot sheet of plastic draped over the paper provided weather

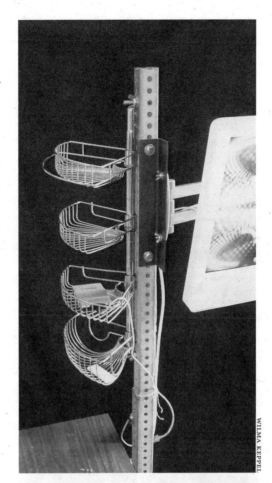

13.18: *A simple angle iron adapter mounts a computer wall mount arm on the Recliner Workstation II. A wire rack held by wing nuts holds peripherals.*

13.19: *Model of a 4 x 5 foot roadside sign. Diagonally brace the legs with string or wire.*

protection. More grid beam held it in place.

This design worked well. The paper signs were inexpensive, could be re-used, and required minimal storage space. Jack later adapted his design into a bulletin board, chalkboard, marker board and rear projection screen.

13.20: *Toy car by Richard.*

WILMA KEPPEL

Toys

Kids love grid beam. Very young children can use the smaller sticks as blocks. Soon they'll start building their own toys and play structures. Isn't a life-size Erector Set every kid's dream? Grid beam can truly grow with your child.

Avoid giving small hardware such as hex nuts to young children who might swallow the pieces. Remember that if *your* kids are having fun, younger children may join them. Once kids reach a hardware-safe age, we recommend joint connector bolts and weld nuts tightened with T-handled Allen wrenches. These wrenches are easy to hold, and easy to find when dropped. If you don't have access to joint connector bolts, use carriage bolts, which have square shoulders that bite into wood to keep them from turning, or hex bolts and washers. Fasten them with wing nuts, which kids can hand-tighten without tools.

Grid beam playhouses are quick to assemble and can grow with your child. All but the youngest children can assemble simple play structures.

For structures kids will be climbing on, make sure the design is safe, and check all joints to make sure they are tight. Unlike most building toys, grid beam can make projects big enough to climb onto, drive or jump from. Think of grid beam as equivalent to letting your kids build a tree house, and supervise accordingly.

13.21: *Elijah Mosher on stilts Richard made by bolting foot rests made of two-by-four to grid beam sticks.*

WILMA KEPPEL

Dr. Jack Martin used a length of 1½-inch wooden grid beam as the frame for a radio-controlled grid beam submarine! The buoyancy of the stick just balanced the weight of the other components. The holes allowed him to adjust the position of the motor and control surfaces to get the balance and steering just right.

With grid beam, you can easily make your own tools and time-saving gadgets. It's like having a hardware store and welding shop right next door!

More McProjects

- Temporary kitchen, Figure 20.2.
- One-hour stair rail, page 64.

13.22: *Maraya Buono with the teeter-totter her father George built. An aluminum frame supports wooden seat rails. The pivot point adjusts to accommodate users of different weights.*

13.23: *Rona Jergenson, age four, in a grid beam playhouse she built.*

PHIL AND RICHARD JERGENSON

PHIL AND RICHARD JERGENSON

Part 3

Working with Grid Beam

WHAT WOULD GRANDPA HAVE DONE?

Basic Components

In this chapter we discuss basic components — sticks, panels and hardware. These are the standard interchangeable parts of the grid beam system. You'll learn how to buy and cut panels and sticks, how to drill panel mounting holes, and where to buy the hardware you want. The next chapter discusses non-standard components and how to adapt them to grid beam.

The easiest way to build with grid beam is to start with a kit. Components are pre-selected. All you have to do is put them together.

That said, the whole point of grid beam is that you get what *you* want. If what you want isn't sold in kit form, you'll need components to build it.

Buying components locally has many advantages. Reduced shipping helps the environment. Prices are often lower. Buying from locally-owned businesses keeps money in your local economy,

where it continues to benefit you. You get to inspect conditions and policies where you do business. If you don't like how a supplier operates, vote with your wallet and take your business elsewhere.

Buying grid beam sticks

As we write this, pre-made wooden, aluminum and steel grid beam is available in a limited number of US sizes. (Check our websites for updates.) You'll find supplier contact information — plus sources for grid beam kits, sticks and a wide variety of useful components — in the Suppliers chapter starting on page 245.

Wooden sticks

Wooden QuikStix brand grid beam measures 1½-inches square, with holes every 1½-inches. Holes ⁵⁄₁₆ inch in diameter fit ¼-inch bolts. Weight varies from ½ to 1 pound (0.22 to 0.45 kilogram) per foot. Buy from QuikStix.

Aluminum sticks

80/20 Inc. makes 1½-inch square tubing with ⅛-inch wall thickness and holes every 1½ inches. Called "HT Series Framing," it is made of alloy number 6105-T5, which is similar in strength to the 6061-T6 Phil used to hand-drill for his vehicles. Holes ²¹/₆₄ inch in diameter fit ⁵/₁₆-inch grade 8 bolts. Tubes are available in lengths of 97 inches and 145 inches. Flanged tubes are also available. Fittings made to work with these tubes include brackets, casters, feet, leveling legs, hinges and flanged bolts and nuts that need no washers when used on stationary projects.

Buy these tubes from 80/20 Inc., or through industrial suppliers. McMaster-Carr sells some of the brackets and accessories, plus tubes in 4, 6 and 8 foot lengths.

Steel sticks

Square steel tubes with holes punched every inch on all four sides are made in several types and finishes. Most are manufactured for the US traffic sign industry, and have ⁷/₁₆-inch holes which accommodate both ⁷/₁₆-inch and ³/₈-inch bolts. Widths range from 1 inch to 2½ inches. Because of the 1-inch hole spacing, **only the 1-inch and 2-inch tubes make tri-joints.**

Traffic sign support tubes with 12-gauge (0.105 inch) or 14-gauge (0.083 inch walls nest inside each other — just use a tube ¼ inch larger or smaller (Figure 1.5). Use 1¾-inch sticks for internal splices, 2¼-inch sleeves for building legs. The brands are interchangeable. We use 12-gauge tubes that nest snugly; the 14-gauge tubes have thinner, weaker walls and wiggle more. Tubes with 10-gauge (0.135 inch) walls are too thick to nest.

Traffic sign post manufacturers make 20- and 24-foot tubes. These are cut ¼ inch to 1 inch or more over-length — a good thing, since they are cut by length, not hole placement. At least one supplier (Northwest Pipe) also stocks 8, 10, 12, 14 and 16 foot tubes. Since they are not cut on a hole, they may end up short after correcting the end cuts. We recommend buying the longest tubes you can, and cutting them to length yourself.

Bare steel tubes must be painted to prevent rust. Factory-painted tubes are fairly easy to scratch, and start to rust after a few years outdoors. We strongly recommend buying galvanized tubes. For just a few cents more per foot, you get a beam that is impervious to dings, scratches and weather, and will last 40-plus years outdoors. For even more protection, powder coat on top of the galvanized finish.

Types of steel grid beam:

S-Square sign support posts with 12-gauge walls are made in five nesting sizes measuring 1½, 1¾, 2, 2¼ and 2½ inches. A few sizes are also available with 14-gauge walls. This manufacturer ships small orders virtually anywhere in North America. Buy from S-Square Tube Products.

POZ-LOC Performance Posts are made in the same nesting sizes as S-Square. Most sizes are available with 12- or 14-gauge walls. These sign support posts are sold in plain galvanized steel, or with an additional powder coat layer available in several colors. Buy from Northwest Pipe Company.

Telespar sign support posts with 12-gauge walls are made in the same nesting sizes as S-Square and POZ-LOC. A few sizes are also available with 10-gauge or 14-gauge walls. Buy through Allied Tube and Conduit's Telespar Division, or order from Unistrut. McMaster-Carr sells lengths up to 12 feet.

Ulti-Mate sign support posts with 12-gauge walls are made in the same nesting sizes as S-Square, POZ-LOC and Telespar. A few sizes are also made with 14-gauge walls. This tube's galvanized coating is extra-thick. Buy from Ultimate Highway Products.

Square-Fit tubes identical to Telespar are made in seven sizes — the five listed above, plus 1 inch and 1¼ inch (31.7 millimeter) — and two wall thicknesses, 12 and 10 gauge. Hole diameter is $7/16$ inch except for the 1-inch and 1¼-inch tubes, which have $1/32$-inch holes that fit $5/16$-inch bolts. Buy through Allied Tube and Conduit's Mechanical Tube Division.

Qwik-Punch resembles the tubes above, but has knockouts rather than holes. Remove the knockout with a punch wherever you want to put a bolt. Use Qwik-Punch where dirt or chip buildup inside the tubes would be a problem. It has 14-gauge walls and comes in two sizes,

1¾ inch and 2 inch. Buy through Allied Tube and Conduit's Telespar Division.

McMaster-Carr sells pre-punched steel tubes 6 feet long with holes every 1 inch. The electroplated zinc finish is prettier but less durable than the galvanized finish used on sign posts. The 1-inch and 2-inch sizes work as grid beam. The 2-inch size has $7/16$-inch diameter holes, and 12- or 14-gauge walls. The 1-inch size has $1/32$-inch diameter holes that fit $5/16$-inch bolts, and walls 0.079 inch or 0.109 inch thick. The part number on the thinner tube, which is used by middle school electric car clubs, is 6535K21.

Avoid Telestrut, a $1^7/8$-inch tube with holes every $1^7/8$ inch made by Allied. It makes tri-joints, but the odd size requires tremendous waste when you cut materials. Few components bolt to this hole spacing. And where will you find $5/16$ inch tubing for half-size sticks?

Dealers from each of Allied's divisions can order products from other divisions. Since shipping is a major cost when ordering steel tube, find the Telespar, Square-Fit and Unistrut dealers nearest to you, and price your order through the closest one. Then compare to the other manufacturers. Local dealers may discount short pieces left over from cutting other orders if you ask.

By the time you read this, other commercial grid beam products and sizes may be available. Remember, any potential grid beam stick must make tri-joints. That requires one hole every one stick width.

We discuss recommended stick widths and materials in the "Homemade Sticks" chapter. If no one manufactures a particular stick size or material you want, consider drilling your own.

Cutting sticks

Cutting sticks is straightforward, and involves:

1. Measuring
2. Marking
3. Cutting
4. Smoothing the cut edges

Measuring and marking

When cutting sticks for a specific project, have a clear idea of what you want to build before you begin. It helps to cut the longest pieces first.

Plan your cuts. Standard grid beam gets cut *between* the holes. Double-hole grid beam gets cut *on* a hole. Double-check by measuring the total length of the stick.

To measure accurately, you must use accurate tools. Most of the inaccuracies in tape measures and rulers are at the ends, which get worn or bent. Make sure the

Basic shop safety

1. **Wear eye protection while using power tools** or doing anything that can fling chips, fragments or dust. If you wear glasses, add side protectors, goggles or a face shield to keep chips and sawdust from getting past the sides of the lenses and into your eye area.

2. **Wear ear protection** when using loud tools.

3. **Keep loose clothing, long hair and dangling jewelry out of the shop and away from power tools.** Power tool shafts turn very quickly, and will yank anything that gets caught into the machine in a fraction of a second. Even one strand of hair caught in a machine will quickly pull in other loose hairs. Braid or tie back long hair and tuck it into your shirt, or pin it up tightly. Make sure it cannot work loose. Remove ties and dangling necklaces, and roll up or remove loose sleeves.

4. **Run drill presses bare-handed.** Anything that could snag on turning parts — including rings, watches and gloves — is a risk.

5. Do wear gloves when welding, grinding or using a chop saw — these operations throw hot sparks.

6. Wear shoes or boots, and other protective clothing as appropriate.

7. Keep power cords out of the way, where no one will cut or trip over them.

8. Know how to use tools safely. If necessary, get someone experienced to show you.

9. Before using power tools, check your setup. Are the tool and its guards adjusted appropriately? Are you wearing the right safety gear (such as goggles)? Make sure the tool can complete its entire operation (drilling a hole, making a cut) without running into anything, running out of power cord, or cutting anything it shouldn't. If a machine has clamps and guards, use them.

10. Unplug power tools or remove their batteries before changing or working on their blades.

11. Always keep your hands and body away from the blades and moving parts of any tool.

end of your measuring device is accurate, or use the 1-inch, 2-inch or 1½-inch mark (or the appropriate metric mark) as zero, and count from there. This is easiest if you fasten your tape measure to the stick with masking tape (Figure 16.2).

The traditional shop rule is **"Measure twice, cut once."** Measuring six times isn't too many if it saves you from making a costly mistake.

Avoid errors by writing down any number you have to remember for more than a few seconds. We often write on the material itself. A light pencil mark will erase off most surfaces. Bare steel is dark, so mark it with a silver pencil which you can buy from welding supply shops or art stores.

Mark your cut with a fine, accurate line. Make sure the mark is placed correctly, then use a square to extend it across the stick. When cutting a stick into several lengths, save time and make all the marks at once.

A saw blade cuts a slot slightly wider than itself, called the *kerf*. Don't try to compensate for kerf by cutting your sticks the exact "right" length. This could leave you short of material for the last piece. Instead, mark each cut as if kerf didn't exist, then cut down the middle of the mark.

Cutting

Tools are as accurate as you make them. Practice on scraps until you can make square, accurate cuts.

Use every bit of good beam. Even very short pieces are useful. A two-hole section

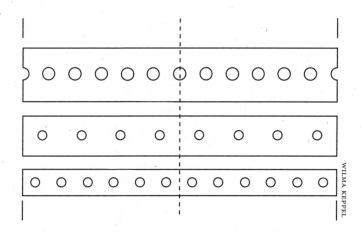

of standard beam, or a three-hole section of double-hole, is all you need to turn a two-stick joint into a tri-joint. Even one-hole pieces are useful as stops and spacers.

Hand cutting

When freehand cutting with any type of hand saw, mark the piece on all four sides. Hold it well-braced as you cut. If your blade starts to wander, simply flip the piece 90 degrees and start a new cut. Practice hand cutting scrap until you get accurate.

Our favorite hand saws for wood are the Japanese type with hardened teeth that cut in both directions. You get a fast, easy cut — just keep your knuckles out of the way. If you use European-style saws, a cross cut saw (designed to cut across the grain) will give you a better results than a rip saw (designed to cut along the grain). Use a miter box for straighter, faster cuts.

To hand-cut metal, use a hacksaw with a sharp blade. Fine teeth cut hard or thin material, coarser teeth cut soft aluminum. Use a lubricant.

14.1: *Cut grid beam with the standard hole pattern* between *holes. Cut double-hole beam on its extra holes.*

WILMA KEPPEL

Lubricants for cutting and drilling

Use a lubricant when you saw or drill metal. Lubricants make cutting easier, help your tools stay sharp, and help chips exit the cut. **Do not use lubricants with abrasive blades or grinding wheels.**

Hardware stores sell "cutting fluid" for cutting and drilling. This works well on steel, poorly on aluminum. Buy cutting fluid for aluminum from a machine shop supplier. A small brush applies cutting fluid to blades and drill bits. In a pinch we've used WD-40 spray lubricant.

14.2: *A power miter saw — our favorite tool for cutting wood and aluminum.*

PHIL AND RICHARD JERGENSON

14.3: *To get straight cuts on a table saw, clamp long sticks to the miter guide. The hand screw shown here won't mar your sticks.*

WILMA KEPPEL

Power cutting

Most power saws have a table. To get straight cuts, your stick must lay flat on it. Before you turn the saw on, put your eye at table height and check that there is no gap beneath the stick. Long sticks will require end support. If you use a hand-held power saw, make sure the sole plate of the saw stays flat on your stick while you cut.

Cutting wooden sticks

Our favorite tool for cutting wood is a power miter saw. This is the safest circular saw we know of. Most miter saws have a clamp to hold your work. Use it.

When cutting wood using any type of circular saw (including miter, table and radial arm saws), use a cross cut or combination blade. Carbide tipped blades stay sharp longer, unless they hit a nail. That strips the teeth off. If your wood contains nails, use a flooring blade.

To make a straight cut on a table or band saw, use the miter guide. As you saw, push both the miter guide and the stick to help keep everything square. Sticks over 3 feet long will creep out of square unless you clamp them to the guide. A small hand screw works well — you can operate it with one hand, and it won't mar the stick like a C-clamp.

When cutting wooden sticks away from the shop, we use a battery-powered hand-held circular saw. These saws are fast and inexpensive, but dangerous. Support the work firmly (*don't* use your leg). Set the blade depth so it is just slightly deeper than the thickness of your stick. Double-check before you cut to make sure you won't saw into your support surface.

To keep your cut straight, align a square against the side of the stick, then put your saw's sole plate against the square. A bolt dropped through a hole drilled in the square will perfectly position the square on your beam every time. Drill the hole to match your saw's sole plate — they're all different.

Cutting aluminum sticks

A band saw makes a very narrow cut, which keeps your tubes close to optimum length. We cut aluminum with the smallest band saw on the market — it costs under $200. Use a lubricant — cutting fluid made for aluminum works best.

We used to cut aluminum with a power miter saw, which makes a wider kerf. The best blades are designed to cut aluminum. You can also get good cuts using a fine-tooth plywood blade (eight or ten teeth per inch; three or four teeth per centimeter). **NEVER use a regular wood blade to cut aluminum on a power tool.** The blade will probably grab the work and could seriously injure someone! Before starting a cut, put a little lubricant on each side of the blade. As your blade gets dull its teeth will clog more easily. Remove the chips with a stiff brush.

Most woodworking saws will cut aluminum if you use an aluminum-cutting blade. Its smaller teeth cut slower than a wood blade.

Cutting steel sticks

The best power tool for cutting steel tubing is a band saw — the same one that works for aluminum. Use a lubricant made for steel on the blade. Bare steel tubes are nicer to handle if you remove the oily anti-rust coating before you cut, using a rag and degreaser.

You can also cut steel with an abrasive cutoff saw. This specialized tool is designed to cut steel at high speed using a special abrasive blade. **NEVER use a toothed blade on an abrasive cutoff saw!**

An abrasive cutoff saw turns so fast that your tubing will get red-hot. Sparks can fly up to 20 feet (6 meters), so clear the area of flammable materials before cutting. Degrease oiled tubing before you cut it. **Never use cutting fluid with an abrasive blade.** It could cause a fire.

Wear ear protection and a face shield. (Even safety glasses can't always keep fast-moving sparks from bouncing off your cheeks into your eye area.) Use leather gloves to protect your hands from the hot metal. A tightly woven long-sleeved shirt keeps sparks off your skin. Work in a well-ventilated area, and if you're doing a lot of cutting, wear a dust mask. **Always use the clamp on your saw to hold your work.**

14.4: *A band saw is the best tool to cut metal grid beam.*

PHIL AND RICHARD JERGENSON

Smoothing

Smooth the cut ends of your sticks so they're friendly to bare hands. **Make sure you smooth inside metal sticks** — people often reach into the ends to pick them up.

- **Wood.** To prevent splinters, smooth toward the end of your stick. Power sanders are fast, but can remove too much wood if used carelessly. For hand-sanding, wrap sandpaper around a short length of lumber or grid beam to make a sanding block. (Sandpaper will tear along a straight line if you crease it first.) Or lay sandpaper face-up on your workbench or shop floor, and rub the stick over it.
- **Aluminum.** Deburr the sharp edges of your sticks with a hand-held file or sandpaper. Phil likes 100-grit aluminum oxide cloth.
- **Steel.** Abrasive blades leave nasty sharp edges on steel. (Richard calls them "alligators" because they bite.) A flat metal file removes them almost as quickly as a power grinder, and can also smooth inside the stick.

Skin materials

We briefly reviewed skin materials on page 29. This section explains what to get, where to purchase it, and how to work with it.

Almost all panels used by the US construction industry are made in 4 x 8-foot sheets that you can cut into standard grid beam sizes with no waste. Some materials such as sheet metal are available in larger sizes that also allow waste-free cutting.

Since grid beam components get used again and again, it makes sense to invest in high-quality materials. Think versatility. How might you re-use this component? A little forethought can save a lot of money.

Buy most skin materials at a lumberyard (see buying tips on page 176). Purchase wood and wood-fiber panels from stacks that are stored flat and dry. Avoid swollen or delaminated edges, a sign of moisture damage. Reject warped panels, and those with edges damaged by the straps used to bind the stack together.

Many lumberyards will cut panels to size, though accuracy is sometimes a problem. Bring your own tape measure and check. Reject wrongly cut panels, and refuse to pay for them.

Most panels can be stored vertically, leaned against a wall, as long as they stay straight. A panel stored bent may warp permanently. If the floor might get damp, set your panels on spacers or in a rack.

Different skin materials have different characteristics that make them suitable for different projects.

Boards

Wooden boards are very stiff and make great shelves. Buy boards that are straight, flat, have straight fine grain, and lack pitch pockets or big knots. We explain the details of inspecting lumber on page 28.

Nominal US board sizes don't match the actual sizes. A "one-by-twelve" board measures about ¾ x 11¼ inches, a one-by-ten about ¾ x 9¼ inches. These sizes fit US wall standards and brackets (page 161), and work well as shelves in offset frames. If you have a sawmill in your area, consider having locally grown lumber custom cut into sizes you like.

Boards are very strong along the grain, but easy to split across it. Place board cross-braces diagonally for greatest strength.

Hardboard

Hardboard (also called fiberboard, beaverboard or masonite) is made from sawdust bonded into stiff sheets. Inexpensive and widely available, this is the Jergensons' favorite panel for bracing light-duty projects such as furniture. Tempered hardboard is stronger than untempered. Keep it dry or it will warp.

Hardboard is available is several thicknesses and various specialty finishes. The Jergensons use ¼-inch tempered side panels for furniture. White-coated bathroom paneling of ⅛-inch tempered hardboard makes a great dry-erase whiteboard. Wilma uses it under loft decks and behind shelves to reflect light. Hardboard isn't stiff enough for load-bearing surfaces such as shelves or decks.

Inadequately bolted hardboard panels can bow away from projects. Bowed panels make much weaker cross-braces. Use enough bolts to keep panels flat.

Pegboard

Pegboard is hardboard with holes every 1 inch. (We have not tested metal or plastic versions.) Metric versions have holes every 20 or 25 millimeters. A wide variety of hooks, trays and shelves plug right in. Many people use pegboard for workbench backs so they can hang their tools. Since the holes almost never match a project's frame, we treat it like solid panels and drill wherever we want to put a bolt.

Plywood

Easy to use, reasonably priced, and available everywhere, plywood is one of our favorite skin materials. It comes in 4 x 8-foot sheets ⅛ inch to 1⅛ inch thick. Its strength makes it a good choice for floors, loft decks and structural skin panels that brace your project. Thin plywood (¼-inch or less) makes furniture side panels that are much stiffer and stronger than hardboard.

Plywood is made from glued-together sheets of wood called veneers or plies. The more plies, the stiffer the plywood. The glue determines how weatherproof plywood is. Interior plywood that gets wet will sag and delaminate. Exterior plywood can withstand more moisture. Marine plywood is made for use on boats and is *really* tough, but expensive.

The quality of most plywood's outside veneers (the ones you see) is measured by grades. Grade A is smooth, strong and beautiful; Grade D is rough and weakened by large knotholes and splits. Since a sheet of plywood has two sides, it has two grades. The "CDX" plywood used in building construction is Grade C on one side, Grade D on the other, and uses exterior glue.

Used as shelves, most plywoods will sag over time unless supported lengthwise. The exception is "high-ply" types that have extra layers. For indoor shelves and desktops we use high-ply birch and apple, which are very sag resistant, reasonably priced and look beautiful. Where dampness is an issue, we use signboard.

Signboard

Signboard (also called Medium Density Overlay, or MDO) is a type of high-ply exterior plywood used for outdoor signs. It is extremely resistant to sagging and weather. The surface is covered with a smooth, durable, paintable layer that has no grain. (Make sure this surface covers *both* sides.) An oil finish will turn the tan panels a beautiful dark brown. They also take paint well. Buy it at lumberyards or sign suppliers.

Signboard ½ inch thick makes stiff, durable shelves and desktops. It costs more than birch or apple plywood, so we use it only when a project might get damp.

Alucobond and Dibond

Our favorite panel material for vehicles is Alucobond, a panel used for signs and skin panels on skyscrapers. A 0.02 inch (0.5 millimeter) sheet of aluminum is bonded to each side of a hard plastic core. Alucobond can be drilled easily, cut with simple woodworking tools, and formed to create rounded corners. It is durable and resists cracking. Unfortunately it's expensive and can't be recycled. It is available in thicknesses of 3 millimeters (0.12 inches), 4 millimeters (0.16 inches) and 6 millimeters (0.24 inches), in panel sizes up to 5 x 16 feet.

The same manufacturer makes a lighter, less expensive sign material called Dibond. Construction is the same as Alucobond, but the metal is only 0.01 inch thick. Total sheet thickness is 2 millimeters (0.08 inches), 3 millimeters (0.12 inches) or 4 millimeters (0.16 inches). Dibond promises to be an excellent alternative to Alucobond. Both are available through sign supply stores. Contact Alucobond Technologies to find a dealer near you.

Sheet metal

Widely available in many thicknesses, sheet metal is easily formed. Thicker plate

Salvage

You can save a lot of money by salvaging materials. Re-use also helps the environment.

Prices at salvage yards and military surplus stores range from wonderful to ridiculously high, so shop around. Also check your local dump. Some allow salvage; others collect and resell dumped building materials. Prices are often excellent. Ask neighbors if they have unused building materials they'd like to get rid of, and check your own scrap pile.

Construction site dumpsters are often a great source of lumber and panels less than 8 feet long. In 1981, Richard salvaged $5,000 of Alucobond from a construction site dumpster, and we're still using those panels. Always get permission to salvage or dumpster-dive, and leave the place neat so you'll be welcomed back.

metal makes excellent workbench tops. Buy both from a metal dealer unless you can find what you need in the junkyard or a metal shop's scrap bin.

Sheet steel is inexpensive and strong. We usually buy it with a galvanized finish so we don't have to paint it.

Sheet aluminum is much lighter than steel and doesn't require painting. Different alloys possess vastly different structural qualities — some are soft and formable, while others are hard and brittle. One of Phil's favorite materials is aluminum diamond plate, available in $1/16$ or $1/8$ inch thickness. A raised surface texture adds strength and prevents loads from sliding around.

Specular (mirror-polished) aluminum and stainless steel are used for solar reflectors and concentrators. Specular aluminum must have a plastic coating to keep the surface from oxidizing. It still gets dull after a while. Specular stainless steel is expensive, but stays bright for decades.

Wire mesh

Wire mesh varies from fine screen to heavy-duty welded wire panels that will stop a bull. To minimize waste, buy and cut mesh in whole-foot widths. Join panels by splicing with wire rings, or sew them together with a piece of wire.

Welded wire is stiff enough to use for storage shelves if well supported. Bolt it to the project frame so it can't sag. The 1 x 2-inch mesh is a good compromise of weight and stiffness.

Fiberglass

Fiberglass is made of fine glass fibers set in resin. Extremely strong and tough, fiberglass can be shaped only once, and cannot be recycled.

Phil has used flat fiberglass sheets to cover small shelters, including his Portable House. He likes Filon brand, which is used for greenhouse glazing. UV stabilizers keep it from turning fuzzy and opaque in sunlight.

Sheets of fiberglass cloth can be laid up by hand into very streamlined shapes, such as the nose on Phil's X-Wing. The process is so labor-intensive that Phil switched to Alucobond for vehicle bodies.

ABS plastic

ABS plastic is widely used for automobile bodies and molded parts. It is light, tough, flexible, resistant to vibration damage,

14.5: *Electric Moose Club battery safe with welded wire mesh panels. Plastic wire ties attach them to the 1-inch frame.*

WILMA KEPPEL

impervious to battery acid, and can be recycled. Severe impacts can split it. To weld cracks, use a soldering iron and scrap ABS for filler.

ABS cuts easily with woodworking tools, and can be heat-vacuum formed to create compound curves. If you have time to make molds, it makes dynamite streamlining. Phil made the battery boxes on the Solar Bear from 1/8-inch white ABS, using a simple strip heater to make the bends.

Plexiglass (acrylic plastic)

Plexiglass can be used for windows, view ports and vehicle windows. Don't use it for windshields: it scratches easily, and becomes difficult to see through. We buy flat sheet stock, which is available in opaque white or clear. The thinner sheets can be bent into curves.

Plexiglass is prone to crack if improperly mounted. Use a rubber gasket under the bolt head in place of a washer, then tighten lightly. If you need a plastic panel in a breakage-prone area, use Lexan instead.

Lexan (polycarbonate plastic)

Lexan is the durable version of acrylic plastic, at two to three times the cost. It is much more resistant to breakage than acrylic, and stands up well to weather without discoloring or degrading. It scratches more easily than glass.

Glass

Very clear and hard to scratch, glass makes excellent windshields. We used safety glass windshields for the Vanda and Sol Train. **Never use window glass in a vehicle.** It breaks into sharp pieces in a crash.

For buildings, the glass from sliding glass doors is the least expensive way we know of to buy window-quality glass in large sheets. Many glass dealers sell low-priced single panes salvaged from repair jobs.

Doors

A door with a flat surface makes a great desk or table top. Slightly damaged doors are often available for a few dollars at lumberyards, or free at the dump.

Solid-core doors are made from a chipboard core covered with veneer. Very heavy, they are also quite strong. Hollow-core doors are strong enough for desks and sewing tables, but too weak to use as workbench tops. A screwdriver can punch right through the veneer! You can often buy slightly damaged hollow-core doors inexpensively at lumberyards. Avoid ones that are warped, delaminating, or have large areas of damaged veneer — check both sides! Water stains are usually okay. Much of the door's strength is in its solid rim, so don't cut there. Thread computer cords through the lock hole, or use a sliding closet door with no hole.

Fabric

Our fabric-skinned projects have turned out so well, we probably haven't used this material enough. Light-weight, portable and compact to store, fabric is great for tents, awnings, beds, seating and more. Offering limited weather projection, fabric vehicle skins weigh very little. We stretched white Lycra over grid beam frames to make diffusers and reflectors used for photographing this book.

Use fabric rectangles with sleeves sewed onto each end for room divider panels, seating and storage. Or omit the sleeve, and wind an extra-long piece of fabric several times around the support beams. You'll find many innovative fabric ideas in the *Nomadic Furniture* books, and in *Systems of Living Space,* both reviewed in the Resources chapter.

Rope and cord

Parallel or woven rope or cord can substitute for panels, as on Chris Koveleski's folding chair (Figure 5.11). Netting shelves for clothes cost far less than plywood (but they don't cross-brace your project).

Working with panels
Cutting panels

Panel materials that come in 4 x 8-foot sheets can be cut to fit grid beam projects with no waste. By using standard sizes (Figure 4.1), you can re-use panels on project after project.

To mark straight cutting lines, use a chalk line, straight edge, or a straight piece of metal or wood. For greatest accuracy, lightly clamp the ends of your guide before marking. Panels must be cut square.

To notch panels, use a saber saw (power jigsaw). This nifty tool cuts wood, steel, aluminum, Alucobond, Dibond and plastic; just use the right blade for the job. The pieces left over from notching plywood and hardboard make handy shims to level projects on uneven floors.

Cutting wooden panels

Always cut plywood so the grain runs lengthwise on the panel (Figure 4.4). Panels with crosswise grain are prone to sag.

We use power saws to cut plywood, signboard and hardboard. You can also cut panels with a hand saw. We recommend power saws for hardboard, which is difficult to cut and dulls blades fast.

A portable power saw cuts a much straighter line if you improvise a saw guide. Use a straight, rigid piece of material — metal grid beam or angle iron is ideal. Clamp it at both ends to keep it parallel to your cut line. Put your saw guide the same distance from the cut line as your saw's

14.6: *Richard cuts a panel with a portable circular saw. The saw guide is a piece of aluminum grid beam clamped to the plywood.*

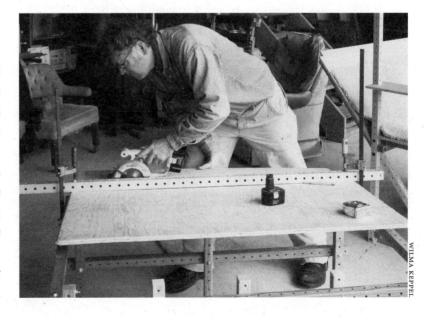

WILMA KEPPEL

blade is from the side of its sole plate. With the saw placed against the saw guide, the blade should touch your cut line.

When trimming off scrap or a damaged edge, clamp the saw guide to your good material. If your blade wanders, it will cut the part you don't want.

Sand cut surfaces smooth. Slightly round the corners of all panel edges to prevent them from chipping or splintering.

Cutting metal panels

The budget method for cutting thin sheet metal is to use hand-held sheet metal shears. For thicker material, use a saber saw (power jigsaw). Clamp your work piece to the edge of something solid so it can't jump up and down with the blade — we use clamps and locking pliers. Make sure you don't cut into the brace. Thin metal cuts most neatly if you back it with a softer material such as plywood or hardboard, then cut through both.

Plate steel $3/16$ inch or thicker can be cut with an oxyacetylene cutting torch. Thinner steel will warp from a torch's heat, so cut it with a saw or plasma cutter.

Smooth the cut edges of sheet metal with emery cloth or a metal file. On plate steel, grind off any burrs with an angle grinder, then use its power wire brush attachment to smooth and polish the corners.

Cutting sheet plastic

Easily scratched and somewhat brittle, plexiglass and Lexan require special care when cutting, drilling or mounting. Thin material can be cut by scoring where you want to cut, using a straight edge and a sharp blade such as a utility knife. Lay the cut over the edge of a table to snap it. This yields a very clean cut.

You can also cut these plastics with standard woodworking power tools such as a table saw or portable circular saw. Run masking tape down both sides on top of the protective paper, then cut right down the tape. Use a sanding block and emery cloth to smooth the edge.

Most other plastics can be cut with woodworking blades. Check with your plastics supplier.

Cutting fabric

A rotary cutter, self-healing mat and quilter's ruler will cut fabric much faster and more accurately than scissors. Buy these tools in a quilt shop or fabric store.

Once cut, most woven fabrics will fray at the edges. Stop fraying by lock stitching, zigzagging or seaming the cut edge.

Panel mounting holes

The fastest way to mount a panel is to clamp it to your project's frame, making sure everything is square. Using the holes in the grid beam as drill guides, use a hand-held power drill to drill the panel. If your sticks are under-sized or have off-center holes, or you plan to move the panel around a lot, drill the panels before mounting to ensure accurate hole placement.

Position panel holes to match the middle of the sticks they will mount to — 1 inch from the edge for 2-inch sticks, ¾ inch from the edge for 1½-inch sticks. Most projects have tri-joints at the corners, so put panel holes elsewhere.

Drill panel mounting holes in a regular pattern that will make it easy to re-use the panel. If you are mounting something to the middle of a panel, put the holes where a future stick *could* go.

A warped panel loses a lot of its bracing power. Use enough bolts to keep your panels flat against the project frame. We usually bolt side panels to a project's vertical posts. Most projects have posts on or near the outside corners. Add a spacer block wherever you want to bolt to a horizontal stick.

To get panels to lie flat over hex bolts, chisel a pocket for each bolt head on the back side of the panel. Or drill holes through the panel that are slightly larger than the heads on the frame bolts.

Making panel holes

Most panel materials can be drilled with a hand-held power drill and ordinary bits. For hard materials or large bit sizes, use a drill press.

For large holes, drill a smaller pilot hole first. The pilot holes acts as guide for the larger bit.

To reduce splintering on wood and wood fiber panels, reduce pressure on the bit just as it starts to exit the far side of the material. Or drill into a firm backing such as scrap wood, plywood or hardboard. Also use a backing when drilling plastics. Keep plexiglass and Lexan flat to prevent them from splitting.

Center-punch metal panels before you drill to keep the bit from wandering. When drilling sheet metal, either drill into a backing, or use a step drill bit — our preferred tool for drilling thin metal or plastic. Designed to drill sheet materials, it's much faster than a standard bit. On sheet metal it needs no backing — just center punch and drill. Each step makes a different standard hole size, so one $40 step drill bit can replace 5 to 14 standard bits. Step drill bits designed to cut thicker materials make fewer hole sizes.

Panel cutouts

Reinhold Ziegler's MATRIX lofts used square hardboard bracing panels 2 feet square, with decorative round cutouts. The Jergensons use similar panels to brace the ends of desks and workbenches where solid panels would make the inside of a project too dark.

You can buy a saber saw attachment for cutting accurate round holes quickly in panels. Or mark a circle, then use a drill to make a hole (or several overlapping holes) big enough to admit the saw blade in the part of the panel you plan to remove. Freehand cut along your mark with a saber saw or keyhole saw. That's how Phil cut the window holes for the Sol Train and Vanda, rounding the corners so the gaskets could follow the curves without crimping.

Hardware

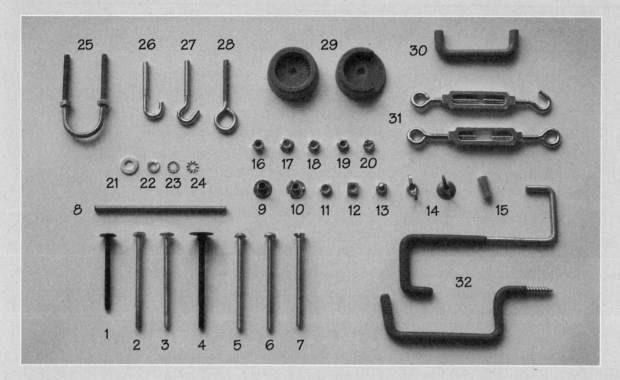

Bolts

1. **Joint connector bolt.** Our favorite bolt for wood frames (it's not strong enough for metal). Its Allen head is easy to tighten, and super-flat so panels bolt right over it. Use with weld nuts. We recommend plated (silver-colored) hardware; the black oxide shown here can stain your sticks. Buy by mail order.

2. **Hex bolt.** Available everywhere, strong, easy to tighten. Strongest with a washer under the head to spread the load.

3. **Carriage bolt.** Semi-flat, panels can bolt over it. Widely available. The shoulder under the bolt head, which keeps it from turning, requires wood or a soft panel to dig into. Can be difficult to get tight if the hole is worn.

4. **Elevator bolt.** Super flat. Panels bolt over it. Shoulder version requires a wood frame or panel. Can be difficult to get tight if the hole is worn.

5. **Slot-head machine screw.** Semi-flat bolt for metal. Difficult to get tight; prone to stripped head. Sometimes called a **stove bolt.**

6. **Pan-head machine screw.** Semi-flat bolt for metal. Difficult to get tight; prone to stripped head.

7. **Flat-head machine screw.** Requires countersunk (tapered) hole. Difficult to get tight and prone to stripping except for the Allen head versions. Tapered head acts like a wedge and may split wood if over-tightened.

8. **Threaded rod.** Bolt thread with no head. It's significantly weaker than a bolt with a shank.

Nuts

9. **Weld nut.** Our favorite nut for wood. Usually used with joint connector bolts. Weaker than hex-type nuts. Buy by mail order.

10. **T-nut.** Like a weld nut, but with fangs that dig into the wood, making it difficult to remove. Not recommended.

11. **Hex nut.** Strong, inexpensive, available everywhere, easy to get tight. Strongest with a washer to spread the load.

12. **Square nut.** Useful where a slot keeps it from turning.

13. **Cap (acorn) nut.** Less likely to snag clothing than hex nuts, but somewhat weaker. You may need to shorten the bolt to keep it from breaking the nut's cap.

14. **Wing nut.** Easy to tighten by hand. Good for components that need frequent adjustment, but difficult to get really tight. Flanged version doesn't need a washer.

15. **Coupling nut.** Used to join sections of threaded rod, or to join threaded rod to another fastener such as a hook.

Lock nuts

Use lock nuts on top of a flat washer that spreads the load.

16. **Nylon-insert lock nut.** Excellent vibration resistance. Reusable one or two times before the nylon wears. Unsuitable for high-heat areas such as engines or brakes.

17. **Flange lock nut.** Large holding area, high-torque, heat-proof. Reusable until the serrations start to dull.

18. **K-lock nut.** Inexpensive. Don't reuse on a vehicle.

19. **Flex-type lock nut.** Reusable many times, heat-proof, but expensive.

20. **Castle nut.** Very secure; used to fasten axles. Requires a drilled bolt. Insert a cotter pin through a notch in the nut, through the bolt, then bend the pin.

Washers

21. **Flat washer.** Spreads loads, which makes joints stronger and protects beams from crushing. Use under lock washers.

22. **Split-ring lock washer.** Okay for stationary loads; not secure enough for vehicles or trailers.

23. **Internal-tooth lock washer.** Effective against vibration, good on vehicles, but not reusable (the teeth crush).

24. **External-tooth lock washer.** Effective against vibration, good on vehicles, reusable.

Liquid thread locker (not shown). The chemical equivalent of a good lock nut. We use blue Loctite. Red Loctite requires extreme heat to remove. Re-apply each time you move the nut.

Specialty hardware

25. **U-bolt.** Use to attach pipe or rod.

26. **J-bolt.** Use to attach cargo nets, welded-wire panels, pipes or cables.

27. **Hook.** Use nut and washer on the hook side to adjust its height from stick.

28. **Eye.** For greater strength, weld the eye closed. For high-strength applications, use forged hooks and eyes.

29. **Clothes rod hangers.** Attach with a tapered machine screw and weld nut.

30. **Drawer pull.** This one's hole spacing matches grid beam. It attaches with screws.

31. **Turnbuckle.** Use to tighten cables or threaded rod. The type shown here works on furniture-sized projects. For decks and buildings, use a heavy-duty turnbuckle with forged hardware.

32. **Hooks.** Top hook is designed to fit over two-by lumber; bottom hook screws into wood's frame holes.

Pegboard hardware (not shown): A wide variety of hooks, tool holders and shelf supports plug into pegboard. Many also work with metal grid beam that has 1-inch hole spacing.

Hardware

We show a wide variety of fasteners on page 150. Most are available in hardware stores, lumberyards, and farm supply stores. Buy joint connector bolts and weld nuts by mail order.

Where to buy hardware

Grid beam projects gobble hardware. Virtually all projects use two or more bolts and nuts per stick. Even a simple cube requires 24 frame bolts, plus nuts and washers. Save yourself emergency trips to the store and buy extra.

Vendors with the best prices sell hardware by the pound or by the box. Next best is paying by the piece. A store that carries hardware in little packages of four to eight pieces has to charge extra. Excess packaging is also hard on the environment.

Farm supply stores such as Tractor Supply Company that sell hardware by the pound often charge less than lumberyards. Some hardware manufacturers, such as Fastenal, have retail outlets in major cities where you can buy in quantity. Or order bulk hardware direct from manufacturers. Prices vary enormously, so shop around.

What hardware to get

A good hardware store stocks a bewildering array of fasteners in different sizes, metals and finishes. Here's what to look for.

Rust protection

Don't waste your money on unplated steel hardware — it will rust even indoors, staining your sticks and panels.

Black oxide looks nice, but rusts outdoors. Indoors it sometimes stains wood, especially if humidity is very high or it gets wet. We used black oxide hardware to build projects for this book because it's easy to see in photographs, but we don't recommend it.

Most hardware is coated with shiny blue-gray zinc chromate. A dull gray hot-dipped galvanized coating is thicker and more durable. Cadmium makes a durable shiny yellowish finish, but is toxic to the environment. Don't use cadmium around kids or food.

Even coated hardware will eventually rust if left outdoors. Store yours in a dry place, preferably indoors to prevent condensation caused by temperature fluctuations.

Plated steel in contact with aluminum creates an electrolytic reaction when the metal gets wet. After about five years outdoors, this strips the plating from steel hardware, and it rusts. The ultimate in outdoor durability, stainless steel costs several times more. Most fasteners used in the grid beam system are available in stainless from Fastenal.

Threads

Some US hardware is available in coarse or fine thread (abbreviated NC and NF). A lot more types of hardware are available in the coarse thread, so that's what we use.

For wooden projects, we like tap bolts, which have threads their full length. Cut them to any length you need.

Metal grid beam can mash bolt threads, especially if there is vibration or pounding.

On metal-framed projects and vehicles, we use bolts with a shank. A shank is stronger than threads, and less prone to crack under extreme loads.

Hardness

Bolts are available in different hardnesses, called grades. Harder bolts are stronger but cost more. Phil always uses hardware store bolts (soft Grade 1 or 2) on grid beam projects because he considers the wall of the grid beam tube to be the weakest point. Most builders prefer to use Grade 5 hardware for vehicles. 80/20 Inc.'s aluminum tubes are designed for use with Grade 8 hardware. 80/20 sells flanged Grade 8 bolts with flanged nuts. On stationary projects, they need no washers. (On vehicles, substitute washers and lock nuts or washers.) **Use nuts as hard as your bolts.**

Most non-metric hex bolts indicate grade with lines on the head — count the lines and add two to get the grade number. Bolts with no lines are mild steel (Grade 1 or 2). Metric bolts use a different grading system, with the number written on the head. A metric 8.8 bolt is made of soft steel equivalent to a US Grade 1 or 2.

Bolt diameter

On most projects, use a bolt a bit smaller than your hole size. This gives you enough slack to make assembly easy. We list the bolt diameters we prefer on page 27.

On steel-framed projects subject to shock, vibration or very heavy loads, use

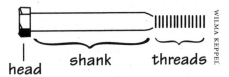

head   shank   threads

14.8: *Tap bolt (top) can be cut to any length. Bolt with a shank is a bit stronger, and less likely to get its threads mashed.*

WILMA KEPPEL

bolts the same size as the holes. Line up the frame holes with a drift (a tapered tool for aligning holes) or screwdriver. As you insert the bolt, wiggle the frame while *lightly* tapping the bolt to get it in without bending the threads.

Most galvanized steel double-hole tubes have 7/16-inch holes designed for both 3/8-inch and 7/16-inch bolts. We use 3/8-inch bolts for most projects, 7/16-inch bolts for building legs and trailers.

Bolt length

Bolt length includes only the shaft, not the head. Most US non-metric bolts jump half an inch between sizes. The joint connector bolts we use are made shorter so they won't stick out of the nut.

Bolts should go all the way through hex nuts, engaging all the threads. Bolts should go most of the way through weld nuts. Washers, lock washers and panels require extra length. **Use washers *plus* a lock washer or lock nut on all vehicle and trailer bolts.**

Tightening a bolt with a shoulder requires forcing the shoulder into the wood. Turning the nut that hard may scuff the stick or even make it dig into the wood, so use a washer.

We used to build frames using 3½-inch carriage bolts, washers and hex nuts. Today we use 2¾-inch joint connector bolts and weld nuts. Our metal projects use hex bolts 3½ inches long for 1½-inch aluminum, and 4½ inches long for 2-inch steel. The length of the bolts you use to fasten panels depends on the panel thickness and whether you are bolting through one stick or two.

Sometimes projects require bolting so many pieces of beam together that a bolt won't reach. Instead, use threaded rod, which is bolt thread with no head. Hardware stores sell pieces up to 6 feet long. The threads make it weaker than a bolt with a shank. Cut it to the length you need, then use a nut and washer on each end.

Bolt heads and nut types

Grid beam projects are easiest to assemble if you use low-profile hardware (Figure 2.14). Hex bolts and nuts with washers are much stronger than flat bolts, which is why we use them for all metal-framed projects. Strength isn't an issue on 1½-inch wood, because even flat hardware is so strong compared to the sticks.

Joint connector bolts with weld nuts lie flat on both sides of the joints. Carriage bolts aren't as flat, and the nut end projects. Flat bolts that don't have a shoulder, such as pan- and slot-head machine screws, also have a projecting nut end. All but the Allen head versions are much harder to tighten than carriage bolts, and the heads may strip.

For big timbers such as four-by-fours, use hex bolts and nuts with washers, and counterbore (recess) the ends of the holes so panels will lie flat on the sticks. Counterboring is too much bother to use on small sticks, and weakens them a lot.

Cutting bolts and threaded rod

Put a nut on bolts and threaded rod *before* you cut them. After you cut, file the sharp edges, then back the nut off over the cut to realign the threads.

We usually cut bolts to length right on the project, using a hacksaw with a metal-cutting blade. Start by attaching the bolt to your project or another piece of beam, and tighten the nut. Using the nut as a blade guide, hacksaw through the bolt, cutting on the first thread after the nut. A light yet direct push-pull will cut through a Grade 2 bolt in seconds. Slow down near the end of your cut to avoid cutting into your stick. Now remove the nut, and deburr the end of the bolt with a metal file. You can also cut bolts using a hand-held angle grinder or an abrasive cutoff saw.

The toughest part of cutting threaded rod is holding onto it without mashing the threads. Tighten two nuts against each other next to your cut. Thread another nut on the rod a short distance away. Clamp the nuts in a vise, and proceed as above. If threads *do* get mashed, a type of file called a thread restorer will quickly fix them.

Accessories and Adapters

Accessories are components and assemblies that can be used with grid beam, but aren't actually part of the system. Almost anything can be a grid beam accessory: lamps, wheels, motors, sinks, solar panels, even fireplaces. **Adapters** are parts that let you bolt non-standard accessories to grid beam. Since accessories and adapters work together, this chapter describes both.

You can buy many accessories at your local lumberyard, hardware store, electrical or plumbing store, or hobby shop. 80/20 Inc. sells a variety of brackets, feet, wheels, hinges and other components that fit their 1½-inch grid beam; most also fit 1½-inch wood. Accessories available by mail order include alternative energy, electric vehicle, go-kart, automotive and industrial components. (The "Suppliers" chapter lists our favorite sources.) Salvage yards sell industrial, automotive and motorcycle components; military surplus

shops may sell virtually anything. Some salvage yards and military surplus stores charge more than buying new, so shop around.

WILMA KEPPEL

15.1: *Many items designed to mount on walls or doors bolt to grid beam with little or no modification.*

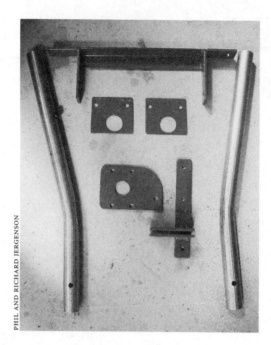

15.2: *Simple adapters mate a wide variety of parts to grid beam. These components built the Yard Truck in Figure 10.7.*

PHIL AND RICHARD JERGENSON

WILMA KEPPEL

15.3: *Allied Tube's locking pin for double-hole is handy for quick-adjust legs and posts.*

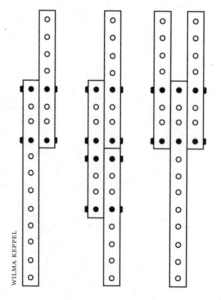

WILMA KEPPEL

15.4: *Left to right: lap joint; double lap joint; telescoping leg made with lap joints.*

As we write this, few adapters for mating accessories to grid beam are commercially available. Fortunately, most adapters can be fabricated from ordinary materials in a simple home shop. You'll find directions for making them at the end of this chapter.

If you discover more components, adapters or materials that work with grid beam, or additional suppliers, please write or call us so we can add them to future editions of this book. You'll find our contact information on page 244.

Splices and extensions

Splicing makes two shorter pieces of grid beam into one longer piece. Use splices for adjustable legs, and to create custom-length sticks. These are useful when you need to fit projects into odd-sized spaces.

Splice steel double-hole by inserting a tube one size smaller and at least 1 foot long inside your beams where they join. Bolt each end.

Phil extends building legs that hold thousands of pounds with a sleeve one size larger, and uses several $7/16$-inch bolts. Diagonally brace the legs if they extend more than 2 feet.

Internal splices for 1½-inch aluminum can be purchased from 80/20 Inc. Buy the "extended tube insert" for HT Series tubes.

Splice wood and 1-inch aluminum with a single or double lap joint, putting a bolt at each end of the lap. Or use an external sleeve of double-hole or steel. Aluminum-on-aluminum sleeves tend to stick or jam unless there is a lot of extra space between the tubes.

Mounting hole position and spacing

Some commercial components have holes that match grid beam. If the holes *almost* work, enlarge them using a round file. Or use an existing hole, and drill one or more new holes to match grid beam. You can also buy components designed to be welded, such as blank hinges, and drill your own holes.

If re-drilling your component's holes won't work, use an adapter with two sets of holes — one for your component, and one for grid beam. Holes spaced at multiples of 3 inches bolt to four standard US sizes of grid beam (page 27). We fabricate most of our adapters from plate steel or angle iron. Where light weight is necessary, use aluminum plate or angle.

Furniture wheels and casters

Wheels and casters make furniture, workbenches and shop equipment portable. The bigger the wheel, the bigger the hole or bump it can roll over. Use small wheels indoors or on flat surfaces such as concrete.

Our favorite furniture casters have a 5/16-inch steel shank that press-fits snugly into the holes in 1½-inch wooden grid beam. Most are sold with a larger sleeve for the shank. Discard it.

We have also used lawn mower wheels for furniture and light-duty shop use. Use a bolt for the axle.

15.5: *Holes 4 inches apart bolt an industrial caster to a 2-inch steel workbench frame. Use two or more bolts and support both sides of the mounting plate to keep it from bending.*

WILMA KEPPEL

Heavy shop loads will jam or break furniture casters. Instead, use quality industrial hardware that can roll a loaded tool chest, welder or shop table. Plain wheels on one end make items easier for one person to steer; casters everywhere make them more maneuverable. Use two locking casters or wheels to keep equipment from moving once you position it. Locking wheels shift less than locking casters.

In the shop, use metal or hard rubber wheels that won't pick up embedded grit and then jam. To avoid marking tile and wood indoor floors, use plastic or soft rubber wheels

Most hardware stores and lumberyards stock only a few types of industrial wheels. They rarely match grid beam. We usually buy from McMaster-Carr, which has an excellent selection. Industrial salvage yards sometimes have deals, but some overcharge. Check new prices before you buy.

Feet

For furniture-sized projects, bolts make decent feet. Protect the floor beneath metal feet with rubber caps sold for furniture legs, or scraps of wood or carpet. We discuss feet for scaffolds and buildings on page 72.

The feet on Ken Isaacs's Storage Grid were sections of two-by-two, 8 inches long. For mounts, use two-by-twos or short pieces of grid beam, and drill a hole in one end. Mounts should overlap the Storage Grid's posts by at least 6 inches.

Shims

Grid beam projects are naturally square — but what if the building isn't? The scraps left over from notching the corners of plywood and hardboard panels make

15.6: *Bolts tipped with rubber feet protect the floor under Jean Tantra's La-Z-Nerd Workstation.*

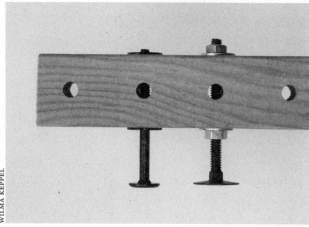

15.7: *Leveling feet made with a joint connector bolt and weld nut (left) and an elevator bolt, hex nuts and washers (right).*

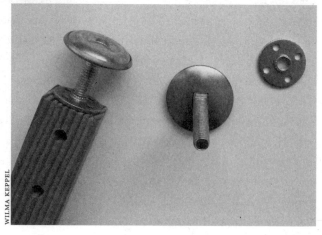

15.8: *This screw-adjust foot fits a hole drilled into the end of the stick. Attach the plate with one or more small screws if you wish.*

great shims. Place them under project legs to accommodate uneven floors. You can also use plastic furniture feet sold in hardware stores. If the floor is one or more stick widths off level, use adjustable legs. Screw-adjust leveling feet that fit 1½-inch aluminum can be purchased from 80/20 Inc.

Screws

We use screws when connecting grid beam to conventional construction, and when fabricating some components.

Lag screws are large, hex-head screws that make strong attachments to wooden building frames. Phil lag-screws scaffolds directly to the building he's working on. Earthquake-proof tall bookcases by lag screwing the top to the nearest wall. Drill holes in the building's wall studs the same size as the screw shaft or slightly smaller, so that the full depth of the threads bite into wood.

Deck and **drywall screws** drill their own holes in wood or drywall. They're useful for assembling wooden frames for Filon windows, and similar projects. Install using a power screwdriver or a drill fitted with a drywall (Phillips screwdriver) bit. Reverse your drill to unscrew them. To make drilling and removal easier, rub a bar of soap on the threads before you drill.

Drywall screws are intended for one-time use indoors. They soon rust immovably to outdoor projects. Plated deck screws last longer; stainless steel lasts virtually forever.

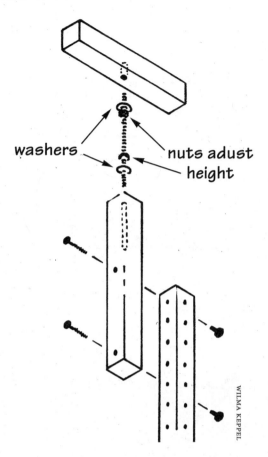

washers **nuts adust height**

WILMA KEPPEL

Screw **liners** are plastic sleeves that fit in the holes of wooden grid beam. Screwing in a drywall screw expands the liner against the walls of the hole, locking it in place. Use this system for attaching light-duty panels in a hurry. Panels install from one side — handy if you can't reach the other side of the sticks.

Butt joint brackets

Butt joints look like a letter L or T. While not as strong as tri-joints, they are useful where you need a flat joint. Phil uses them underneath cargo beds on his work vehicles.

15.9: *Ken Isaacs used feet similar to this to clamp his Storage Grid between floor and ceiling. A pad of felt or inner tube protects the ceiling and keeps the foot from sliding. Nuts on the threaded rod adjust the height.*

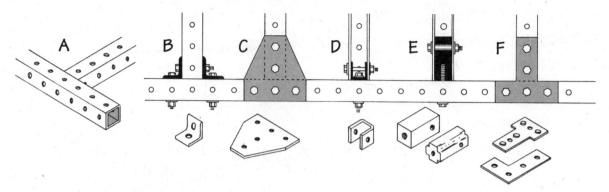

15.10: *A butt joint (**A**) requires special hardware.*

B: *L-brackets made from steel or aluminum angle*

C: *Mounting plate made from plate steel or aluminum.*

D: *Internal U-bracket fabricated from bent plate steel (drill after bending), channel iron, or aluminum.*

E: *Threaded internal block. Square version is fabricated from aluminum bar stock.*

F: *T and L-brackets made by Allied for double-hole. 80/20 Inc. makes B, C, and the cross-shaped block E to fit their 1½-inch aluminum tubes.*

15.11: *Heavy-duty plastic bins make excellent drawers.*

PHIL AND RICHARD JERGENSON

Lamps

We sometimes remove the clamp from swing-arm lamps, and either slip the pivot post into our grid beam's holes, or mount it in a drilled block of wood that bolts to the project's frame. Unlike clamps, these methods make secure connections that won't work loose.

For diffuse light under lofts, Wilma winds strings of Christmas tree lights around the overhead frame members. LED lights use one-tenth the power of incandescents and last many times longer.

Incandescent and halogen bulbs produce a lot of heat. Always make sure lamps can't cause a fire.

Power strips

We recommend plugging all electronic components into a power strip or surge protector with a switch. This lets you turn components off when you're not using them. (Many appliances run power supplies or electronics all the time unless you unplug them.) With only one cord to plug in, portable desks and workbenches become easy to move. If your power strip won't bolt directly to grid beam, attach it to a piece of plywood, then bolt the plywood to your project.

Drawers

The simplest drawers for grid beam are ready-made trays, bins or wire baskets that slide on grid beam side rails. These drawers needs no hardware. Use a stiff bin that won't collapse when loaded. Most plastic bins are not designed to hang from their rims. Ken Isaacs built similar plywood drawers for his Microdorm.

We feel the ideal drawer for grid beam would be just like the rest of the system — made from standard modular pieces that could be reused. If you come up with a design, please let us know!

Shelves and shelf brackets

Many commercially available shelves adapt to grid beam. Richard used particle board shelves coated with plastic laminate for several mini-desks. Cut them to size, then use an iron to apply strip laminate to cover the edges. Wilma likes the coated-wire closet shelves sold at home improvement centers. They are strong, light-weight, and don't block light like a solid shelf. Cut them to length with a hacksaw, then use like boards or hang from your project's frame with wire.

Button Shelves™

Button Shelves are round shelves developed by Phil that attach to a project's frame using a single bolt. Tighten securely by rotating the shelf, or leave them looser to make a comfortable leg rest. A similar half-round design attaches with two bolts. Buy from QuikStix.

Shelf standards and brackets

Standards and brackets are modular shelf supports designed to screw into wall studs. They are strong enough to support shelves of books. Like grid beam, this system is modular, reusable, and stores in a tiny space. Most US standards have mounting holes spaced every foot except for one end hole, so they bolt to grid beam.

15.12: *Wooden dowels support a notched shelf on the Conversation Lounge.*

15.13: *Button Shelf on a mini-desk.*

Mount standards on vertical sticks, putting the unusable hole at the bottom. Use flat-head machine bolts so the heads don't project, with a washer under each nut. Standards work best on the ends or back of a larger project. They concentrate a lot of stress on their support sticks, so make sure yours are well-braced.

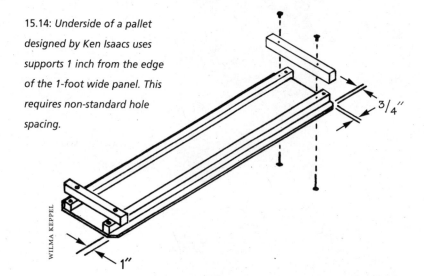

15.14: *Underside of a pallet designed by Ken Isaacs uses supports 1 inch from the edge of the 1-foot wide panel. This requires non-standard hole spacing.*

WILMA KEPPEL

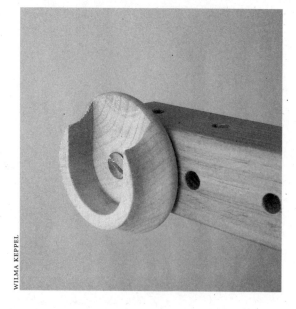

15.15: *Wooden clothes pole support on Richard's free-standing closet attaches with a tapered machine screw and weld nut.*

WILMA KEPPEL

Pallets

Pallets are modular, movable surfaces that sit on the horizontal rails of a project's frame. Ken Isaacs began using them in the 1960s, and soon incorporated them into a number of his Living Structures. Usually one foot wide, pallets can be used as benches or shelves, or grouped to make desks, dining tables and sleeping platforms.

Ken's pallets were ¼-inch hardboard stiffened by a pair of two-by-twos underneath. Two-by-two crossbars kept the pallets from sliding sideways off their supports. Cutting ¾ inches off each corner makes pallets easier to grab, especially when they form a deck inside a project. For use inside projects with side walls, Ken shortened his pallets by ¼ inch and narrowed them by ⅛ inch so they wouldn't jam.

Since pallets are modular, you can make their supports from either grid beam or undrilled two-by-twos. Use fasteners that don't project. Ken used flat-head machine screws and counterbored the bottom holes. We prefer joint connector bolts and weld nuts.

Clothes poles

On some projects we use 1½-inch wooden grid beam for clothes poles. On spans 5 feet and longer, a round pole bends less. Support it using the hangers sold in hardware stores. These bolt right to your frame using machine screws and weld nuts. The pole itself can be wood, metal conduit or pipe.

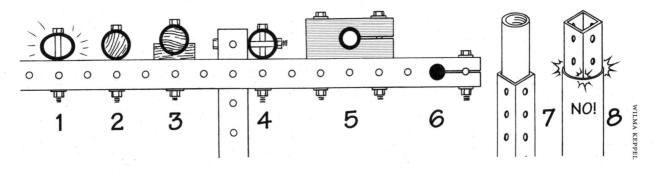

WILMA KEPPEL

Round tubes

When you need to attach a round tube to your project, you have several options.

1. A tube simply bolted to grid beam can crush if the bolt is over-tightened. Phil has successfully used this method to mount 1¼-inch conduit crossbar-style handles on Yard Trucks.

2. A plug of wood, hard plastic or metal protects the tube against crushing. (You can also reinforce square tubes with square plugs.)

3. A plug and saddle spread and stabilize the load.

4. Tubes bolted into a tri-joint pattern are quite strong. Phil has mounted wheelbarrow-style Yard Truck handles of 1¼-inch conduit this way.

5. A pinch block makes the strongest mount. Make it from metal, wood, or hard plastic. Drill all holes before you cut the slot.

6. Phil sometimes makes his grid beam into a pinch block.

7. Put round tube inside square tube, where it will bear against the flat sides.

15.16: *Ways to attach stationary (non-rotating) round tubes and rods to square grid beam. Weakest methods are on left, strongest on right. Avoid method #8.*

KEN ISAACS

Square tube inside round tube makes a weak connection with stress points at the corners.

15.17: *Pivoting reading support on Ken Isaacs's Superchair. Four hardboard pallets make the seat.*

Pivots

A bolt holding a washer or two between two sticks makes a simple pivot. Instead of tightening the nut against your sticks, tighten it against a second nut, leaving a bit of slack. Richard used this method to pivot the desk on his awning chair.

The reading shelf on Ken Isaacs' Superchair was a piece of ¼-inch plexiglass mounted to an aluminum support with pinch blocks made from sections of two-by-two. Ken's ½-inch support rod goes through the frame. Today we would fabricate an adapter to avoid drilling nonstandard holes in our sticks.

Motor mounts

Phil makes his own pivoting motor mounts (Figure 15.18). On most, the weight of the motor automatically tensions the drive belt.

Phil's simplest motor mounts are fabricated from plate steel welded to a shaft (page 165). The ends of the shaft pivot in the project's frame holes. Washers fine-tune the mount's position and keep it from rubbing on the frame.

Where a motor sits on the mount affects belt or chain tension. A chain will skip if a small gear is placed too close to a large one, because the chain won't wrap around enough teeth to hold it. A pulley on a small wheel close to a large one will slip for the same reason. Phil puts the mount in the frame and tests motor posi-

Grid beam adapters

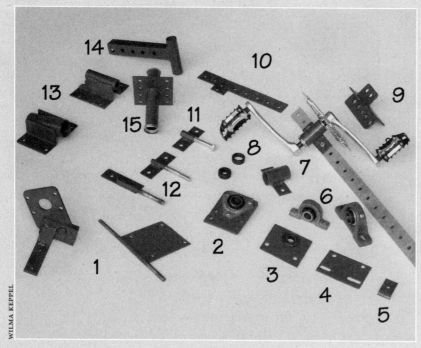

WILMA KEPPEL

15.18: *Grid beam adapters.*

Simple grid beam adapters:

1. Two types of motor mounts fabricated from plate steel.

2. A self-adjusting bearing held between bearing hangers, which bolt to a fabricated steel mounting plate.

3. A round hole in this plate holds a flanged bearing. Use a shaft clamp on the axle to hold the bearing in place.

4. Plate steel mount for the bearing on the end of the Electric Tote Goat's rear axle. The slot allows adjustment to tighten the drive chain.

tion before drilling the motor mounting holes.

Wheel mounts

Phil fabricates simple wheel mounts to attach garden cart wheels to low-speed projects such as handcarts and his Electric Mower (Figure 15.18). The axle is a bolt.

Rotating shafts

Bearings and bushings allow rotating shafts such as axles to turn freely (Figure 15.18). Buy the self-adjusting type — they pivot a bit to compensate when parts don't line up exactly (they never do).

The mounting holes on some pillow-block bearings and bearing hangers match grid beam. If holes don't quite match, file them larger. We discuss specialty pivots, shafts, and other vehicle components in the Vehicle Design chapter, and show a variety of shaft and wheel mounts in Figure 21.7.

Fabricating adapters

As we write this, few adapters that mate non-grid beam components to grid beam

5. Bracket for mounting a solar panel without drilling it, made from a thin piece of plate steel slightly curved at one end. Don't use on vehicles or anywhere the panel will vibrate a lot, because the steel will wear the panel.

6. Commercial pillow blocks, which support a rotating shaft, bolt directly to grid beam. If the holes don't quite match your sticks, file them larger.

7. Bicycle bottom bracket mounts, made by welding a bottom bracket shell to a strip of thin plate steel.

8. Shaft clamps. Buy the type that work like a pinch block. Avoid the type with a set screw; they mar the shaft, making it difficult to slide parts on and off.

9. A bracket from Phil's Portable House, fabricated from two pieces of angle iron.

10. Mounting bracket for a transmission, fabricated from plate steel.

11. Garden cart wheel mount fabricated from a steel plate welded to a coupling nut. The bolt screwed into the nut is the axle. This arrangement does not permit a lock nut. Use only for low-weight, low-speed applications (in case the wheel comes off), never for vehicles.

12. Garden cart mounts made from bolts welded to steel plates. They attach wheels to the side (above) or end (below) of a beam. To keep the nut from unscrewing, tighten two nuts against each other (use a lock nut on the outside), or drill the bolt shaft outside the nut and install a cotter pin.

13. Head tube mounts attach a motorcycle fork (lower) and homemade fork (upper).

14. Head tube mount for a bicycle. The fork angle is built in.

15. Bicycle head tube mount with the tube attached at 90 degrees to the plate. The frame angle sets the fork angle.

Many of these adapters are available from QuikStix™.

are commercially available. (Check our website for updates.) In most cases you will have to make your own adapters or get someone to make them for you.

Most adapters can be fabricated in a simple home shop, using drilled or slotted plate steel, angle iron or pipe. To save weight, Phil sometimes uses aluminum plate or angle, especially on vehicles and carts. A few adapters require bending or welding (Figure 15.18).

We usually avoid welding directly to grid beam. Once a piece is welded, it is no longer standard and interchangeable. Since it will no longer fit every project, its future is limited. Often adjustments must be made after a part is welded. That involves cutting, grinding, cursing, and all the problems grid beam was designed to solve. As Michael Hackleman says, "Once a welded piece doesn't work a little bit, it won't work at all."

Adapter fabrication basics

Start with steel or aluminum plate or angle at least as thick as the thinnest item you are bolting to. This is usually the wall of your tubing. For most purposes you want material thicker than that. Phil uses $1/8$-inch steel for most adapters. He never uses steel thicker than $1/4$ inch because it would exceed the strength of his other materials, including the grid beam he bolts it to.

Fabrication equipment

In addition to the standard measuring and marking equipment, for fabricating you will want:

- A center punch and hammer for marking holes to be drilled. For greatest accuracy, use an automatic center punch to mark the hole. Use the standard center punch to enlarge the dimple if needed.

- A set of center finders (optional). These inexpensive tools let you use an item that already has holes as a template for making more holes.

- A way to cut plate metal, such as a hacksaw or saber saw. Steel can also be cut with a cutting torch or abrasive cutoff saw.

- A way to smooth metal edges and corners. We use a metal file for steel, emery cloth for aluminum.

- A drill press or heavy-duty power drill for making holes. Drills make more accurate holes if clamped in a drill stand. To keep the drill bit from grabbing and spinning your work piece, clamp it down or use a drill press vise.

- Drill bits. For smooth, fast holes in sheet metal, use a step drill bit.

- When bending steel, it is helpful to have a bench-mounted vise in which you can clamp your work, and a torch to heat the area to be bent. (Heating is only necessary for thick stock.) Clamp heated metal in the vise, then pound with a mallet to make a sharp corner.

- Some adapters require welding, which a welding shop can do for you. Tricky to weld, and prone to crack afterward, aluminum should be welded by a professional.

Of course the ideal fabrication accessory is a friendly neighbor who is a retired machinist and welder with a fully equipped shop.

Simple adapters are the quickest to make and tend to be the most versatile. Mounting holes spaced at multiples of 3 inches allow your bracket to bolt to the four US sizes of grid beam. Where you need to fine-tune the position of critical parts, use slots rather than holes.

For most adapters, we use the same cutting techniques used for panels. Aluminum and steel plate can be cut with a saber saw, hacksaw or plasma cutter. You can also cut plate steel with an oxyacetylene torch. Cut sheet metal with a plasma cutter or sheet metal shears, or clamp it to a piece of scrap wood plywood or hardboard, then saber saw through both materials.

Always weld and torch-cut where you have good ventilation. Grind off paint or galvanizing around the area you will heat *before* you torch-cut or weld. These coatings make cutting torches spit, weaken welds, and give off toxic fumes when they burn.

We use a drill press to make most holes in metal. See page 172 for tips on drilling technique, and Figure 16.5 for drill speeds.

To make a neat slot, drill a hole the width of the slot at each end. Then cut from one hole to the other using a hacksaw, saber saw or cutting torch. If your saw blade won't fit through one hole, drill several holes that overlap. You can also cut straight slots with a hand-held grinder or chop saw. Clamp the work piece to keep it from moving. Make a second cut from the back side of your plate to trim the ends of the slot. A cutting torch can quickly cut virtually any slot shape in steel plate.

Welded parts tend to flex and distort slightly as they cool. Plan your order of operations. If your part will be hard to drill after it's welded, or if welding won't affect the drilled holes, drill first. If welding is likely to distort the part and drilling will be easy after you weld, weld first.

For pivots, Phil avoids plain steel rod. Available only in $1/8$-inch or $1/16$-inch increments, it is sometimes oval rather than round. Instead, Phil uses drill rod, a type of steel rod used to make drill bits. Available in $1/64$-inch increments, it has an exact, machined surface. Drill rod steel gets extremely hard when heated — so hard you can't even file it! Abrasive blades and cutting torches will heat the rod enough to harden it. Instead, cut drill rod using a hacksaw, metal-cutting (horizontal) band saw, or cold saw (a special 10 rpm chop saw with a carbide blade). If you plan to cut, thread, notch, drill, machine or file your pivot, make sure you complete all machining operations *before* you weld!

After fabricating your adapter, smooth the edges with a metal file or emery cloth. When fabricating large numbers of steel parts, Wilma grinds off large burrs with a hand-held power grinder, then power wire-brushes all edges and corners. This creates a smooth surface that is pleasant to handle.

Paint steel to prevent rust. We usually spray paint small parts. Powder coating is extremely durable and more environmentally friendly. Aluminum can be left bare.

The next two chapters explain drilling your own sticks and list grid beam parts providers. If you prefer to look at more projects or learn more about building with grid beam, turn to "Frame types" on page 185.

Homemade Sticks

If you can use a drill and tape measure, you can make your own grid beam. Okay, maybe it isn't *quite* that simple, but it's close. If you lack the necessary skills, get a friend to help you, or take a shop class. Many high schools, technical schools and colleges offer night courses for adults.

Should you drill your own?

If you have time, access to the necessary tools, and possess modest shop skills or are willing to learn, drilling your own sticks is a great way to save money. We won't lie to you; it is not the entertainment sensation of the decade. Impatient people may find it mind-numbingly boring. With the right attitude, however, it is very satisfying work. The best part is when you finish drilling and get to build something!

If you have no prior shop experience, drilling your own sticks is a good way to learn the basics — how to accurately measure, mark, drill and cut. With a little practice, you will soon be able to fabricate a variety of simple components that enhance your grid beam creations.

What's involved

Aluminum is the simplest material to process. You only need to mark, drill and deburr it. Marking and drilling are similar for wood, aluminum and steel.

Steel requires degreasing before you drill, and some sort of finish afterward to keep it from rusting.

Wood is easy to work with, but requires the most processing. You must select quality sticks, then cut out any crooked or weak portions. Wood needs smoothing to remove splinters, and benefits from a finish to protect the sticks from stains and ground-in dirt.

Time requirements

Drilling your own grid beam is slow. With a decent shop setup and drill press, plus a little experience, marking and drilling 50 feet (15 meters) of 1½-inch (40-millimeter) wood is an easy day. Figure on spending at least another half day on those sticks — ripping boards to size, smoothing corners, sanding surfaces, applying a finish. This sounds like a lot of work, and it is — but remember, you only have to do it once! The next fifty times you build, your sticks will be pre-cut, drilled and ready to go.

You can save a lot of time by using a drill jig — check our website for availability. A jig eliminates most measuring and marking, and lets you position sticks under the drill bit much faster. Using a jig, you can drill up to 100 feet of wood in a day, though it's a long, hard day and you won't want to do it again tomorrow.

With aluminum, there's a constant problem with long chips getting tangled around the drill bit. You can drill 20 feet in an easy day, 24 to 30 feet if you push yourself, and as much as 40 feet using a drill jig.

Do you really need to drill all the holes?

To make standard 1½-inch grid beam, you must drill 16 holes for every linear foot of stick. That's a lot of holes!

In the 1970s we experimented with a bunch of hole patterns (Figure 2.13), trying to minimize drilling. As we recycled the sticks through dozens of projects, each hole we'd skipped became an obstacle. "It seemed like every time I put together a project I had to get out the hand drill and make at least one more hole," Richard

remembers. "And my hand-drilled holes weren't always straight. That made them a hassle to use on later builds."

Today we avoid those hassles by pre-drilling all holes. Although it takes more time in the beginning, drilling all holes will save you significant time and frustration *every single time you build*, over years or decades.

Required tools

Invest in the best tools you can afford. You'll continue to benefit from faster work and fewer hassles long after you've forgotten the purchase price.

No tools or shop? Many shop classes let you work on personal projects. Or perhaps a neighbor with a shop would like to barter.

To make your own sticks, you'll need basic tools for measuring and marking: a tape measure, fine pencil, masking tape and a square (we prefer a combination square). Fine sandpaper removes sharp burrs from your drill holes, and smooths the cut ends of your sticks. Use a flat metal file to smooth steel.

Drilling tools

Do not try to make grid beam using a hand-held power drill. They are not accurate enough. You'll spend your time fighting crooked holes instead of building projects.

You *can* make wooden grid beam by clamping a drill in a drill stand (Figure 2.3). Inexpensive miniature drill presses now cost less and do a better job.

A full-size drill press is even better. A good one will drill accurate holes on miles of grid beam without overheating, breaking or wearing out. Get one with a motor of at least ¼ horsepower (185 watts) for drilling wood, at least ½ horsepower (370 watts) for drilling aluminum. A 1 horsepower (750 watt) motor is better.

Work space

We like drilling and sanding outdoors. You have room to work, and cleanup is easy. Sweep up all metal chips — they can cut pets and bare feet.

Indoors the main requirements are dryness (so your tools don't rust and your wood doesn't rot or swell), room to work, adequate light and ventilation, and bearable temperature.

With tarps covering doors, floors and furniture, you can drill right in your living room. Put plywood under the drill press to provide a level surface and protect the floor. Better yet, turn a bedroom into a temporary shop. Move the furniture out, protect the floor, and keep the door closed. You'll have a nice place to work, and the mess will stay in one room. Sweep or vacuum frequently to keep sawdust and chips from getting tracked around.

Stick specifications

No matter what size sticks you make, all grid beam has standard proportions that make tri-joints possible. Here are the basics:

- **All hole measurements specify the CENTER of the hole.**

- **The end holes are half a stick width from the ends of the stick.** If the stick is 1½ inches wide, the end holes are ¾ inch from the ends.

- **Holes are spaced one stick width apart.** If the stick is 1½ inches wide, the second set of holes is 1½ inches from the first set, and 2¼ inches from the end of the stick (1½ + ¾ inch).

- **The stick length is a multiple of its width,** almost always an *even* multiple.

- **Most stick lengths are a multiple of a larger basic unit.** Our US sticks are mostly multiples of 6 inches or 1 foot.

Stick width

The wider the stick, the stiffer it is. Twice the width means *eight times* more bending resistance.

Wider sticks also make much stiffer tri-joints. A tri-joint built with 1-inch sticks has only 3 square inches of contact area stiffening it. Using 1½-inch sticks more than doubles the contact area to 6¾ square inches , and 2-inch sticks nearly double it again to 12 square inches.

This means that you can make your project a *lot* stiffer by increasing the stick size even a little. Phil discovered this with his first two vehicles. Built with 1-inch steel tubes, the EVTB's frame flexed under load from its ¾-horsepower (560-watt) motor. For the 1-horsepower (750-watt) Scamp, Phil switched to a 1½-inch aircraft aluminum frame. It weighs the same per foot as 1-inch steel, but is much stiffer due to its larger size and thicker walls. Scamp's frame was so much stronger that Phil has built vehicles with 1½-inch aluminum ever since.

Sticks that big are overkill for children's small, low-speed go-karts. The Electric Moose Club builds with 1-inch aluminum or steel. Phil uses 1-inch aluminum for bicycle trailers, and for non-structural framing on larger projects, such as the solar panel mounts on the Sol Train.

Four-by-four wooden beams 3½ inches square make extremely rigid frames that are tremendously strong. At this size, grid beam provides the benefits of conventional post-and-beam construction in a modular, reusable system.

Hole size

For most uses, holes should be a bit larger than the bolts you intend to use — see the chart on page 27. The extra space makes getting bolts in and out much easier. This is most important on wooden beam, where low humidity can shrink the wood, and the holes. Wood grain tends to make drill bits wander, so holes may not line up exactly. The slack provided by larger holes makes assembly much easier.

If you are building a heavy-duty metal-framed project that will carry a lot of weight and suffer jolts or vibration (such as a trailer or scaffold), use bolts the same size as your holes.

16.1

PHIL AND RICHARD JERGENSON

Drill-it-yourself aluminum

Aluminum is the simplest material to process, requiring only a few ordinary tools and a drill press. Its main disadvantage is that the tube material is expensive, costing several dollars per foot. To avoid mistakes, double-check your measurements before you drill.

For our demonstration, we'll drill 1½-inch aluminum tubes. A similar drilling method works on wood and steel.

1. Acquire your materials. Aluminum tube can be ordered through your nearest metal dealer, or a local welding, metal fabrication or machine shop. It usually comes in pieces 20 feet long. Vendors may give you a deal on short tubes left over after cutting orders, especially if you ask.

   Aluminum alloys range from soft and bendable to extremely strong and stiff. Phil uses aircraft alloy with ⅛-inch (3-millimeter) walls. Alloy 6061–T6 is by far the cheapest aircraft aluminum we have found. Expect to pay several dollars per foot. **Softer alloys such as 6063 are okay for furniture, but may bend or break if used in a vehicle.** A tube with rounded corners is stronger than a tube with sharp corners.

2. Cut your tubes to manageable lengths, such as 8 or 10 feet. If an end isn't square in both directions, re-cut it.

3. Using a square, carefully line up the ends of three or four pieces of aluminum.

4. Mark the center of your first hole ¾ inch from the end of one stick. Make a thin, crisp line. Phil uses a 0.5 or 0.7 milllimeter mechanical pencil with a soft HB lead. A sharp wooden pencil works also.

   If you mark wrong, erase inaccurate lines and try again. A tiny amount of WD-40 on a rag removes the old lines. Wipe all the fluid off so your new lines won't smear. (On wood, remove marks with an eraser.)

5. Fasten your tape measure to the work — this helps accuracy a lot! We use masking tape. Line up the 1½-inch mark on the tape measure with the mark for the first hole. This makes counting the hole spacing easier. Double-check your tape measure placement by making sure the ¾-inch mark lines up with the end of your tube.

6. Carefully place marks every 1½ inches down the length of the pieces. The numbers must be a multiple of 3 inches every other hole. This tells you that you're counting accurately.

7. Remove the tape measure. At each mark you made, use the square to draw one clear line across all your parts. Be exact.

8. Next, flip all the pieces on their sides and line them up with the square. Use your original marks as guides to mark the second side of your tubes. Your marks must line up on both sides of

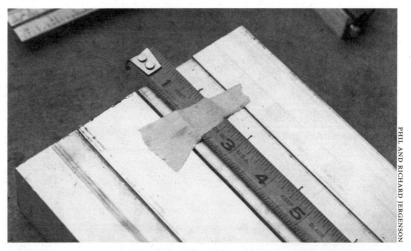

16.2

16.3

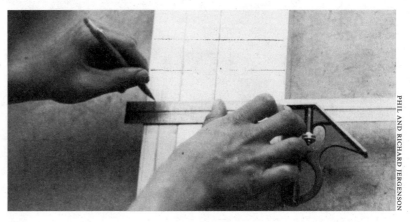

16.4

all the pieces, or your hole placement will be off.

9. Check your clothing. Drill presses are safe shop machines as long as you

Drill speeds (rpm)				
Bit Size	**Aluminum and Wood**		**Steel**	
⁵/₁₆"	7,330	14,660	920	3,670
¹¹/₃₂" ³/₈" ¹³/₃₂"	6,110	12,220	760	3,050
⁷/₁₆"	5,240	10,490	660	2,620
Bit Type:	steel	carbide	steel	carbide

16.5: *Run nitrided (gold color) bits twice as fast as carbide bits.*

16.6: *Drill press with a steel backstop. The support arms keep sticks flat on the table as you drill. To drill wood, add the hardboard backing and spacers shown here.*

ALWAYS wear eye protection, and make sure NO clothing, jewelry or hair can get drawn into the machine. Remove all jewelry, including rings and watches. Loose long hair is very dangerous around a drill press — if even one hair gets caught, it will pull in more hairs within a split second, causing a serious injury. Tie back or braid every bit of long hair, then pin it up or tuck it into your clothing where it cannot work loose. Remove loose or dangling clothing and necklaces, and tuck in shirt tails. Gloves can get snagged on the machine, so **work bare-handed.**

10. Set up your drill press. Put the correct bit in the chuck and adjust the machine's speed (Figure 16.5).

    Set the depth gauge and table height so your bit clears your sticks in the up position, and in the down position drills completely through your stick and out the other side. The easiest way to do this is to set a piece of tube *beside* the bit while you make adjustments. The bit should go through the center hole in the table with a bit of space on each side. Make sure the bit stops before the chuck touches your stick.

11. Now position a backstop on the drill press table. This can be any straight, square material — we like 2-inch double-hole. Stack a few washers under each end to make a space for chips to escape.

Arrange your backstop so that when a tube lies against it, the point of the drill bit touches the exact center of the tube. Bolt or clamp your backstop to the table, then drill a piece of scrap to make sure your holes are centered.

Now arrange supports for your sticks. They must stay flat on the table as you drill, or you'll get crooked holes. We usually bolt support arms on our double-hole backstop, then use floor stands to support the projecting ends.

12. Always use a lubricant (page 140) when drilling metal. Brush, rub or spray the lubricant on the turning bit before you drill, and reapply every few holes.

13. Position a marked stick against the backstop, with the point of the drill above the first mark. **Use one hand to firmly hold the stick against the backstop as you drill.** This keeps the bit from pulling the stick off the table. A fairly light but steady pressure on the bit will give the best results. (Steel requires heavy pressure.) Drill each hole all the way through the tube and out the other side. To get smoother holes, decrease the pressure as you push through the far side of the piece.

14. Leave the machine on as you position the stick for the next hole. Continue along the stick, drilling the first set of holes all the way through the material. Long, curly aluminum chips will tangle around the bit. You'll have to stop the machine periodically to remove them.

PHIL AND RICHARD JERGENSON

16.7

To prevent off-center holes, brush off chips before they build up against your table or backstop. Brush your bit if it starts to clog.

15. Flip your tube on its side and drill the other set of holes.

16. After drilling about 100 feet of tubing you'll need to replace or resharpen the drill bit. As the bit gets dull, aluminum will melt to the cutting edge. **Keep a batch of sharp bits on hand, and replace them frequently.** Drilling with a dull bit is slower, more tiring, and makes messier holes.

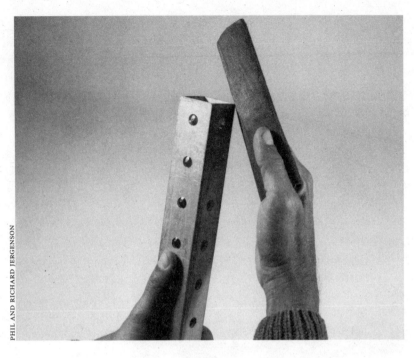

PHIL AND RICHARD JERGENSON

16.8

17. You will notice a lot of curly aluminum chips inside the finished tube. Removing them by pushing a piece of pipe or rebar through the tube.

18. Deburr the cut ends and sharp hole edges with sandpaper. Phil likes 100-grit aluminum oxide cloth.

It is fun to check your accuracy by making a tri-joint with your first three sticks.

Drill-it-yourself steel

We feel commercial steel grid beam is better than anything we can make. We only drill our own steel when a project requires a special size.

Use degreaser and a rag to remove the protective coating on the bare steel before you mark or drill. A silver pencil (available from art and welding supply stores) makes an easy-to-see mark. Use a slow drill speed (page 174), heavy pressure, and lubrication (page 140).

After drilling, use sandpaper, a metal file or a small angle grinder to remove large burrs. Then fit a wire brush attachment on the grinder, and use it to smooth the hole edges. **Always wear a face shield and ear protection when using a grinder or wire brush.**

Once your tubes are drilled, apply a finish to protect them from rust (page 152).

Drill-it-yourself wood

Drilling wood is similar to drilling aluminum. Stick selection, preparing and finishing involves extra steps. For our demonstration, we'll use 1½-inch sticks.

Buying lumber

Start by buying the lumber you need.

A large proportion of the sticks you'll need are short — 4 feet and under. Using free lumber to make these short pieces can save considerable money. Check your lumber pile, and ask neighbors for short pieces. Some builders let people salvage lumber.

You can help the environment and your local economy by buying wood harvested in your area. It often costs significantly less than buying from a lumberyard. There are thousands of small mills all over the country. Many will custom-cut sticks to your specifications. If you own trees, a portable sawmill operator can cut and mill one right on your property — often for a share of the wood.

When buying from a lumberyard, always select your materials in person. Yards sell their worst materials to people who order by phone.

What to get

Richard's first choice is Douglas fir, sometimes sold as "fir." He has also used pine. The construction industry uses these woods for building frames. They are available almost everywhere at reasonable prices.

In lumber-producing areas you may be able to buy green (undried) lumber. It is much cheaper than dry lumber, and drilling it causes fewer splintering problems. It also dulls drill bits faster, and the chips are harder to get out of the holes. Drill and dry it right away so it doesn't mildew.

Save yourself some work and purchase wood that is smoothed on all four sides — "S4S" in industry jargon. Smoothing rough lumber takes so much wood off that it's easy to end up with undersized sticks.

Two-by-twos (actually 1½ x 1½ inches) take the least work to process. Wood quality is usually better if you buy wider lumber and rip it to size. You'll get two 1½-inch sticks out of a two-by-four, three out of a two-by-six, and so on. You must have extra wood to compensate for the width of the saw cut (called kerf). Take your calculator to the lumberyard so you can figure out what's cheapest per length of finished beam.

US lumber sizes	
Nominal size	**Actual size**
one-by-two	¾ x 1½ inches
two-by-two	1½ x 1½ inches
two-by-three	1½ x 2½ inches
two-by-four	1½ x 3½ inches
two-by-six	1½ x 5½ inches
two-by-eight	1½ x 7¼ inches
two-by-ten	1½ x 9¼ inches
two-by-twelve	1½ x 11¼ inches

16.9: *US lumber sizes*

Lumber size

Bring a tape measure when you buy. Tree farm lumber shrinks a lot when it dries. We have measured "two-by" lumber as narrow as $1^3/8$ inches. This is about the usable limit. A 1¼-inch stick is too small for 1½-inch grid beam, and should be ripped down to 1 inch instead.

Green wood will shrink as it dries, so buy as large as you can — 1½ inch or even $1^5/8$ inch if you can get it. Green sticks $1^3/8$ inches or less will be too small to use when dry.

Buy 8-foot, 10-foot or 12-foot sticks that let you cut whole-foot lengths of grid beam with zero waste. Avoid "stud-length" lumber, which is a bit less than 8 feet long. You'll need to cut off split ends. Buy longer pieces if necessary.

Stick selection

Wood selection is critical to producing good grid beam. You want strong, straight sticks. Inspect the lumberyard's piles before making your purchase. Avoid warped, mildewed and knotty piles. You

16.10: *Problems to look for. Curves are easier to see if you sight down the board from one end. Reject sticks that are off-square or have crown, twist, cup or bow — they produce crooked sticks. Cut away sharp changes of direction, crosswise grain, wane, pitch pockets, large or loose knots, and splits. Small, tight knots are usually okay. Small checks and shakes have little effect on strength; treat large ones like splits. Denser grain is stronger.*

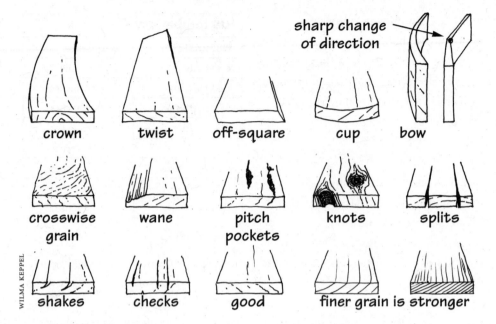

can waste a lot of time cutting the bad sections out of lumber. It is worth paying extra for good wood. Shop around.

Once you get on good terms with the lumberyard crew, they may let you select your own sticks. Neatly re-stack the pile when you're done so you'll be welcome back next time.

Select the straightest sticks you can find by sighting down them lengthwise. Avoid crooked, twisted and badly split pieces. Are the ends square? Buy fine-grained sticks when you can; they're stronger and less prone to split.

Many yards have stopped letting customers select their own sticks because too many people left messy piles. If your local yard has done this, politely explain to the yard crew what you need, and if the quality of what they bring you is too low, reject it.

Used lumber

Used lumber is often too damaged or full of nail holes to be worth bothering with, but sometimes you can get good wood at a great price. Check for flaws, and avoid mildewed, soft or rotten wood. You may need to remove damaged ends.

Salvaged lumber often contains hidden nails that have broken off in the wood. Rip the sticks using a flooring blade, which is designed to cut nails, then sand them smooth. Planer and router blades will chip or shatter if they hit a nail.

Drilling your sticks

We list the rest of the steps for drilling wood assuming you'll use a hand-held power sander or sandpaper to smooth your sticks. If you plan to use a power planer, remember that it can't plane short sticks. Change the order of operations so that you drill first,

Storing Lumber

When you get your wood home, protect it from warping and rot by storing it flat and dry, out of weather and sun. Keep it off the ground or floor by stacking the pile on a few stickers (short pieces of lumber laid crosswise) no more than 4 feet apart. Make sure the stack is flat so the boards won't warp.

In many shops the best storage space is overhead — between the joists in a basement shop, or on the rafters of a garage. Use common sense and don't overload the beams.

Storing green lumber

To prevent mildew and warping, stack green wood with air spaces until it is dry. If you ripped wider boards to make two-by-twos, use your leftover waste strips for stickers (lumber spacers) between each layer of sticks. Support your sticks at least every 4 feet, and put weights on top to keep the upper sticks from warping.

Drying may take weeks or months. Drying time is reduced by warmth, low humidity, and good air circulation. Drilled sticks dry faster than undrilled. Drying wood too fast can cause checks (small splits).

Dry sticks feel light and are dry to the touch. When you sand one, the sawdust stays loose rather than gumming up in little balls. Check a stick from the middle of your stack, where drying is slowest.

dry the wood if green, plane, and rout the corners *before* cutting out flawed portions.

1. If you bought wide stock such as two-by-fours or two-by-sixes, use a radial arm saw or table saw to rip them into two-by-twos. Allow for saw kerf when planning your cuts — you must end up with full-size sticks — and test on scrap first. **Use a flooring blade to rip or cut used lumber.** It is designed to cut through nails, which can shatter a standard wood-cutting blade.

2. Round the long edges of your sticks. This reduces your chances of getting splinters while drilling. We use a router to put a $^3/_{16}$-inch (5-millimeter) radius on the corners of our sticks. You can also use a power sander, hand plane, power jointer, or sandpaper and a sanding block.

PHIL AND RICHARD JERGENSON

16.11: *Always wear a face shield and ear protection when routing.*

Never rout used lumber! A router blade turns at 20,000 rpm. If it hits a nail it will shatter, sending shards of metal all over the shop. Nails also destroy planer and jointer blades. Sand the corners of used lumber.

3. Cut out the bad portions of your sticks. Discard severe bends, knots, pitch pockets, splits and weak grain. If this will leave your pieces too short to grab while drilling, mark the bad sections and cut them off after you drill.

    Use badly warped sticks for something other than grid beam. If you must use a bad stick, discard the worst sections and cut the rest into short pieces.

4. Make sure one end on each piece is square. You will drill this end first.

5. Make your clothing and hair safe for the drill press (page 174).

6. Set up your drill press as described on page 174. Or use a power drill in a drill stand (Figure 2.3). Clamp the drill stand to a work surface you don't mind drilling holes in, such as a piece of stiff plywood.

    To minimize splinters as the drill exits your wood, drill through the wood into a firm backing such as a scrap of hardboard or thin plywood. Move the backing as the holes in it get fuzzy.

7. Drill your holes. Either measure and mark as we demonstrated for aluminum, or use a drill jig. Help the bit eject chips by raising it repeatedly as you drill the hole. Clogging is a worse problem with green wood, which also dulls bits faster.

8. Expect to replace or sharpen your bit after drilling around 100 feet (30

meters) of sticks. Keep a supply of sharp bits on hand and change them frequently. Drilling with a dull bit is hard on your equipment, much more tiring, and more likely to produce splintery holes.

9. If you bought dry wood from the lumberyard, it should not need further drying. Dry green wood as described on page 179.

10. Smooth your sticks with sandpaper on a sanding block, a power sander (much faster), a hand plane or a power planer (extremely fast). All these tools work along the grain, not across it.

    Planing gives a satiny-smooth finish, and is ideal for removing ripping marks. It takes off a bit more material than sanding. If your sticks are already a bit small, sand them. **Never plane used lumber.** Nails destroy planer blades.

11. Cut your sticks into standard lengths, then use sandpaper or a power sander to round off the sharp corners. To minimize splintering, round toward the end of the stick.

12. Apply a finish (see below). Bare wood is easily damaged by moisture, and will absorb dirt and stains.

Finishing your sticks

Finishes protect steel grid beam from rusting, and wooden grid beam from moisture, stains and ground-in dirt.

Because of grid beam's holes, liquid finishes that sit on the surface (such as paints and varnishes) are prone to drip and run. Light spraying works fairly well. Or apply thin coats with a roller. Brushes are a disaster!

Some paints and varnishes are prone to a problem called *blocking,* where the finish on two different pieces sticks together. Blocking is most likely where sticks are clamped together in a tri-joint. Blocked paint can pull right off the stick when the joint is disassembled. Blocking is worse when pieces get bolted together before they are completely dry. Finishes that quickly dry to the touch may take weeks or months to harden completely. Check with the manufacturer.

Finishes for steel

Hot-dip galvanizing is hard on the environment, but creates a finish that is impervious to dings and impacts and lasts for decades outdoors (less near salt water). It also protects the inside of the stick.

Powder coating is one of the most environmentally friendly painting technologies. Heat fuses a plastic layer to the metal. The plastic is fairly resistant to impact and abrasion, and impervious to salt water and most chemicals. It does not protect the inside of the stick very well. For an applicator near you, check under "Paint" and "Powder Coating" in your Yellow Pages.

You can spray paint grid beam if you apply the paint thinly, in several coats. A thicker coat of paint will build up in the holes and cause drips and runs. Start with a coat or two of primer, then apply the finish coats. Depending on the type, spray paint is mildly to extremely toxic, and fairly hard on the environment. **Spray only in a well-ventilated area, and use the breathing protection recommended by the paint's manufacturer.**

Finishes for wood

Phil leaves his wooden sticks bare. If a stick gets a spot, he sands it off with 100-grit sandpaper.

Richard and Wilma perfer oil finishes that protect sticks from stains and dirt.

Oily rags are a fire hazard

A common cause of shop fires is oily rags. After sitting for a while, **oily rags or paper towels can burst into flames all by themselves.** Linseed oil is the worst. A rag soaked with linseed oil can burn underwater! We have two friends whose shops burned down due to rags soaked with linseed oil. Another found the smoldering pile just in time.

Oily rags ignite due to a heat-producing reaction with oxygen in the air. If heat can't build up, the rags can't ignite. Crumpled or folded rags act as their own insulation. Clip unfolded rags to a wire over bare concrete to prevent heat buildup and ignition, or store them in a metal container with a tight-fitting metal lid — a wood stove is ideal. Phil has used rocks to weight rags safely in the middle of a parking lot, but don't do this during fire season. **Never leave oily rags lying around your shop,** especially if people live in the same building.

Made from oils that harden in air, they do not feel oily when dry.

Oil finishes soak into the wood, so you get no globs, drips or runs. Since the finish is *in* the wood, not on it, it cannot be chipped or scraped off. Oil looks great, is super-durable, and gives excellent protection. More can be applied at any time, an advantage for outdoor projects. If you cut a stick, you can brush or dip more finish onto the freshly cut ends. (We don't bother.)

The main disadvantages of oil finishes are solvent toxicity during application, air pollution as the finishes dry, and fire hazard in the shop due to oily rags (see page 181).

Richard's favorite oil finish is one coat of Watco Danish Oil, available in clear and several stain colors. After 30 years, his oldest Watco-finished sticks still look fantastic. Watco is top-quality, but expensive. It has a distinctive scent that some people can smell years after application.

Wilma prefers boiled linseed oil because it costs less and she can't smell it after it dries. She applies it in two coats. The first coat is ⅓ linseed oil and ⅔ thinner. The thinner can be mineral spirits, naphtha, paint thinner, etc. Thinner helps the oil penetrate deeply into the wood. After the sticks are dry to the touch (4 to 24 hours, depending on temperature), she applies a second coat of ½ linseed oil and ½ thinner. The sticks then dry for at least a week while the thinner evaporates.

Safer wood finishes

These are low-toxicity, environmentally friendly alternatives to conventional oil finishes. We've heard good reports about:

- BioShield Hard Oil #9, a low-toxicity, low-odor, environmentally friendly oil finish for indoor use. It does not need thinning except on exceptionally dense woods. Dip, wait 15 minutes, then wipe off any excess with a rag. Requires a week to cure.
- AFM Naturals Clear Penetrating Oil, a low-toxicity, environmentally friendly oil finish for indoor and outdoor use. It has more of an odor than the BioShield Hard Oil, and doesn't penetrate as well. For the first coat, thin as much as four to one with AFM Naturals Dilutent/Reducer 4099. Thin each successive coat less.
- Timber Pro UV Internal Wood Stabilizer, a very low-toxicity, environmentally friendly outdoor finish that's used for edible landscape planter boxes. Soaks in and then reacts with the wood to form a glass-like layer like petrified wood under the surface, which keeps out mold and moisture. May turn the wood black as it pushes impurities out. Wipe off the black layer, then add a stain or clearcoat on the outside if desired.
- BioShield Aqua-Resin, a low-toxicity, environmentally friendly, water-based wood stain and finish for indoor and outdoor use. It is washable and provides moisture protection. In heavy-wear areas like kitchen cabinet doors or floors, add a wax finish.
- Livos finishes have a reputation for quality. You may need to mail order them. Auroand Tried & True also make environmentally friendly, low-toxicity finishes. We don't yet have details about these products.

A number of less toxic substitutes for conventional oil finishes have come on the market in recent years (see box page 182). We'll be testing several brands after this book goes to press, so check our websites for updates.

You can dip, spray, roll or sponge on oil finishes. Wear plastic gloves and ensure good ventilation. Dipping is fast and protects even the insides of the holes, but uses more finish. Richard uses a section of gutter as a dip vat. Wilma prefers to spray her sticks using a hand-held sprayer charged with compressed air. This uses less finish but makes more fumes, so she works outdoors. Hang finished sticks up by their holes to dry in a well-ventilated area.

Recently, low-temperature powder coating has been developed for wood. The plastic finish soaks into the grain, much like an oil finish. This process is much more ecologically friendly than most paints and stains.

WILMA KEPPEL

16.12: *Applying an oil finish using a spray bottle charged with compressed air. Spray short pieces on top of longer ones so the overspray hits your sticks.*

Part 4

Project Design

Frame Types

In the next five chapters you'll learn the basics of grid beam project assembly and design. To help you build, we've included simplified explanations of a few construction basics. We'll start with project frame types.

Most grid beam projects start with the frame. Frames fall into three general types:

1. **Box frames** look like an outline of a box. Shelves are notched at the corners to accommodate the frame posts. Vertical panels bolt to the posts.

2. **Offset frames** are like a box with the posts offset from the corners. Shelves fit inside the frame, and are not notched.

3. **Stem frames** are skeletal and use a minimum number of sticks, like signposts or clotheslines.

Box frames

The frame of a box-frame project resembles a line drawing of a box. It is made of rectangles and has tri-joints at or near the corners. This type of construction is inherently strong and rigid. Cross-brace box frames by bolting on a skin of stiff panels such as plywood. Good box-type projects include shelves, desks, workbenches, buildings and vehicles.

Most box-frame projects have posts on their outside corners. This gives you several options for putting shelves inside a frame:

17.1: *A ¼-inch plywood skin turns a box frame closet organizer into a 2 x 4 x 6-foot free-standing closet. This type of frame can bear very heavy loads.*

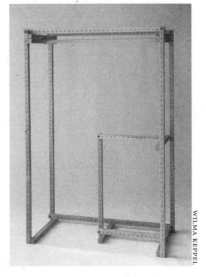

WILMA KEPPEL

WILMA KEPPEL

WILMA KEPPEL

17.2: *Wilma's offset frame pantry shelves use 1 x 3 foot shelf panels of high-ply exterior plywood. Frame is 1 foot deep, 8 feet tall, and 39 inches wide. All sticks are standard lengths.*

PHIL JERGENSON

17.3: *Shelves sit in front of an offset frame's rear legs and project in front. This version of the workbench Phil built in Chapter 1 is shorter and has the small shelf on top (not shown).*

1. Use shelves in standard sizes such as 2 x 4 feet, and notch the corners. A panel with posts on all corners is locked securely into the project's frame.

2. Use smaller panels that will fit between posts without notching. Shortening the long dimension of a panel creates a slide-out shelf.

3. On projects where the shelves go only partway across the project, position the middle posts so they will support your shelves with no notching (Figure 6.3).

Offset frames

Offset frames have their legs offset from the corners. Wilma developed these frames while visiting Willits in 1995. "I needed a computer desk, but I didn't want to notch the Jergensons' panels to build a project that might only exist for a few weeks. Instead, I figured out a way to build a frame *around* the shelves, using standard-length sticks. Once home, I realized I could use the same method with board shelves that I didn't want to notch. It worked so well that 10 years later, I'm still building this way."

An offset frame's rear legs stand *behind* the shelves, which project slightly in front. The project's front legs stand *beside* the shelves. The shelves slide out, so it's easy to adjust their height. Offset frames make good shelves, desks and workbenches.

Assembling an offset frame

Assembling an offset frame is a bit different than building a box frame. Wilma

WILMA KEPPEL

17.4: *Bookcase components. All the sticks and panels are standard lengths: 4 sticks 3 inches long; 8 sticks 1 foot long; 4 sticks 5 feet long; 4 sticks 3½ feet long; 4 shelves 3½ feet long*

PHIL JERGENSON

17.5

PHIL JERGENSON

17.6

demonstrates with a bookcase. The shelves are wooden boards 3½ feet long.

1. Tall projects are often easiest to assemble lying on their backs. Lay the rear legs on the floor. Now bolt on the top and bottom crosspieces. Leave one stick width projecting to each side, and one at the top.

    Due to humidity changes, wooden projects occasionally need their bolts tightened. Position the bolts so you can tighten them without removing panels. On metal-framed projects, put the nut ends of your bolts where people are least likely to bump into them. Leave the bolts a bit loose; this makes it easier to align the frame holes as you add more sticks.

2. Add the top and bottom side rails outside the rear legs, below the crosspieces. This creates tri-joints.

3. Bolt the front crosspieces to the top side of the side rails.

4. Now add front legs. There are two ways to do this:

Method 1: Bolt a 2-hole piece to each side rail just behind the front joint, then bolt the leg to these 2-hole pieces (Figure 17.7) . Since this doesn't create tri-joints, you will need to add at least one more side rail on each side. Use 2-hole sticks to make tri-joints at each end of it. The legs are at the front of the frame, making this method useful for very shallow shelves (Figure 6.5).

Method 2: Bolt the front legs to the side rails, one stick width from the front of the project. Now use a two-hole piece to make a tri-joint behind the leg at each joint. The front legs stand one stick width behind the front of the frame (Figure 17.8). This method makes the strongest frame.

5. Tip the frame upright, and add the rest of the shelf supports.

6. Tighten all bolts.

7. Add a back panel if your project has one. It will project one stick width on each side of the rear legs. Use the gap

17.7a-b

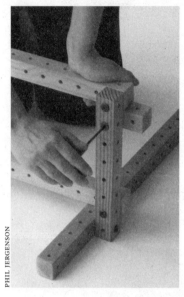
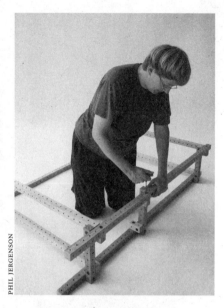

PHIL JERGENSON

PHIL JERGENSON

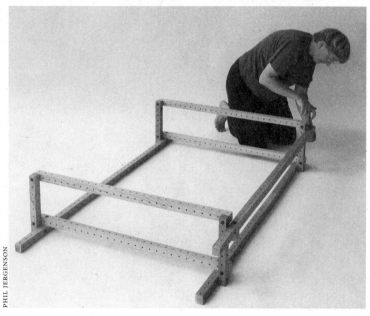

17.8

PHIL JERGENSON

17.9

WILMA KEPPEL

17.10

17.11a

17.11a-c: *A single-post stem frame such as this indoor clothesline (a) needs diagonal bracing under any significant load. Double crossbeams (b) or double posts (c) make a much stiffer frame, as Richard demonstrates by hanging from a clothes rack he designed.*

between the rear panels and the back of the shelves to run power cords.

8. Slide in the shelves.

The finished bookcase measures 45 inches wide — 3½ feet plus the two 1½-inch (40-millimeter) outside legs. The inside of the frame is 10½ inches deep — 1 foot minus the 1½-inch rear legs. Reduced depth makes offset frames good for use with wooden boards, which are narrower than their nominal (named) sizes. The "one-by-twelve" pine boards used here measure 11¼ inches wide.

Stem frames

Stem frames use the minimum number of sticks to get the job done. Resembling a tree or window frame more than a box, they are especially useful for lifting or hanging loads.

Stem frames concentrate a lot of stress at their joints, especially when beam spans

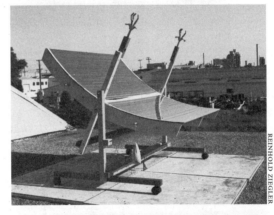

17.11b

17.11c

are long. "I learned about bracing stem frames the hard way," Wilma says. "Previous books about grid beam show mainly box-frame projects, most braced

WILMA KEPPEL

17.12: *Steel frame of Wilma's unbraced stick-drying rack bending under 600 feet (180 meters) of wooden grid beam — about 300 pounds (135 kilograms) — despite tri-joints at all corners.*

with panels. The Jergensons' first book said they only used cross-bracing on very large projects with spans of 8 feet or more. But when I started building stem-style projects, whether wood or steel, I got frames that leaned crazily when loaded, or that bent or crushed the tubes at the corners. A few projects almost collapsed. Adding tri-joints to all the corners didn't help much. Adding diagonal braces made these projects very strong."

Wilma's stick-drying rack demonstrates the problem. With single posts and no bottom crossbar, this frame design is very weak. Despite tri-joints at every corner, the 300 pound (135 kg) load pulled the single-post frame out of square, and visibly bowed the vertical posts. (They straightened once she removed the load.)

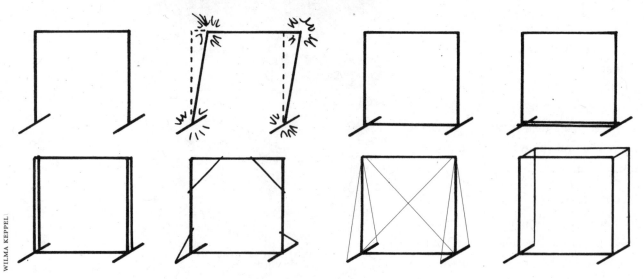

WILMA KEPPEL

17.13: *Unbraced stem frames tend to rack at the corners when loaded. With no bottom bar, the top left design is particularly weak. A frame with crossbar is somewhat stronger. Brace stem frames by adding double crossbars or double posts, adding diagonal sticks or gussets (triangular panels), bracing with cables or strings in opposing pairs, or adding a partial box.*

PHIL AND RICHARD JERGENSON

17.14: A *stem-frame desk braced by adding a partial box at the* *rear.*

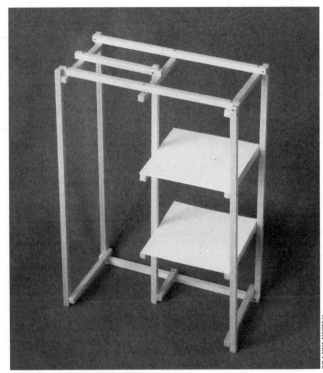

WILMA KEPPEL

For something holding this much weight, double posts or diagonal braces are a must, even with a steel frame.

To brace a weak or wobbly stem frame, add double posts or crossbeams, build a partial box frame, or cross-brace the project using diagonal sticks, cables, wires, threaded rod or perforated metal strap. String is adequate to brace light-weight projects such as yard sale signs. Brace the frame in every direction in which it experiences heavy loads.

Good stem-type projects include closet organizers, sawhorses, roadside signs, wind turbine towers, Savonius and helical rotor frames, and some types of trailers.

When to use which frame type

Many projects can be built several ways. In general:

- Use stem frames for lifting, hanging, or tall, narrow loads. If side loads are significant, add diagonal braces.

- Use offset frames when you don't want to notch shelf or desk panels.

- Use box frames for everything else.

17.15: *Stay flexible when you plan projects. This closet frame has both box and stem elements. Wilma built a similar design in 1995 as a combination computer desk and closet.*

 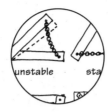 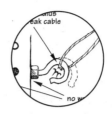 

Bracing

One of the questions we always get at trade shows is, "Why don't you use diagonal braces?" Actually, we do — but most small grid beam projects don't need them. The tri-joints at the corners of desks and bookcases are usually enough to keep them square. If not, we bolt on one or more panels that cross-brace the frame.

Bracing turns a wobbly frame into one that's strong and stable. **Bracing cannot substitute for adequate structure.** If you are trying to hold up a battleship on four legs of 2-inch steel, no amount of bracing is going to do the job because the frame itself is not strong enough.

What bracing *can* do is help you get the most strength out of the fewest and lightest-weight materials. Let's find out how.

Bracing basics

What makes a strong, rigid structure? Let's experiment with some boards to find out. (We are indebted to *The Dome*

Builder's Handbook by John Prenis for this simplified discussion of structure.)

1. One board won't build much.

2. Two boards bolted together can hinge around the bolt and collapse.

3. Adding a third board to brace the other two creates a rigid structure. This triangle can't be distorted without bending or breaking the boards or pulling a joint apart.

4. Four boards are no more rigid than two. This type of collapse is called *racking*.

18.1: *Only shapes braced with triangles stay rigid when loaded.*

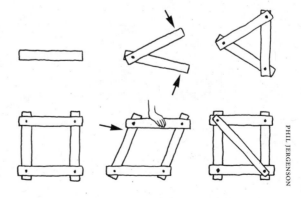

PHIL JERGENSON

193

18.2

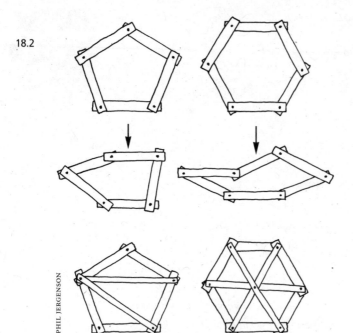

PHIL JERGENSON

5. Use a fifth board to turn the square into two triangles, and it becomes rigid.

6. Are more boards better? No.

7. Only when you divide the new shapes into triangles do they become rigid.

The triangle is the only flat shape you can build with straight boards or beams that is rigid! Triangles are the basis for most built structures.

Rigid structures are being braced by triangles whether you can see them or not. This includes "unbraced" items such as chairs and table legs. The triangles are *inside* the joints and frame members. We believe that grid beam frames are so rigid because the triangles inside tri-joints are much larger than in other types of construction, and also overlap and interlock more. The wider your sticks, the bigger the bracing triangles inside the joints.

Cross-bracing

A diagonal brace that turns a rectangle into stable triangles is called *cross-bracing*.

Let's go back to our two-board structure. What if you make the third side from something flexible, such as a length of chain (Figure 18.4)? You may have seen folding tables made this way. Notice that in order to work, the chain must be in *tension* (with the ends being pulled apart). If the chain is in *compression* (with the ends pushed toward each other), the triangle can collapse.

You can use chain, cable, wire, rope, perforated metal strap or threaded rod to make a rectangle rigid, using two diagonal

WILMA KEPPEL

18.3: *Gate, railroad bridge and building all use triangles to make them stiff and strong.*

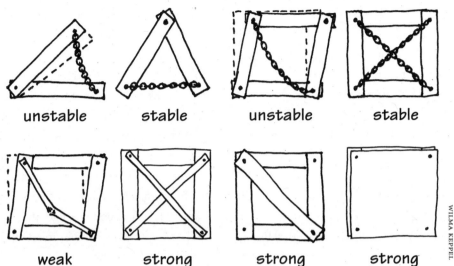

unstable   stable   unstable   stable

weak   strong   strong   strong

18.4: *Types of cross-bracing.*

braces that cross each other. These braces work only while they are in tension. Keep the braces tight to keep your project square.

A board brace works whether pulled or compressed. But a brace made from a *narrow* board can collapse just like a chain. Instead use a thicker board, two crossed boards, or a panel.

A panel works for cross-bracing because of the hidden triangles inside it. To prove this, cut out pieces of the panel, leaving triangular braces joining the frame pieces. This panel can still brace the rectangular frame. If you cut away the panel in any way that destroys the triangles connecting the frame pieces, the frame can collapse.

Even wooden building frames are floppy until panels get attached. Sheathing and siding brace the outside; drywall panels stiffen the interior. On construction sites you can often see diagonal braces holding a building frame square before its panels get added.

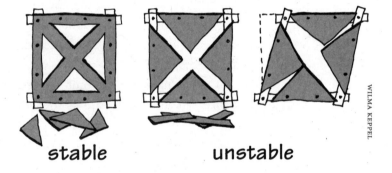

stable   unstable

18.5: *Triangles must connect frame pieces.*

We've just demonstrated three easy options for cross-bracing grid beam projects: panels, rigid diagonal braces such as grid beam sticks, and tension braces such as wire or cable.

Panel braces

Our favorite bracing method is a bolt-on skin made of stiff panels such as plywood, signboard, pegboard or hardboard. A partial back is often all the bracing a project needs.

Panels used for cross-bracing are called *shear wall*. We like shear wall because it's easy to apply, strong and looks great. Disadvantages include the cost of the panels and their weight.

For maximum bracing effect, panels must stay flat on the frame of your project. Use enough bolts that your panel can't bow. Stiff panels such as thin plywood have more bracing power than flexible panels like hardboard.

On most projects we add skin right over the frame bolts. The flatter the hardware, the easier this is. If your frame needs the strength of hex bolts, chisel a pocket on the back of your panel to make room for the bolt heads, or drill a hole bigger than the bolt head right through the panel.

Cutting parts out of your project's panels can actually increase its strength. (A heavy project may use most of its strength carrying its own weight.) We use square panels with decorative round holes to brace furniture, a technique developed by Reinhold Ziegler in the early 1970s. The holes provide light and ventilation, and the corner triangles brace the frame.

Sometimes you can get rid of the middle of the panel entirely, and use a separate piece to brace each corner. These triangles are called *gussets*.

Diagonal braces

Diagonal braces give your project the structural advantages of a rigid skin without the weight. Diagonals don't need to connect exactly at the corners to work; an almost-triangle works fine.

It's usually impossible to use both end holes on a grid beam diagonal brace and get a square corner. Instead, you'll need to fasten one end using a hole *near* the end. Start by bolting one end hole of your stick to the project near a tri-joint. Now pivot the stick until a hole near the other end of the brace matches a hole in the project's frame. Slip in a bolt to hold the brace while you check whether the project's frame is square. Move the attachment point until you get a square corner, then tighten the bolts.

You can make diagonal braces from boards, pipe or anything stiff, strong and reasonably straight. The floppier your brace material, the more important it is to use braces in pairs. *Securely* attach the ends to your frame. Remember, the end bolt on a diagonal brace is taking the load shared by *all* the bolts attaching a panel.

Tension braces

Tension braces are thin, strong braces such as wire, cable or threaded rod that are kept tight, like a guitar string or bicycle spoke. They combine high strength with low weight, which is why they are used on airplanes, broadcast towers, bridges and boats. The use of tension elements to lift and brace is called *rigging*.

Tension braces are easy to use at furniture scale, tricky when scaled up to building size or larger. The tension tips we present here are very basic. A good rigging handbook or experienced professional rigger will help you use tension safely.

- **Use tension elements in opposing pairs.** On rectangular frames, cross tension elements in an X. To hold a pole upright, use pairs of cables pulling in opposite directions.

- **Tension elements must stay tight at all times** A loose tension element has ZERO bracing power! A slack cable is not bracing your project. An unbraced project might collapse.

- **A tension assembly is only as strong as its weakest part. Each component must be strong enough to take the entire load.** The forces concentrated in and by tension members can be tremendous. Make sure your frame and tension elements are strong enough to take the load.

Ken Isaacs used crossed pairs of steel cables to brace projects such as his Superchair and Microdorm. Depending on the project, you can also use wire, threaded rod, perforated steel strap and even string. Install tension braces in opposed pairs, then tighten them alternately until they are as snug as you want.

Perforated strap

Perforated steel strap is inexpensive and easy to use — just bolt it to the project frame. Since you can't tension it, install it as tight and flat as possible. This light-duty brace is good for stationary projects such as storage locker shelves. It's ugly, so we don't use it on indoor furniture.

18.6: *Tension braces made of threaded rod brace a wood-framed stick rack Wilma built for the Jergensons' shop. Here it holds 300 feet (90 meters) of wooden sticks up to 8 feet long.*

WILMA KEPPEL

Threaded rod

We use ¼-inch threaded rod to brace projects such as bunk beds and storage racks. It is strongest if you attach it so you can get it really tight. Two 6-foot lengths will nicely brace posts 4 feet apart. Use barrel nuts to join sections if you need longer pieces.

The simplest way to install threaded rod is to bend each end to fit through your project's frame holes. (Bending weakens the rod, so don't use this method on high-strength projects.) We insert ¼-inch rod about 2 inches into our furniture's wooden frame, then bend the long part by hand. Now reverse the rod and bend the other end. Make the straight section a little bit short — ½ inch is good — because the frame members will draw together when you tighten the braces. You can also bend threaded rod in a vise. To avoid mashing the threads, clamp the rod between pieces of wood, or thread some nuts on it and clamp the nuts.

Once both ends are bent, insert the rod into your project's frame. It will seem too long; you'll need to twist it. Use a nut and washer on each end to tighten it. You want the rod snug, not loose or floppy. If necessary, move one of the ends to a different hole. Tighten opposing braces alternately, checking often to make sure your structure stays square. Once you have everything the way you want it, you can hacksaw off the rod's projecting ends if they're in the way, using the nut as a saw guide. Smooth the ends with a file.

Threaded rods used to brace large projects such as buildings and bridges are attached like a cable, using forged turn-buckles and rod ends. Consult a rigging handbook for details.

Wire and cable

Wire is useful for bracing small, stationary projects. For heavier loads, use multi-strand steel cable, also called wire rope. It is stronger than solid wire, and can flex repeatedly without cracking.

Install cables in pairs, with a turnbuckle at one end of each cable for tightening. You will need to form an eye (loop) in each end. Use a metal thimble in the eye to protect the cable from fraying, kinking and excessive bending, and secure with cable clips. A rigging handbook will show you how.

When measuring and installing cables, unscrew the turnbuckle hooks and eyes until they are fully extended, with all threads

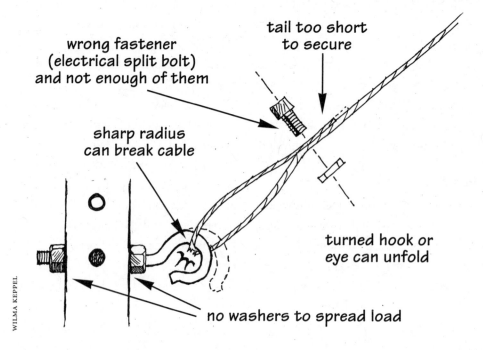

18.7: *How not to terminate a heavily loaded structural cable.*

WILMA KEPPEL

wrong fastener (electrical split bolt) and not enough of them

tail too short to secure

sharp radius can break cable

turned hook or eye can unfold

no washers to spread load

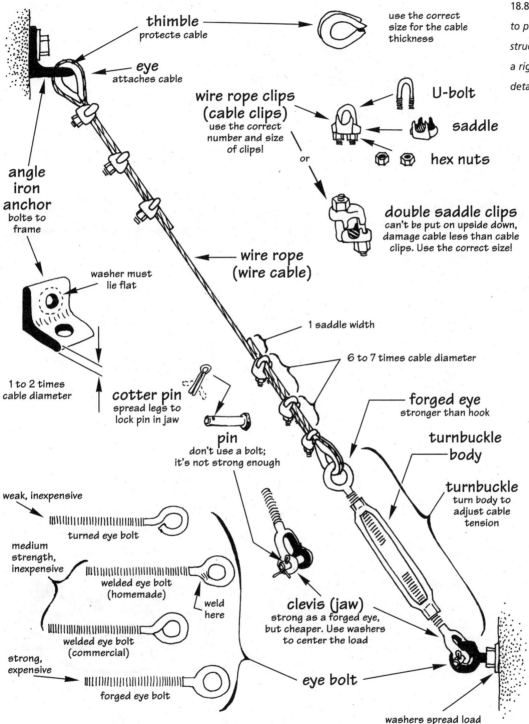

thimble
protects cable

use the correct size for the cable thickness

18.8: *One of several ways to properly terminate a structural cable. Consult a rigging handbook for details.*

eye
attaches cable

wire rope clips (cable clips)
use the correct number and size of clips!

U-bolt

saddle

hex nuts

or

double saddle clips
can't be put on upside down, damage cable less than cable clips. Use the correct size!

angle iron anchor
bolts to frame

washer must lie flat

wire rope (wire cable)

1 to 2 times cable diameter

1 saddle width

6 to 7 times cable diameter

cotter pin
spread legs to lock pin in jaw

pin
don't use a bolt; it's not strong enough

forged eye
stronger than hook

turnbuckle body

turnbuckle
turn body to adjust cable tension

weak, inexpensive

turned eye bolt

medium strength, inexpensive

welded eye bolt (homemade)

weld here

welded eye bolt (commercial)

clevis (jaw)
strong as a forged eye, but cheaper. Use washers to center the load

strong, expensive

forged eye bolt

eye bolt

washers spread load

WILMA KEPPEL

18.9: *The bigger the load-bearing triangles inside a beam, the stiffer it is. A beam half as thick bends eight times more!*

WILMA KEPPEL

in the turnbuckle body engaged by the hooks and eyes. Install the cables, then tighten them by rotating the turnbuckle bodies. This screws both ends in or out. Tighten opposing cables alternately, checking often to make sure your structure is square. You want to preload the cables with enough extra tension that they won't sag under load, plus a bit extra for emergencies. Don't over-tighten or the cable could break.

Beams and trusses

Conventional construction methods use triangle braces to get more strength out of less structure. Triangle tricks adapt elegantly to grid beam.

Let's start with beams and trusses. Beams are those big timbers and I-beams you see holding up roofs and floors. Trusses

do the same job, but are made from multiple pieces. They are often spidery-looking. The most famous example is the Eiffel Tower.

Beam basics

Triangles make beams and trusses strong. Bigger load-bearing triangles make a stiffer structure.

When a load is put upon a beam such as a floor joist, the beam bends. The top side gets shorter and the bottom gets longer (Figure 18.10). Nothing much happens in the middle, which is why we put holes there.

Since the top and bottom of a beam do most of the work of holding up its load, there are two ways to get more strength for less weight:

1   **Add material** to strengthen the load-bearing top and bottom of the beam. This is how railroad rails and I-beams work. Carpenters use a wooden version called a web truss.

2. **Remove material** from the middle of the beam where you don't need it. This

WILMA KEPPEL

18.10: *How a loaded beam bends.*

is how ladder, roof and box trusses work.

Truss tricks

The trick with trusses is to keep strength where you need it. Taking too much material away weakens the truss. Triangles can sag if they're too long. Use triangles small enough to stay rigid.

A truss can only support a load that goes straight across the triangles. A twisted truss can't hold much.

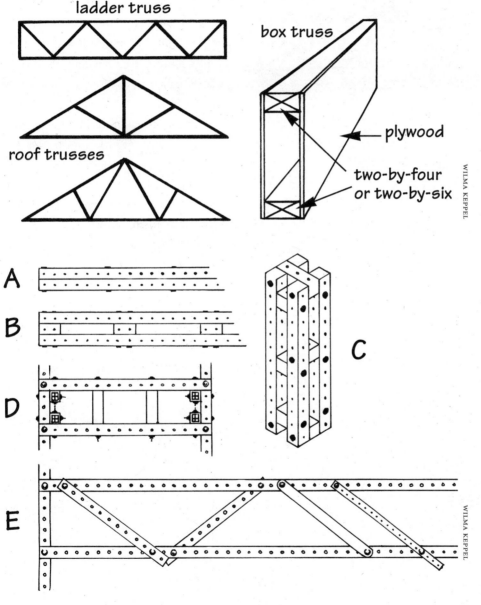

18.11: *Several types of trusses.*

18.12: *A: Bolting two sticks together makes a simple truss. B: Adding spacer blocks makes it stiffer. C: Another way to use spacer blocks. This technique comes from Craftsman furniture. D: On vehicles, Phil uses sections of round aluminum tube to make spacers taller than one stick width. E: Corners of the diagonal sticks on a web truss protrude unless you double the top and bottom horizontal beams, round the corners on the diagonals, or make diagonals from narrower sticks.*

PHIL AND RICHARD JERGENSON

18.13: *Aluminum diamond plate turns each side of this Yard Truck into a truss.*

A vertical truss can hold up huge loads from the top, bottom or ends. If you push from the side, the truss is very weak because the triangles you are bending are small. A beam or truss must either be thick enough to withstand side loads (box truss), or it must have side support from other parts of the structure.

The farther apart the top and bottom of your truss or beam, the stiffer it will be. A tall truss puts a lot of stress on its top and bottom pieces, so make sure they are strong enough.

Knots are weak in tension, and can even fall out of the stick. If you must use knotty lumber, keep the knots on the top side of your truss or beam, where they are compressed.

You can stiffen problem areas on your projects by creating little mini-trusses. For instance, a sagging shelf can be stiffened by adding a piece to the edge. (Wood and angle iron both work well.) This creates bigger triangles to resist the sag.

 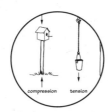  

compression   tension

dynamic load

Building Safe Projects

A family building an underground home during the 1970s got hassled by their building inspector. Unfamiliar with underground construction, he worried about the weight of dirt on the roof, even though the home was wildly overbuilt. The owners waited until all the dirt was in place, then drove the bulldozer across the roof — a load many times heavier than anything it would ever experience from rain or snow. After that demonstration, the inspector was happy to approve the house.

This shows the danger of listening to experts. Sometimes everyone tells you a project won't work just because their thinking is in a rut.

On the other hand, Ken Kern, a widely respected and experienced builder and designer who wrote *The Owner-Built Home* and many other do-it-yourself books, was killed in the collapse of a partially completed experimental building

he'd designed. So use your judgment. If your project is potentially dangerous and you're not sure what you're doing, get help from someone capable, such as an experienced builder or structural engineer. And make sure that person has experience *successfully completing and using* the type of project you are interested in. You don't want someone who only *thinks* they know what you're doing; you want someone who *does* know, and has the experience and success to prove it.

The purpose of this chapter is to give you basic knowledge that will help you safely modify, design and improve projects. We'll cover basic safety, how structures work (and fail), and simple tests and fixes to help you troubleshoot projects and make them work.

Avoiding trouble

The biggest factor in staying out of trouble is "common" sense, which is rarer than you might think. Knowing what you *don't* know takes skill and experience. Some tips:

- Respect your own abilities and build projects within your skill level. If you find a project requires expertise you lack, stop or get help. Vehicles take more know-how than any other type of project.

- If you think something might break, get out of the way *now!* Figure out what to do next *after* you and others are safely out of the way. (And make sure you *can* get out of the way while building and testing your project.)

- If you think there *might* be a problem with your project, there probably *is* one. Figure out how to avoid disaster while you run tests, find the problem, and fix it.

- Assume that what can go wrong, will: plumbing and roofs will leak, beams will rot, a wheel will hit a huge pothole at high speed. How will the problem affect your project? The best projects warn you before they fail, then fail slowly. To some degree you can ensure this by good design. See Stewart Brand's *How Buildings Learn* and any of J. E. Gordon's books about structure for more information.

- The easiest way to find many problems is with a visual inspection, so leave vital parts exposed whenever you can.

- When venturing into uncharted territory, overbuild.

- The smaller the project, the bigger the risks you can afford to take with the design. If your flower pot stand collapses, it's no big deal. But if the wing of an air-plane falls off in midair, that test flight could become *much* too exciting.

- Learn to make smart mistakes. A smart mistake is affordable (the wheel collapsed, but the vehicle was only going 15 miles an hour). A smart mistake is also one you can learn from (use a stronger wheel). Everybody makes mistakes. They are probably the best learning tool that exists! The more *smart* mistakes you make, the faster you will learn.

The best time to find a problem is *before* it gets you into trouble. We'll tell you about simple testing methods after you have an idea of what to look for. Let's start by examining loads.

Loads

The whole point of structure is to withstand loads. Loads are those forces that try to push, pull, twist, stretch and crush something.

Dead load is the weight of the project itself, such as a bunk bed. *Live load* is any other weight added to the project, such as pillows or kids. The less your project weighs, the more of its strength can carry live loads.

Static load is constant and unchanging, such as the teddy bear on the bed. *Dynamic load* is variable, such as kids jumping on the mattress. On a vehicle, the weight of the vehicle itself becomes a dynamic load when it bounces.

The faster a load is applied, the more likely it is to cause problems. A brick is easy to pick up and hold in your hand.

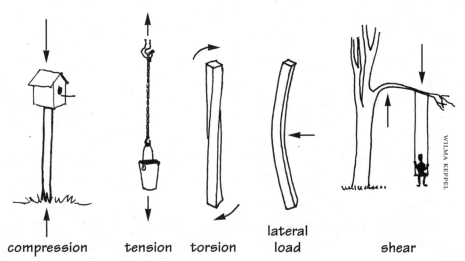

compression   **tension**   **torsion**   **lateral load**   **shear**

19.1: *Types of loads.*

The same brick dropped from an airplane is deadly! A sudden impact such as the falling brick hitting your neighbor's roof is called a *shock load.*

Shock loads are a big problem for vehicles. Hitting a big pothole at walking speed is no big deal. Hitting the same pothole at highway speed might break an axle. Static projects like bookcases are a lot less demanding to build. When was the last time you drove your bookcase into a pothole at highway speed?

Load placement can drastically affect a project's performance. Put heavy loads low and as close to supports as possible. Swaying or bouncing cargo creates huge dynamic loads that can destabilize a marginal project.

A spread-out *distributed load* is much easier for a structure to carry than a concentrated *point load* such as a high-heeled shoe or the strong pull where a cable in tension attaches. Spread loads out when you can.

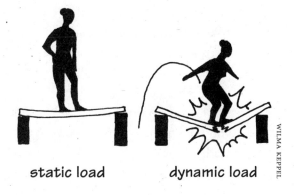

static load   **dynamic load**

19.2: *Static loads are less likely to break a project than dynamic loads.*

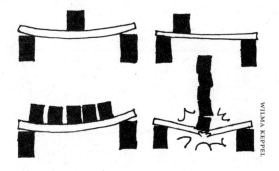

19.3: *Top: A load is easiest to carry when it's over or near supports. Distributed loads (bottom left) stress projects less than point loads (bottom right).*

Failures and fixes

Over the years we've destroyed a number of projects by not bracing them, not building them strong enough, or overloading them. Occasionally we overload projects just to see what they'll do.

Structure has a big effect on strength. We've seen plenty of projects that used way too much material, yet were under-built because the designer didn't understand how to get the most strength from the materials.

Always try to anticipate structural problems. Don't put yourself or others at risk. Apply working loads to projects incrementally, so you can notice and fix problems while they're small, before components bend or break.

The commonest problem we see with grid beam projects is not using washers. Washers spread loads toward the edges of the beams and help cross-brace your project. Fasteners with large heads, such as carriage bolts, joint connector bolts and weld nuts, spread loads the same way. Without washers, small nuts and bolt heads create point loads that can crush sticks.

Another common problem is not enough tri-joints. Tri-joints act as small cross-braces that make your project more rigid.

Common problems and how to fix them

Racking happens when a project goes out of square by flexing at the joints. It is most likely to be a problem where long beams act as levers.

Any grid beam project can rack during construction if its bolts are loose. This is not a problem unless it generates enough force to crush the ends of the sticks. A project with long sticks can put a *lot* of leverage on the frame joints, especially if it is made of heavy materials or is allowed to lean a lot. The thin walls of steel tubes are especially prone to bend when a large project is allowed to rack. Prevent damage to your sticks by limiting how much projects can rack. On large projects, tighten tri-joints as you complete them, and add diagonal braces or structural skin as you build. Brace a building's bottom level before you add a second story or roof.

Wood projects can also rack when low humidity shrinks the sticks. This makes the joints loose. Check wood-framed projects every couple of months and tighten the bolts if needed.

A project that racks *after* its bolts are tight needs more diagonal braces. First, make sure all hex nuts and bolts have

19.4: *Racking*

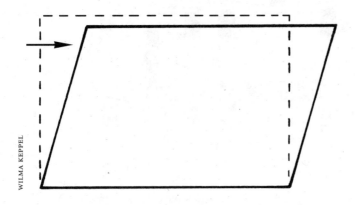

WILMA KEPPEL

washers. Next, add tri-joints, diagonal braces or panels. On furniture, a back panel is often sufficient.

Torsional racking twists the top of a frame out of line with the bottom. Phil has collapsed several projects this way by overloading them. Fix with cross-bracing.

Too much **bending** indicates a component close to collapse. Bent metal components that don't straighten when the load is removed were overloaded.

Don't reuse bent metal tubes or bolts in strength-critical projects such as scaffolding — they may have lost up to half their strength! Cut crooked sections out of tubes, or spray paint them so you'll remember to use them only for low-strength projects. Throw away bent bolts.

To fix a bending project, reduce the load, reinforce with trusses, strengthen components and/or distribute loads, or rethink the project. Sagging shelves can be cured with stiffer shelf materials, better supports, or reinforced edges.

Cracking or breaking components may indicate a load that is too large or too concentrated, weak components, or bad metallurgy. Cracks in or next to a weld are usually heat-related, especially on aluminum. Concentrated loads can break parts on a structure that is otherwise strong enough. Loads tend to concentrate where the structure is either a lot weaker or a lot stronger than elsewhere.

Beam collapse happens when a horizontal support member gets overloaded. The beam will first bend excessively. If

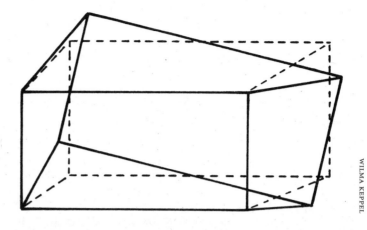

Wilma Keppel

19.5: *Torsional racking.*

overloading continues, it may break. Strengthen the beam, support it in the middle, add more beams, or substitute trusses.

Column collapse. If attached at only one end, a failing column such as a table leg will usually rack. Add diagonal braces. Any load that bends a column away from vertical weakens it a lot.

If attached at both ends, a column may fail by bowing to one side until the middle breaks. Shorter, wider columns are stronger. Horizontal supports such as rails or panels help keep a column straight. Or make the column stiffer by bolting more sticks to it to make a truss (Figure C.12).

A column that collapses straight down is overloaded. Skyscrapers prevent overloading by having more columns toward the bottom of the building where the load is greatest. You can use the same technique on multi-story structures.

Panels don't support much compression load, so vertical loads concentrate on the upright frame members. Make sure your projects have enough uprights.

Shock loads from bumps and potholes can destroy a vehicle's wheels, axles or frame. A suspension's main function is reducing shock loads. Plan on putting a suspension on any vehicle that goes much over 10 mph (16 km/h). (A bicycle can go faster because *you* provide the suspension by standing on the pedals and flexing your knees and elbows.)

Tubes crushed or distorted at the corners indicate concentrated stress from not using washers, over-tightening bolts, or frame racking.

Ominous noises such as creaking, groaning or cracking are symptoms of overload. Reduce the load or strengthen the project.

A project showing any of the above symptoms is seriously overloaded and could fail at any time. Brace or rebuild it, and avoid getting under or inside it while doing so.

Weather, corrosion, or anything else that destroys the strength of your materials can cause problems. That's one reason we like galvanized steel double-hole. Unless exposed to salt, it will last 40 years outdoors.

Insects sometimes invade wood that is close to or directly on the ground, especially if the wood is damp or the humidity is high. Dampness also promotes rot. Elevating wooden buildings 2 feet or more off the ground minimizes rot damage caused by splashing raindrops. Consult *How Buildings Learn* for more information about making buildings last.

Testing your projects

Any project that places people's safety at risk must be strong enough to do its job. This means projects people sit in, climb upon, walk on or under, drive, or ride. The greater the risk of a serious accident, the more careful you must be. Don't wait until you park a grand piano overhead or are traveling down the road at highway speed to find out a project isn't strong enough. Figure out how to test your projects before the safety of you or your loved ones is at stake. Below are some simple tests to get you started.

Initial inspection

If you see significant deflection anywhere (bending, racking or torsional racking), the frame bolts are loose or the project needs reinforcement. Tighten the frame bolts and check again. Your project should now look square, and feel stiff and strong when you grab a frame member and shake it. The frame should not flop around and won't bend much. Wood flexes more than metal.

What constitutes too much bending or racking depends on the project, the frame material, and how heavily the project is loaded. A long horizontal support under a shelf will bend more than a short one. Under most loads, horizontal metal beams will either stay straight, or the curve will barely be visible. Wood will sag more, but should become straight again when you take the load off. Vertical members should always remain straight and vertical when the project is loaded.

Push test

This simple test can quickly tell an experienced person whether a structure without diagonal bracing is close to collapse.

Get all frame bolts snug, but do *not* over-tighten them. Now push on or jiggle the structure.

- A high-frequency vibration (humming or a quick, small shudder) is okay. The faster it dies out, the better.
- A large, low-frequency oscillation means trouble. This is the sort of swaying that can build up and destroy a structure. Vibration that takes a long time to die out is another bad sign. Add shear wall or diagonal bracing.
- Visually examine the structure as it is swaying or vibrating. If you see much bending or torsional racking, add reinforcements.
- Re-check the bolts. If they have loosened, the frame members are probably getting crushed at the corners as the structure flexes. Add bracing. It's best to run this test two or three times because the bolts and joints may not have been fully tight the first time.

Loading

Test-load static projects with jugs of water, sandbags or firewood. These are small enough to arrange easily, yet heavy enough to provide an adequate test. Water is *not* a good load for road tests, because its sloshing can create huge dynamic loads the vehicle would never experience in real life.

WHAT WOULD GRANDPA HAVE DONE?

LARRY TODD

Load projects incrementally. Set up your test so that if problems arise, you can unload the project without getting in, on or under it. Make sure that a failure, or a vehicle or trailer stopping suddenly, can't send pieces flying, or shift or drop the load where it might hurt someone. (Tip: Cargo nets can attach right to your project's frame.)

The tests described below involve trailers and vehicles. If you're not building or driving that type of project yet, you may want to skip to the next chapter.

Jump test

This test is very useful on trailers and vehicles. Use another method where a collapse could dump someone far enough for serious injury.

Jump up and down vigorously. You want solid support and minimal vibration or shuddering that dies out quickly. The project should not sag or sway to one side. Excessive flexing is another bad sign.

On vehicles and trailers, regular bouncing that takes a long time to die away may just mean the shock absorbers are worn out. Replace them and try again.

Try to rock the project side to side. You should feel firm support and minimal swaying that dies out quickly. Excessive swaying on a trailer or vehicle may mean you need to move the shock absorbers closer to the wheels.

Inspecting a vehicle

Before you test-drive your vehicle, it should be in good working order. Brakes that work are especially important. Check these items:

- Make sure all bolts are tight, have washers under both ends, and are secured with lock nuts, lock washers or cotter pins. Many vehicle builders think all frame bolts should be Grade 5 or harder, especially on higher-speed vehicles. Phil's vehicles, which travel a maximum of about 30 mph (50 km/h) use $^3/_8$-inch Grade 1 or 2 bolts in home-drilled sticks, and he hasn't had problems.

- Tube, panel and component edges should be smooth, with no sharp edges.

- Motor, drive train, steering and wheels should be securely mounted.

- There should be guards around moving parts such as drive belts and chains that people in the vehicle could potentially touch, especially if they could do so by accident. Make sure people and their clothes can't get caught in the drive train.

- Seating must be secure. If seats aren't installed yet, make sure you can sit securely on the frame without falling off, and have secure places to put your feet and hands. Brad Booth requires Electric Moose cars to have floorboards to prevent kids from using their feet as brakes, and potentially getting a leg caught under the vehicle.

- All wires should be insulated and secured to the chassis. Make sure the control and power switches are securely mounted and accessible to the driver. All circuits or the battery should have fuses. It's best to have a master switch that turns off all vehicle power.

- Meters, if any, should be in the driver's direct line of sight. Switch and meter placement must not interfere with the vehicle controls, especially steering and brakes.

- Seat belts and any roll cage or roll bar should be attached to the frame, not to sheet metal.

- Brakes should be strong enough to lock the wheels. The brake pedal or lever should be firm under pressure. If hydraulic brakes feel mushy, they may leak, need fluid, or have air in the system and need bleeding. Check for leaks around the brake calipers and brake lines.

The emergency brake is your backup if the hydraulic brakes fail, so make sure it works.

- Check oil and coolant levels. Oil leaking from the transmission, clutch or engine may indicate serious problems.
- Walk around the vehicle and push the fenders down one at a time. Good shock absorbers will return without a lot of bouncing.
- Wheels and tires should be in good condition, with adequate tread. Make sure wheels are fastened securely, and tires are inflated.
- Visually inspect alignment by pointing the front wheels straight forward, then sighting across the front and rear edges of the rear tire on each side of the vehicle. On a motorcycle, sight along the rear tire from in front of the bike. The vehicle should be symmetrical and tires should be in line with each other.
- When the vehicle is loaded, the weight should be well distributed. Both steered and drive wheels need good traction.
- Check the steering. Steering should move freely and not bind at any point, yet should not be loose or sloppy. When you turn the steering wheel or handlebar, the vehicle's steered wheel should turn immediately, with no slack or slop.
- Turning radius should be adequate for what you're going to do. Some vehicles need steering stops to keep the steered wheels from turning too sharply — make sure they are in place and secure.

- Sitting in the driver's seat, make sure you can see adequately and have the mirrors you need. Will you be able to see in rain? At night?
- Are the vehicle's controls adequate? Can you reach them? Make sure controls can't interfere with each other.
- If you'll be testing an experimental vehicle in traffic, make sure it has a loud horn.
- An empty trailer should have some weight on the tongue, more when it is loaded. Rearrange the load if necessary.
- Before you road-test a vehicle you didn't build, make sure the builder is competent. This is especially important if there is welding on the vehicle, since you can't look inside a weld to inspect it. If a finished vehicle intended for on-road use fails the tests listed above, the builder probably isn't competent and you should not trust the vehicle.

Driving tests

When testing experimental vehicles, start your tests on a dry, level surface with no traffic. An empty parking lot is ideal. Begin running all tests at low speed. As you get familiar with the vehicle (and as it passes the tests) you can gradually increase the speed and intensity of your tests, plus the steepness of the terrain.

Wear appropriate safety gear, such as a seat belt and helmet. Designing experimental vehicles is loads of fun, but failures can be dangerous, especially at higher speeds. Here are some simple tests:

Brakes. Beginning at low speed, do hard stops. The vehicle should stop quickly in a straight line, without pulling to the side. Make sure you have good control of steering even during a panic stop.

Jerking or vibration indicates a warped brake rotor. A clunking noise when the brakes are applied may mean a warped brake drum, or a bad ball joint that will affect steering. If parts collapse or tear off during sudden braking or other stress, the vehicle is seriously under-built.

Steering must be predictable. When the vehicle hits a bump, the steering should not oscillate, nor should the vehicle change direction or pull to the side. Test this when driving straight and also on curves.

Clunks in the steering indicate looseness that can strongly affect the handling. Vibration may be caused by bad tires, faulty alignment, or serious problems in the steering system. A vehicle that pulls to one side on level pavement has an alignment problem. If it pulls in different directions as you drive, it may have a bad tie rod.

When weaving the vehicle, oscillations should die out rather than increase. Test this at *low* speed on a dry, empty road or parking lot.

Suspension. Vehicles with three or more wheels should not lean at rest or underway. Excessive bouncing is bad. Bouncing that throws the vehicle to the side can be dangerous.

Frame. The frame should not oscillate a lot when you hit bumps. Make sure you have good traction on all wheels under all normal driving conditions. Poor weight distribution in Phil's Welded Bear (page 95) caused the front wheel to lose traction when driving heavy loads uphill.

Now that you understand some structure and troubleshooting basics, let's look at techniques for designing your own projects.

 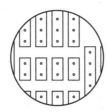  

Designing Your Own Projects

In this chapter you'll learn easy techniques to help you design your own projects. We'll also show you how to solve common design problems, such as attaching a round shaft to your project's square sticks.

While some techniques in this chapter will help you build vehicles, vehicle design is for the advanced builder and gets its own chapter.

Project planning

When planning a project, the most obvious points to determine are:

- **Purpose of the project.**
- **Frame material.** We use galvanized steel outdoors for durability, and everywhere for heavy-duty projects. Wood is light and portable, but best used where it will stay dry. Aluminum is weatherproof but expensive, so we use it where high strength and low weight are critical — mostly on vehicles.

- **Frame type.** Box frames are good for furniture, structures and vehicles. Offset frames are useful for desks and shelves. Stem frames work well for hanging loads, signs and wind turbine towers.
- **Approximate size of project.** This determines the length of your longest sticks.

Ask yourself:

- **What job or jobs will this project do?**
- **What loads will it carry?** What will they weigh? How much room will they require? Remember to include live loads such as wind, snow and bouncing kids.
- **What will the project's environment be?** Will it get wet? Be outside in the weather?
- **Are there other important design considerations,** such as low cost, light weight, or appearance?
- **How long will the project be in use?** If you expect to use a project a lot, or over a long period, it makes sense to invest in good-quality materials.

Thinking through a big or complex project before you build can save time in the long run. With simple projects it's often faster to design as you build.

Design by imitation

The easiest way to design most projects is to look at how other people built similar things. You can often modify an existing design with very little work. Many projects in this book readily adapt to other functions. For instance, the workbench in Chapter 1 also works as a computer desk and potting bench. Copy grid beam designs from the photographs in this book by counting the holes to determine dimensions.

When building a type of project you have not built before, it often helps to examine what is already on the market. If you want to build a bed, visit a furniture store. Notice features you like. Look for triangles, trusses and tension elements. What problems did the designers solve, and how did they do it?

Think function. Your project doesn't have to look conventional to get the job done. That bed frame has to hold the mattress off the floor, but what if you put drawers or storage tubs underneath? Could you store larger or heavier things if you replaced the tubs with pull-out platforms or boxes on wheels? What about raising the mattress to make room for more storage? Play around. If you build something you dislike, disassemble it and try again. With grid beam, projects can evolve until you get what you want.

Drawings

Sometimes the easiest way to think through a design problem is to draw it. You don't have to be an artist — just use graph paper! Paper with ¼-inch squares is easy to work with. Cheap tablets work fine; Clearprint paper from art supply and stationery stores can be erased many times.

If you are just starting to play with your idea, use a small scale such as $1/12$ (US) or $1/10$ (metric). At $1/12$ scale, 1 inch equals 1 foot. In other words, 1 inch on your ruler (four squares on the graph paper) equals 1 foot of real space. To show more detail, try drawing beams one square (¼ inch) wide. This will make your picture $1/16$ scale if you are drawing 1½-inch sticks, or $1/8$ scale if you are drawing 2-inch sticks. You'll probably want to use a large size of graph paper, which you can purchase at art supply stores.

Useful tools include a ruler with a straight edge, and a number 2 or softer mechanical pencil with a fine tip. A kneadable eraser and metal eraser shield from the art supply store lets you erase tiny areas without erasing the lines around them, and won't shed crumbs on your paper. A circle template or compass will help you draw round wheels.

After you draw a side, end and top view of your creation, you can do a perspective drawing. Isometric projection is easiest (use Clearprint isometric paper). True perspective with vanishing points is more like what you actually see. A good basic drawing book will show you how to do it.

20.1: *Photocopy this page and cut out the sticks to make scale models.*

PHIL AND RICHARD JERGENSON

Scale models

Another simple technique for designing projects is to make scale models. Models allow you to refine designs much faster than building full-size projects. Once you have a design you think will work, build it full-size to test it.

The simplest models are paper cutouts. We've included a page you can photocopy to make your own miniature sticks. To keep the pieces from sliding, assemble them on a piece of cardboard or rigid foam, and attach them with pins. The tear-off strips on most form-feed computer paper also makes decent grid beam templates. Strips must have 1 hole for every 1 stick width.

In the 1970s Reinhold Ziegler made three-dimensional scale models using fir sticks ¼ inch (6-millimeter) wide, drilled with ¹⁄₁₆-inch (1.5-millimeter) holes. He assembled them using small brass brads. Panels were cardboard. Reinhold designed his four-by-four cabin frame using a scale model of ½-inch sticks (Figure 8.16). While beautiful, these models required drilling just as many holes as the full-scale sticks!

A much easier technique uses balsa wood sticks lightly marked or scored where the holes would go. When it's time to assemble a project, simply push pins, brads or railroad track nails right through your sticks (Figure 17.5). Panels are mat board purchased from an art supply or picture framing shop.

Mock-ups

Mock-ups are full-size models that allow you to test an idea. Grid beam frames can approximate cabinets, appliances and equipment when you plan a kitchen or workshop. Use inexpensive wood sticks to do the basic design on a vehicle before cutting expensive aluminum. You can even use grid beam to sketch a building in three dimensions, making sure window, door and wall placements are right. When you're done, the components can be used for the scaffolding or building.

Project assembly

It usually takes two or three tries to get a project the way you want it. Grid beam frames are so easy to put together that we often try several designs before building a complete version.

Establish your corner verticals and main surface, such as a desk top, as early as possible. Work up and down from there until your frame is complete.

If you're not sure of your project's final dimensions, assemble the frame using long sticks. Leave the ends projecting while you tweak the project to get it just right. Finalize everything to standard beam lengths. Snap a few photos, then take the frame apart to cut or replace the long pieces.

20.2: *Mock-ups like Phil's temporary stove and sink cabinet can help you place fixtures and appliances.*

PHIL AND RICHARD JERGENSON

Designing Vehicles

Of all the projects you can design yourself, vehicles may be the most fun. They are also the most difficult and the most safety-critical. Even auto manufacturers with teams of experienced engineers and enormous budgets sometimes produce unsafe vehicles.

A basic course on how to design and build your own vehicle would take its own book. All we've done in this chapter is cover a few basics. If you're seriously interested in building vehicles, we hope you'll study some of the excellent books on the subject. Our personal favorite is Michael Hackleman's *Electric Vehicles: Design and Build Your Own.* Unfortunately, it is out of print. You may be able to get it through interlibrary loan, or buy it used online.

Safety

We recommend that beginning vehicle builders start with the simplest possible projects and keep them small, light-weight

and slow moving. Walk-behind vehicles such as Phil's Yard Trucks are much safer than vehicles you ride.

Always wear a helmet when driving any experimental vehicle that goes over 5 miles per hour (8 kilometers per hour). Gloves, sturdy boots, and a motorcycle jumpsuit with crash pads offer additional protection. On-road vehicles that people ride inside should have seat belts.

Today's streets and highways are terribly unsafe. Cars mix with trucks, buses, motorcycles and bicycles. When an accident occurs, the smaller vehicle usually suffers most or all of the damage. To compensate, today's cars are built with crush zones, air bags and roll cages. Despite that, over 40,000 people per year die on US roads.

Driving even the safest home-built buggy on the road risks a crash with Jane Citizen's monster SUV. Do everything possible to make your on-road vehicles safe and visible. Gain as much building and driving experience as possible on private property and little-traveled roads before you and your home-built vehicle venture into traffic.

If your vehicle stays close to the curb because it can't keep up with traffic, impatient drivers passing on a narrow road could force you into an accident. Says Phil, "Either build a vehicle that's fast enough to keep up with traffic, and wide enough to take up the lane so people won't try to share it, or build a narrow vehicle that cars can pass easily, the way they pass a bicycle."

Vehicle basics

With a few glaring exceptions, there are good engineering reasons for most of the design details you see in commercially produced vehicles. They work, and the alternatives didn't. You can learn a tremendous amount by studying existing designs. In many cases your safest course is to copy commercial products, or salvage their parts from the junkyard and re-use them on your own projects.

Go-kart and Electrathon clubs offer a wealth of proven designs for the do-it-yourselfer. Most go-kart parts are available via mail order.

Wheel arrangements

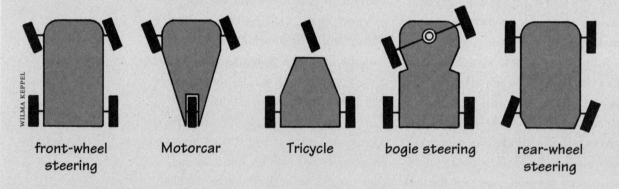

WILMA KEPPEL

front-wheel steering   Motorcar   Tricycle   bogie steering   rear-wheel steering

21.1: *Common steering layouts.*

The best wheel arrangement for your vehicle depends on what you'll use it for. We won't consider two-wheeled vehicles here, since bicycles, scooters and motorcycles provide examples to learn from.

More stable wheel layouts

All vehicles are shown turning left:

1. Four wheels with front-wheel steering is stable at speed and gives you cargo space behind the driver. Put your drive wheels where the weight is.

Fundamental forces will affect any vehicle you build for any purpose. Let's take a look at a few of the most important design factors you'll need to keep in mind.

Stability

A badly designed vehicle can become uncontrollable or even roll over. Stability is greatly affected by your vehicle's center of gravity, the distance between its wheels, and the wheel arrangement.

- A low load is more stable. For maximum stability, keep your center of gravity (where the weight is) low and centered.

- The greater the distance between your vehicle's wheels, the more stable it is likely to be. This distance is called wheelbase (length) and track (width). Generally the faster the vehicle goes, the larger your wheelbase and track should be. In other words, for higher speeds build longer, lower and wider.

- Some wheel arrangements are well-suited to doing certain kinds of work (see sidebar). Others are inherently unsafe. **All vehicles with rear-wheel steering become unstable at higher speeds!** That's why only slow-moving vehicles like fork lifts have steered rear wheels.

Paired wheels rotate at different speeds when you turn a corner. With two driven (powered) wheels, you'll need a differential to keep your tires from scrubbing.

2. A motorcar layout with one rear wheel and two steered front wheels is very stable if you put the weight near the front wheels. This is a good layout for on-road vehicles. Getting power to the rear wheel is simple — no differential! Or use front-wheel drive.

3. A tricycle with one steered front wheel works well on low-speed cargo vehicles such as Phil's Solar Bear. The load sits behind the driver and over the drive wheels.

   Tricycles are much easier to flip than motorcars or four-wheeled vehicles, especially at high speeds or going downhill. Three-wheeled ATVs got taken off the market because of rollover problems. Keep a tricycle's center of gravity low.

Less stable wheel layouts
Some wheel arrangements are inherently unstable!

4. "Bogie" steering is used on pulled wagons. It is unstable on a driven vehicle because the farther the wheels turn, the narrower the front track becomes. A sharp turn makes the vehicle into a tip-prone triangle. Bogie steering can be used safely at low speeds if wheel stops prevent the steering from turning too far.

5. Rear wheel steering is used on forklifts because it gives excellent maneuverability. Forklifts operate at low speeds, have low centers of gravity, and carry thousands of pounds of ballast. All vehicles with rear-wheel steering are unstable at moderate and high speeds. Unless you are building a forklift, avoid this wheel configuration.

Steering and suspension design have huge effects on stability. We suggest you learn from a knowledgeable person with practical experience, and also study books on the subject.

Speed, power and range

Vehicle design involves many trade-offs. For instance, a heavy frame takes more power to move. More power means a larger, heavier and more expensive motor. A bigger motor drinks more fuel or needs more battery capacity. More batteries require the support of a heavier frame and suspension, which takes more power to move.

For the last hundred years, designers have addressed problems with speed, power and range with brute force: bigger engines, higher fuel consumption, larger gas tanks. The social, environmental and personal costs have been enormous. We think it's more practical, and a lot more fun, to solve these problems with good design.

Generally you get the best performance (whether you measure mileage, payload, acceleration, cost, vehicle range, or other factors) by refining a vehicle to be small and light. This is also a good way to stay inside a reasonable budget.

We prefer to build electric vehicles (EVs) rather than use gasoline or diesel engines because:

- EVs are much simpler, with few parts to break, wear out or maintain. You eliminate from your designs starter motors, fuel pumps, water pumps, radiators, carburetors, mufflers, exhaust pipes and many other parts, and free up the time you used to spend maintaining that stuff.
- An EV only requires one power source: electricity. Engines require fuel, plus an electrical ignition system and often an electric fuel pump.

The hidden costs of automobiles and fossil fuel dependency

The US brags about having the fastest transportation system the world has ever known. But in 1974 Ivan Illich took another look. He divided the number of miles driven by the total time people spent on their automobiles — driving, parking, doing maintenance, working to pay for it all. It turned out the average US car traveled less than five miles an hour — about the same as walking, and less than half the speed of a bicycle.

The average US citizen now wastes more time commuting — over 100 hours per year — than they get for their annual vacation. According to the US Department of Labor, car ownership is now the second-largest household expense, costing almost as much as food and health care combined: over $8,000 per car per year.

Autos are "cheap" because they are heavily subsidized. Their real costs include damage to people, buildings and the environment (including global warming); lowered property values; higher costs for police and fire protection; time spent in traffic; and military policing of oil supply lines. In 1987, welfare for automobiles cost US citizens an

- Fossil-fuel engines typically require model-specific spark plugs, transmissions and other parts. Parts for EVs are much more interchangeable.
- Even if you buy your power, an EV costs less to run and produces less pollution than an onboard engine. With solar panels or a wind generator, you can manufacture your own fuel — important on remote sites like Phil's rural home.
- EVs are quieter, therefore less stressful to use.
- EVs are more environmentally friendly (see sidebar).

The main disadvantage of EVs is that batteries are extremely heavy. The energy in one 64-pound (39 kg) lead-acid car battery is less than the energy in half a cup (0.1 liter) of gasoline weighing a few ounces! Another way of saying this is that the battery has low energy density (power per pound, and power per unit of volume), while gasoline has very high energy density. This makes energy conservation a top priority for EVs.

Designing *any* vehicle involves trade-offs between speed, range and weight:

- The greater the vehicle's range, the more fuel it will need. In an EV, more range requires heavier batteries, but …
- The heavier your vehicle, the more energy it takes to move, especially uphill. This *decreases* its range.
- If you add a bigger motor for faster acceleration, it will use more power, which requires more batteries. The extra battery weight *reduces* your acceleration!
- By making your vehicle lighter, you can accelerate faster and go farther using the same motor and fuel. Or you can switch to a smaller, less expensive motor, and use less energy to accomplish the same task.
- Going faster takes a *lot* more energy, which decreases vehicle range. At 12

estimated $378 to $730 billion per year, with some estimates running as high as $1 trillion. The US now spends over $100 billion yearly just buying petroleum.

This has led to the absurd situation that the US is destroying its renewable resources in order to pay for fossil fuels. In the Willits area, the revenues generated by timber harvesting almost exactly equal the money going out of the county to buy oil. In the farmlands of the Midwest, agricultural production pays for fuel to run tractors, at an enormous cost in soil erosion. In both cases, harvests are far beyond sustainable levels.

Often touted as renewable solutions, biofuels such as alcohol and biodiesel have significant problems, including topsoil erosion and the enormous amount of farmland required to grow fuel.

By contrast, you can easily generate enough power for an energy-conserving house and vehicle using sun and wind, and often save money doing it. Until now, the big bottleneck has been access to the technology, since electric vehicles were scarce and expensive. Grid beam promises to change that.

miles per hour (19 kilometers per hour), the average bicyclist uses more than half their energy overcoming wind resistance. Wind resistance goes up with the cube of the speed (speed x speed x speed). Increasing speed from 12 miles per hour (19 kilometers per hour) to 60 miles per hour (96 kilometers per hour) increases wind resistance *125 times!* That's why most automobile mileage contests are run at speeds under 10 miles per hour (16 kilometers per hour). Even slow vehicles can have wind resistance problems in windy areas.

Streamlining can greatly improve the speed and fuel efficiency of your vehicle. The smaller your power source and the faster you travel, the more benefit streamlining creates. The best streamlined bicycles can go over 60 miles per hour (96 kilometers per hour); the whole vehicle has less wind resistance than a truck mirror! In 2006, several streamlined Electrathon winners used under one kilowatt-hour of electricity — less than a hair drier — to drive over 50 miles (80 km) in one hour. This is equivalent to 1,500 mile per gallon (640 kilometers per liter).

Licensing

If you plan to ride or drive your vehicle on the streets, investigate the applicable licensing laws *before* you build. In most US states:

• A vehicle that never gets driven on the road needs no license. Farm vehicles such as tractors that rarely drive on a road can get special exemptions.

• Vehicles that are strictly human-powered need no license. However, you can still get a ticket for exceeding the speed limit.

• Unlicensed vehicles with a motor have power and speed restrictions. Some vehicles with small motors can be licensed as mopeds with fairly minimal requirements.

• Licensing a two- or three-wheeled vehicle as a modified or experimental motorcycle is fairly easy. Your project must meet applicable laws about headlight height and brightness, signals and so forth.

• Some states now license four-wheeled Neighborhood Electric Vehicles (NEVs) for use on low-speed surface streets only. These glorified golf carts have a mandated top speed of 25 miles per hour (40 kilometers per hour).

• A four-wheeled vehicle that will be licensed as an automobile must meet more stringent standards.

A vehicle that gets licensed will be inspected. Make sure yours has adequate brakes, handling, lights, controls and so forth. It helps if you and your vehicle look clean and competent when you go in for inspection. If your buggy doesn't pass inspection, fix the problems and try again.

First things first

It's important to tackle the toughest parts of your design at the beginning. Before pouring a lot of time and money into a project, make sure you can figure out any unclear areas, and that the parts you need are actually available. Anything weird or complex that you leave until the end is likely to bite back — hard. Finding and fixing problems as early in the design process as possible minimizes rebuilding. It's a lot more fun to test-drive your creation after days or weeks instead of months or years!

Planning your vehicle

Vehicles are so complex that planning ahead can save you enormous amounts of time. Before starting construction, list the requirements that your vehicle must fulfill. A long wish list may make your project unmanageable. You'll be happier with a vehicle that does one thing really well than one that does a dozen things poorly. Determine the following:

1. **Kind of work the vehicle will do.** Will it carry people, cargo or both? How much weight is involved? How many cubic feet of storage are needed?

2. **Terrain and conditions where the vehicle will operate.** Consider the extremes as well as the average. Will your vehicle have to handle rain, mud, dust, snow or extreme temperatures? (Lead-acid batteries lose much of their power when cold.) Will your vehicle operate on dirt, grass, gravel or pavement? How will it handle potholes and traffic?

3. **Number and arrangement of wheels.**

4. **Size and type of tires and wheels,** including number of axles and wheel bearings. Use wide, squishy tires for off-road use, and harder, narrower tires on pavement. Wheel choice and configuration determine a lot about the rest of the vehicle.

5. **Suspension system,** if any. Suspensions are essential for most vehicles that go more than 10 miles per hour (16 kilometers per hour) to prevent bumps from breaking components, but they are a lot of work to scratch build. Look at other people's projects for ideas, check catalogs and junkyards for parts, and keep it simple.

6. **Number of passengers.** Consider seating arrangements and legroom. Putting the passenger behind the driver allows for better streamlining.

7. **Range of travel.** Remember that most trips involve two-way travel. Take the shortcomings of batteries into consideration. Most electric vehicles can run 1 to 4 hours between recharges, but take several hours to recharge from grid power, and more if they rely on solar panels. If your EV doesn't carry a charger, it will need to return home to recharge.

   Hill climbing can drain batteries 2 to 20 times faster than operating on flat ground. Regenerative braking gains back only a small portion of this energy — 10 to 20 percent at most.

8. **Top speed.** As speed increases, vehicle stability decreases and power consumption goes way up.

9. **Approximate vehicle weight,** empty and loaded. To estimate empty weight, list each major component, including frame, motor and transmission, wheels with brakes and tires, suspension, battery pack or full fuel tank, body, interior, etc. Add 10 to 15 percent to the total weight of these components, plus the weight of the driver. Additional loads will include passengers as well as cargo. Keep everything light and strong because batteries are *heavy.*

10. **Power source and amount.** What powers your vehicle? How big a motor do you need? This is a fairly complicated calculation involving your vehicle's weight, top speed, rolling resistance (will you drive narrow hard wheels on pavement, or wide soft wheels on dirt or grass?), drive train efficiency, hills to be climbed, etc. A too-large motor is heavy, expensive and wasteful. A too-small motor overheats and wears out quickly. Hackleman's *Electric Vehicles: Design and Build Your Own* covers the math in simple language for first-time builders.

    Detroit determines horsepower by dividing vehicle weight by 43 pounds per horsepower (25 grams per watt). This yields a power plant often 20 times larger than what you need.

    To rate power, manufacturers run combustion engines at their highest speed. In real life, combustion engines mostly run in the middle of their rpm range. They generate little power at low rpms. Electric motors have power throughout their rpm range. This makes a 1 horsepower (750 watt) electric motor roughly equivalent to a 2 or 3 horsepower (1,500 to 2,250 watt) gasoline engine.

11. **Fuel storage.** This includes type, number and wiring of batteries, plus size and placement of the fuel tank and fuel pump, if any. Currently most EVs use deep-cycle lead-acid batteries. Wire 6- or 12-volt batteries into a 12- or 24-volt system, possibly higher depending on the motor you're using. In general, the smaller and slower the vehicle, the lower the voltage.

    With 24 volts instead of 12, you can use series/parallel switching to get two speeds out of your vehicle without a transmission. Doubling the voltage halves the amperage (amps). This halves the wire and controller size, which reduces controller cost. High amperage current can heat wires and burn electrical contacts, and requires heavy-duty switches. It can also drain lead-acid batteries fast enough to damage them. **Put a fuse on the battery to protect it from short circuits.**

    Some electric cars that run at highway speeds use 110 volts. At this voltage, DC current is quite dangerous. Get someone experienced to show you how to work with it safely.

12. **Drive train.** How will you get power from the motor to the drive wheels? Will you use gears, a chain, or a belt drive? Will your vehicle need a transmission? A clutch is convenient, but a low-speed EV can get by without one if you can stop to change gears.

13. **Fuel source.** For EVs, your choices include DC from batteries or photo-voltaic panels, AC from a wall socket, or a combination. Will the vehicle carry a battery charger?

14. **Licensing.** Get a copy of the applicable rules so you can build your vehicle to comply.

Since all these factors are interrelated, Phil uses a "from the ground up" design approach. After getting a general idea of his vehicle's purpose and wheel arrangement, he looks at the terrain and specifies tire diameter and width. He then determines what wheels the tires will mount on. The mounting hole arrangement and other wheel features affect his choice of bearings, axles and transmission. Next comes the kind of suspension, if any, and on it goes.

The next step is some actual designing. Depending on how you work best, you may wish to start by drawing your proposed vehicle, or use grid beam to approximate your frame design.

Drawings

Drawing on graph paper helps you find and solve design problems before you commit money, materials and energy to a project. It can also help you select components, which will in turn help you determine the vehicle's weight.

Draw a side, end and top view. The more you can figure out while your vehicle is still in the two-dimensional stage, the less design work you'll have when you actually build it. Drawing is also a great way to figure out what your vehicle will look like.

At this stage you may discover that your proposed vehicle won't work. Good!

21.2: Two views of an unbuilt EV Phil drew on ¼-inch graph paper at ¹/₁₂ scale.

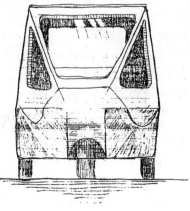

You have just saved yourself countless hours and dollars. Rethink the project and try again.

You can make a template of your own body by marking a large piece of paper with a 6-inch grid. Tape this to a smooth wall. Then set up a single light bulb about 30 feet away, or use the sun if it's low in the sky. Sit in front of the paper as if you're driving your vehicle, and have someone trace your shadow onto the grid. Redraw your outline onto graph paper using the grid marks as guides. You now have an accurate scale drawing of yourself to insert into your plans.

Prototyping

Says Phil, "Prototyping with grid beam is a very useful design technique for building vehicles. I've always had a tough time visualizing projects on paper. This alternate method of freestyle hands-on assembly really makes sense."

Since aluminum is so expensive, you may wish to prototype the frame in wood, and cut your metal sticks to length only after your design is close to final (Figure 21.3).

Begin by sitting on the floor or in your proposed vehicle's seat. Use a box or bucket to approximate the seat height.

Lay down two grid beams of approximately the correct length for the sides, running front to back. Add front and back crosspieces above them. These determine the vehicle's width. Keep a tape measure handy to check length-width dimensions of your vehicle as you build.

Now start adding bolts and sticks. You may want to rough in the design before

21.3a: *Michael Hackleman tests seat position for the Rail Rocket while Kent Jergenson observes. Buckets, wooden sticks and plywood approximate our initial design.*

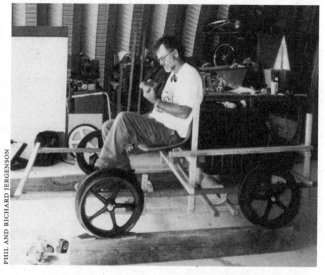

21.3b: *Richard on a wood-frame prototype with two large plastic storage bins in the rear.*

21.3c: Aluminum frame under construction. This version has front pedals and electric drive on the rear wheels.

21.3d: Phil tests the pedal and seat position.

21.3e: Electric drive moved to the front axle.

21.3f: Rail Rocket on the track for testing after we removed the pedal drive.

wrench-tightening the bolts, since in the beginning you will probably make a lot of changes.

At this early stage, don't be overly concerned with details. Instead, try to capture your structural stress points in space by connecting them together. Think trusses. Try different combinations of stacked sticks to strengthen your vehicle's overall structure. Phil says, "I never try to attain the correct geometry on the first prototype. It is just an experiment."

During this stage, you will be making some important decisions about your vehicle's size and shape. To make sure you keep the vehicle's center of gravity as low as possible, visualize its wheel configuration (or prop up pizza boxes), and where to place the inertial masses (all heavy areas, including people). Batteries are usually the heaviest components. They should almost always be placed in the very bottom of your vehicle's pan, right on the floorboard. Put cardboard boxes where your batteries will go.

Now imagine you are driving the finished vehicle, traveling around a corner at speed. Ask yourself, "Does it seem stable?" A top-heavy vehicle can tip over. An unstable vehicle may lose traction at high speeds, or even roll. When in doubt, increase the vehicle's track and wheelbase.

Also think about weather protection, streamlining, and how you will attach the skin. Add support members if necessary. If you have previously sketched your vehicle, you may find your design changing once you start building it in three dimensions.

Draw components you'll need to fabricate or buy, or make mock-ups from wood or styrofoam. Phil glues blocks of wood together to make shapes he needs. This helps him finalize the frame without the time or expense of building or buying the actual component. Redesign or rethink as you encounter problems. Try to get your frame as close to its final form as possible at this stage of the design process.

If you find a design you like, take a picture of it! **Photographs are the easiest and fastest way to record grid beam designs.** The holes automatically record most of the measurements. Take two or three shots from different angles to make sure you get all the details. If you later want to reconstruct something you took apart, you can count holes and rebuild the frame.

Phil's Star Lite is a good example of a vehicle developed first in drawings and preserved in photos. Designed to improve on Vanda's safety and handling, it will have a motorcar wheel layout better

21.4: Sketch for Phil's Star Lite.

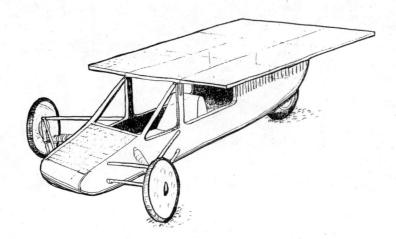

PHIL JERGENSON

adapted to road speeds. The single drive wheel on a swing arm makes the drive train easy to build. The top "wing" is a 5 x 6-foot solar panel. All other body surfaces will be flat or rolled sheet metal. The cab will be 2 feet wide and 9 feet long. To enter, you lift the hinged windshield and step in.

Phil drew the Star Lite in 1987, then partially assembled it in 1991, framing the cab, right suspension arm, and rear swing arm. The swing arm hinged on two pillow blocks. A motorcycle shock absorber connected the swing arm to the frame above.

Needing the space in his shop for another project, Phil photographed the Star Lite, then dismantled it. A box holds special adapters and mounts built for the project. With the photos, they'll allow him to reconstruct the Star Lite exactly. He says, "I would like to put a 2-horsepower (1,500-watt), 24-volt motor in this 350-pound (160-kilogram) vehicle, which will give it a top speed of around 25 miles per hour (40 kilometers per hour) on flat ground. This qualifies as an electric trike, which has simple licensing laws."

Assembly

Once you have a frame design you like, it's time to reproduce it using the correct-length sticks. Next attach components, modifying the frame as needed. If you don't have a part, make sure you can get it before wasting any more design time.

Even before you mount the motor, you can troubleshoot frame and suspension

Star Lite prototype front suspension on partial frame, photo credit: PHIL AND RICHARD JERGENSON

21.5: *Star Lite prototype front suspension on partial frame.*

problems by having friends push your creation while you steer it. This technique is most useful for low-speed vehicles, but can help any project.

As soon as your project is fully drivable, drive it all you can and fix the problems. Low-speed work vehicles will be fastest without the body, which adds weight. The extra speed can help you pinpoint problems. High-speed vehicles will be fastest after you add streamlining. Phil says, "Keep test-driving until you *have* to have a body. It's easiest to make design changes before you add the skin."

Once the body goes on, repeat your driving tests. Does the body perform as intended in varying road, wind and weather conditions? A body that seems weatherproof while parked in the rain may still leak at road speed. Keep checking your vehicle to make sure bolts stay tight and components don't crack, or wear excessively. Fast wear can warn you of potentially serious problems.

Congratulations! You've built your own vehicle!

Design solutions

Here are solutions for common vehicle design problems.

Wiring harness

One of the best things about electric vehicles is that they are so simple. You would think that to build so many EVs, Phil would have to be some kind of electrical genius. In fact, the opposite is true. He says, "I like electric vehicles because they're so simple that even I can understand them."

Most of the wiring on an EV is simple loops. This lets you build your wiring harness up in layers, one loop for each component. You run a wire from the positive battery terminal (+) to a fuse, from the fuse to a switch, and from the switch to your component (motor, headlight, etc.). Another wire returns current to the negative battery terminal (−). Wire lights in parallel (with separate wires from the switch to each light) so that if one bulb fails, the others stay lit.

Fuses

Size fuses so they won't blow during normal operations, but *will* blow if something goes wrong. On a motor, use a fuse with an amperage rating about 50 percent over the motor's rated amperage. This prevents the fuse from blowing during the power surge when the motor starts up. It will still protect your batteries and components from short circuits that could otherwise damage them.

Switches

Think about what job switches will do, and how much they will be exposed to weather, dirt, vibration and impact. A wide variety of automotive, motorcycle and go-kart switches are available via mail order.

Phil's first electric vehicle, the EVTB, used a simple on-off switch to control the motor. "One Sunday I had just driven all over Berkeley, and the batteries were so low that my wheels would no longer carry me. I was only two blocks from home, in an industrial part of town with no traffic. I got the bright idea of walking beside the vehicle, reaching over so I could steer the tiller. I figured that without my weight, we might get up to 5 miles an hour (8 kilometers per hour) or so.

"I smugly turned the switch on. The vehicle's speed kept increasing. Thinking we'd get home that much faster, I started to trot along beside it. Suddenly I was running to keep up, trying desperately to reach the on-off switch, and no longer holding onto the tiller. I chased my vehicle about 100 yards (90 meters) before it veered into the curb, heading straight for a large plate-glass window.

"I dove on the vehicle as it hit the curb, tumbling over and over as both batteries came flying out onto the pavement.

Everything ended up several feet (about a meter) from the window. I had a sprained wrist and a few bumps and bruises. Amazingly, nothing on the vehicle was seriously damaged."

Lesson: **Always control vehicle motors with momentary switches,** which return to the off position when released.

Instruments

A voltmeter will tell you an EV's state of charge, like a gas gauge on a car. An ammeter tells you how fast your batteries are charging or discharging. Discharging a battery slowly nets you more power, like driving conservatively rather than over-revving a gasoline car. Phil likes ammeters with zero in the middle because they show whether your vehicle is using power, or generating it via regen.

Vehicle body

It is our experience that the more a vehicle's body integrates with the grid beam system, the better. Vehicle bodies built from panels are easy to fabricate and attach, and you can easily change your design.

Most plastics will eventually decay from UV damage. Alucobond and Dibond are impervious to UV, and also resist cracking where the bolts attach. Both can be formed into gentle curves.

Formed fiberglass is very labor-intensive, as Phil discovered while building the nose for the X-Wing. Dave Beard enclosed his grid beam go-kart frame in a styrofoam body with a fiberglass outer shell.

When he later decided the frame was too narrow, the body made it difficult to alter. Grid beam used like conventional materials suffers conventional limitations.

Vehicle windows

For the Vanda and Sol Train, Phil cut holes in Alucobond panels, then had a local glass shop fit safety glass in black rubber gaskets. Round your corners so the gasket material can conform to the shape of the glass. **Never use window glass in a vehicle!** In a crash it breaks into deadly shards.

We don't like plastic windshields because they scratch easily. With the sun on it, a scratched windshield can be impossible to see through. Use safety glass for windshields. Use plexiglass and Lexan only for windows whose view isn't essential for safe driving.

Brakes

Put your brakes where the weight is. When you slam a vehicle's brakes on at highway speeds, most of the weight shifts forward onto the front wheels. That's where auto, truck and motorcycle manufacturers put powerful disk brakes. The taller and faster the vehicle, and the faster it stops, the more its weight shifts forward.

At low speeds, weight shifts a lot less. Phil puts the brakes of three-wheeled work vehicles such as the Solar Bear in the back, under the load. A Yard Truck's brakes are on the wheels under the cargo bed. Both use brakes built into the transmission.

Powerful disk brakes are available for vehicles ranging from bicycles to huge trucks. Most of Phil's vehicles use new 8-inch (200 millimeter) hydraulic disk brakes from the go-kart industry. They are much lighter than comparable automotive parts, and bolt on easily. George Buono's SPUV uses motorcycle disk brakes.

For very light-weight vehicles, Phil prefers bicycle disk brakes. The cable-actuated type are extremely light-weight, and having no hydraulics makes them simple to work on. Buy them at a bicycle shop — pro bike shops are best, because they stock lots of custom parts.

Use disk brakes with double-acting cylinders, which squeeze both piston pads against the disk. Single-acting cylinders squeeze only one pad. The other pad may drag on the disk, which wastes energy.

If hydraulic brakes feel weak, first check the brake fluid level. A mushy pedal means air in the brake lines, so bleed them. Make sure the brake pads are worn in. Brake pads ship with a slick coating that takes a while to wear off. If you're still having problems, increase the disk size. A larger disk with the same caliper will increase stopping power. A larger caliper with the same disk can *decrease* stopping power because force is less concentrated.

Regenerative braking can give any EV extra braking power. It's especially useful on steep terrain, where it can extend a utility vehicle's work day by as much as an hour. Regen requires running the motor above its normal speed. This is easiest to do if the vehicle has at least two speeds. Regen has the most stopping power at high speeds. It will slow a vehicle rather than stop it. Use regular brakes to stop a vehicle.

Drive train

Gearing allows a small power source to move a big load — it just moves it slowly. The smaller a vehicle's power source, the more it needs gears to accommodate different loads. A one-speed bicycle and a mountain bike may be equally easy to pedal unloaded on flat terrain, but as soon as you add significant cargo or hills, those extra gears make pedaling the mountain bike a *lot* easier.

Pedal-powering a vehicle requires attaching the pedals to the frame. On a bicycle, this part is called the bottom bracket. It houses the bearings for the crank arms and pedals. Phil's version uses a bottom bracket shell welded to a steel plate (Figure 15.18).

Use gears or pulleys to match electric motors to the load. Phil's Solar-Assisted Mountain Bike used a large pulley that attached to the rear spokes. On most EVs, Phil bolts motors to home-built pivoting motor mounts (page 164). Gears or pulleys reduce the gear ratio. A gear motor, such as Phil used on his simplified Yard Truck (Figure 11.2), has a fixed gear ratio built in. Use gears or pulleys to reduce the gearing even more if necessary.

To move heavier loads, or move them on steep terrain, use a transmission. This supplies low gearing for heavy loads and climbing hills, and higher gears for flat ground and downhill travel. On most of his work vehicles, Phil uses three- or four-speed garden tractor transmissions. Those with helical-cut or straight-cut gears allow you to push the vehicle if it stalls or the battery runs low. Worm gears lock if you try to push the vehicle.

An electric vehicle that can stop to change gears doesn't need a clutch. While slightly inconvenient, this saves weight and money.

A vehicle with paired drive wheels will need a differential to keep the tires from scrubbing on turns. A live split axle is a simple type that can be used with chain gearing, as on Phil's Japanese Bear (Figure 21.6). Phil's Bears and most of his Yard Trucks use transaxles that include built-in differentials.

Wheels

Size vehicle wheels to the job they do. Larger wheels turn more easily and roll over cracks and holes that will stop a small wheel. Wheel size becomes more important as your project gets heavier, goes faster, or crosses rougher terrain.

On most vehicles Phil uses garden tractor wheels purchased from Northern Tool or the Surplus Center. They weigh much less than auto wheels, and mate to light-weight go-kart axles, suspension components, brakes and drive sprockets. We list several sources in the "Suppliers" chapter.

PHIL AND RICHARD JERGENSON

George Buono's SPUV used cast motorcycle wheels modified to accept a large axle that could be supported from one side only. Weighing far less than car wheels, motorcycle wheels are not designed for heavy side loads.

For trailers, ATVs and some Yard Trucks, Phil uses 4-inch trailer hubs with a four-bolt pattern. These attach to a wide variety of rims that mount many types of tires. The hubs, purchased from Northern Tool, have a square spindle designed to be welded into square tubing. For lightweight trailers that get towed *only* at very low speeds and don't require a suspension, Phil sometimes drills a hole in the spindle, then slides it inside a double-hole frame tube and secures it with a bolt. *Never* use this method on a vehicle, or a trailer that will be heavily loaded or used on roads, highways or rough terrain — it's not strong enough.

Any trailer that will be used at road or highway speed must have a suspension to

21.6: *Simple drive train on Phil's Japanese Bear. A chain drive links the 1-horsepower (750-watt) motor to the rear axle, which has a built-in differential that keeps the tires from scrubbing.*

keep jolts from bending or breaking parts. Trailer torsion axles with attached wheels easily modify for use with grid beam (page 237).

For bicycle trailers and similar projects, use bicycle or garden cart wheels. Wheels on trailers and garden carts must take side loads bicycle wheels aren't designed for. On lightly loaded bike trailers this is generally not a problem. A heavily loaded garden cart going across a steep slope will collapse most bicycle wheels. For heavy side loads, use garden cart wheels. We've successfully used plastic wheels on a cart used for transporting young trees across steep, bumpy hillsides. Steel wheels with welded spokes are even stronger. Some garden carts use solid tires that won't go flat when rolled over thorns or broken glass. Pneumatic tires weigh less and are easier to roll.

Simple wheel mounts

Support bicycle wheels on both sides, using brackets bolted to your project's frame. Phil's Solar Bike Trailer used brackets fabricated from aluminum angle.

Garden cart wheels are designed for support from one side only. This lets you

21.7a: *An early version of Phil's Electric Tote Goat mounted the front axle on pillow blocks bolted to grid beam forks.*

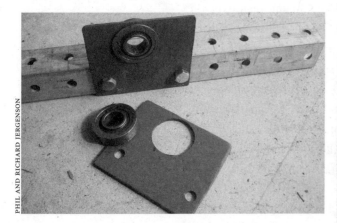

21.7b: *Simple adapter plates hold flanged bearings for a Yard Truck axle. Shaft clamps on the axle hold the bearings in place. Avoid the type with a set screw. Instead, use the type that looks like a round pinch block.*

21.7c : *Rear wheel mount on Phil's Electric Tote Goat. Slots let Phil adjust wheel position to tension the drive chain.*

build a lighter, simpler frame. Phil attaches garden cart wheels using welded adapters (Figure 15.18).

On wooden-frame garden carts, we mount the wheels on short sections of aluminum grid beam bolted to the wooden frame. The metal spreads the load, preventing damage to the wood. Some axles fit through the holes in the aluminum.

Phil sometimes mounts axles in pillow locks bolted directly to the frame. Examples include the front wheel on the Electric Tote Goat prototype, and the rear axle of the Scamp. If bearings are in the wheel(s) and the axle is stationary, Phil may hold it using pinch blocks (Figure 15.16).

Fork adapters

Simple welded adapters mate bicycle forks to grid beam (Figure 15.18). Check our website for availability.

Phil's EVTB used the front fork assembly from an off-road bicycle. The Scamp used a Honda 50 motorcycle front end. In both cases Phil fabricated simple adapters that allowed him to bolt the fork assembly to the frame. Here's how:

Before removing the forks from the original vehicle, measure their angle relative to the ground or to a plumb line. You probably want to duplicate this pretty closely. Now cut the head tube off the old frame, or find a substitute tube. Fabricate mounting flanges or cut them from angle iron (Figure 21.8). Weld or braze these flanges to the head tube. Protect all bearings and seals from overheating—the easiest way is

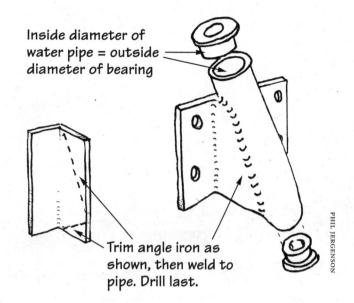

Inside diameter of water pipe = outside diameter of bearing

Trim angle iron as shown, then weld to pipe. Drill last.

PHIL JERGENSON

to remove them. The angle between head tube and flange sets the angle of the forks. Drill mounting holes after you weld to ensure accuracy.

Forks

The forks of Phil's first Electric Tote Goat motorcycle prototype were grid beam tubes attached to the frame with a welded adapter (Figure 21.9). On motorcycles, this assembly is known as a triple-clamp. Phil's triple-clamp was part steel, part grid beam. Pillow blocks with 3-inch hole spacing held the axle.

For several vehicles, Phil fabricated entire front fork assemblies. The head tube is built like Phil's fork adapters. The Solar Bear's head tube was 1-inch inside diameter non-galvanized water pipe 6 inches long. Phil welded this to two pieces of 2 x 2 x $^3/_{16}$-inch angle iron, also 6 inches long. This set the fork angle. When fabricating a

21.8: How Phil builds motorcycle fork adapters and head tubes.

PHIL AND RICHARD JERGENSON

21.9: Triple clamp and grid beam front forks on Phil's first Electric Tote Goat prototype.

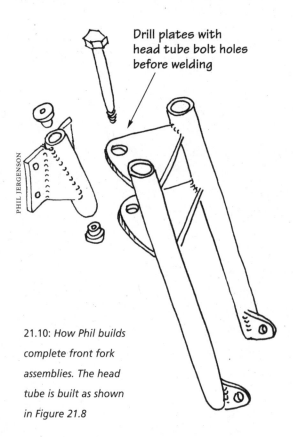

PHIL JERGENSON

Drill plates with
head tube bolt holes
before welding

21.10: How Phil builds complete front fork assemblies. The head tube is built as shown in Figure 21.8

head tube assembly, drill the mounting holes after welding to ensure accuracy.

The handlebars were 1-inch inside diameter water pipe slipped into square tubes welded to two plates $3/16$ inches thick. Drill holes for the head tube bolt in the plates before welding. To connect the head tube to the triple clamp, Phil used bronze bearings with a ¾-inch inside diameter and a 1-inch outside diameter. A large bolt joined fork and head tube, with a lock nut to keep it snug.

Suspensions

Suspensions are necessary on most vehicles traveling over about 10 miles per hour (16

21.11: Solar Bear fork mount, dashboard and headlight. Homemade brake pedal at bottom left pivots on a bolt.

PHIL AND RICHARD JERGENSON

Steering stability and trail

Vehicles that are easy to drive have steered wheels with *trail:* the contact patch (where the wheel touches the ground) is slightly behind where the wheel pivots. Trail gives the wheel a slight tendency to straighten itself out, which makes steering stable.

This is easiest to see on a bicycle. Look at where the handlebar-and-fork assembly rotates in the frame's head tube. The rings around the top and bottom of the head tube contain bearings. Turn the handlebars, and you'll see that the whole wheel and fork assembly pivots on those bearings.

Draw an imaginary line through the centers of the two bearings, and extend it down to the ground. (Use a broom handle or other straight object to help you visualize it.) This line is the *steering axis.* It hits the ground a bit ahead of the tire's contact patch. The distance between the steering axis and the center of the contact patch is the trail. As long as the contact patch trails behind the steering axis, the wheel tends to straighten itself out like a caster on a chair.

Too much trail makes a wheel difficult to steer. Not enough makes steering jumpy: the driver sneezes and cross four lanes. Negative trail (contact patch ahead of the steering axis) makes a vehicle unstable at high speeds. You can sometimes compensate for negative trail with a steering damper, as Phil did on the X-Wing.

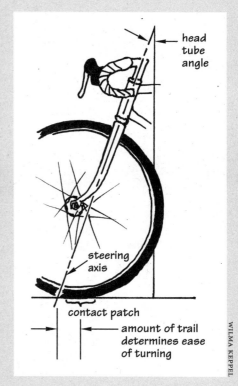

21.12: *Trail on a bicycle.*

kilometers per hour). Although they protect you, your passengers and any payload you carry from uncomfortable jolts, their main function is to protect the vehicle itself from shock loads that could otherwise bend or break the rims, axles or frame.

A rigidly mounted wheel hitting a bump or pothole slams huge forces onto a tiny area of rim or axle, especially at higher speeds. That's why it's so easy to bend the rims on a rigid-framed bicycle by hitting a curb. When you stand on the pedals and bend your knees, your legs and arms act as shock absorbers that protect the bike. All vehicles that travel at highway speed use suspensions.

A suspension saves weight because you don't have to overbuild the rest of the vehicle. There are a number of fairly simple ways to add suspensions to vehicles.

Torsion axles

Torsion axles are simple, low-maintenance suspensions that have been used on RV

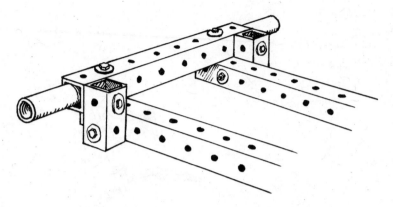

WILMA KEPPEL

21.13: *Grid beam swing arm.*

trailers for over 40 years. Northern Hydraulics sells some with a weld flange. Phil drills the flange to match grid beam, then bolts it on.

Swing arms

A swing arm is what lets the rear drive wheel of a scooter or motorcycle bounce. For low-speed vehicles, Phil uses a hammer and block of wood to pound a piece of 1¼-inch conduit through a piece of 1½-inch aluminum grid beam. He then drills through both pieces and bolts them to lock the shaft in place. The rest of the grid beam swing arm bolts to the square tube. Make sure you include a couple of tri-joints to keep the swing arm from racking. To mount the swing arm, Phil fits 1¼-inch outside bearings or bushings over the end of the conduit.

Front fork suspensions

Motorcycle and some bicycle forks have suspensions. A simple fork adapter (page 235) connects them to grid beam.

For the X-Wing, Phil fabricated a leading-link front suspension. Used on

motorcycles before the invention of telescopic front forks, leading links are fairly easy to scratch-build. By tuning the spring strength and the geometry of the suspension, you can cause the front end of your vehicle to sink, stay level, or rise when you slam on the brakes.

MacPherson struts

MacPherson struts are widely used for car suspensions because they are simple and cheap to build. On some designs the wheel tilts as it bounces up and down, which can affect handling. Phil fabricated MacPherson struts for the rear suspension on his X-Wing. The motors mounted on the strut, keeping chain tension steady as the wheel bounced.

Double wishbone suspension

Also known as double A-arm suspensions, double wishbone suspensions handle better than MacPherson struts because the wheel stays vertical as it bounces. Properly designed, double wishbones allow the wheel to be turned over a wide arc, giving the vehicle a small turning radius.

Dave Beard's vehicle and George Buono's SPUV both use double wishbones. George made all the elements of his double wishbones adjustable. After he had everything tweaked to his satisfaction, he drilled through each rod and sleeve set, then bolted them permanently in place. SPUV has excellent handling and a remarkably small turning radius.

Additional Resources

Below we list our favorite sources of useful information to help you succeed in building.

Books and videos

These are the books and videos we've actually found useful. Your local library can probably get out-of-print books for you via interlibrary loan, or you can buy them used online. Titles followed by * are included in the *Appropriate Technology Library*, even if out of print.

Grid beam

Box Beam Sourcebook. Phil and Richard Jergenson. Suntools, 1994. Out of print. Our original grid beam book, published when we still called the system "box beam." Virtually everything in that book is in this one.

Box Beam Video. Richard Jergenson, Phil Jergenson and Howard Letovsky, 30 minutes. QuikStix, 1993. [DVD] Order

from QuikStix. Narrated by Phil and Richard Jergenson, this DVD walks you through the grid beam basics, from components to wooden furniture to electric vehicles. It shows four grid beam vehicles in action.

How to Build Your Own Living Structures. Ken Isaacs. Harmony, 1974. Out of print. The best book about reusable modular building systems that we've ever seen.

The Politics of the Artificial: Essays on Design and Design Studies. Victor Margolin. University of Chicago Press, 2002. The retrospective of Ken Isaacs's design career includes no how-to information.

Building and design

Appropriate Technology Library. A collection of 1,050 titles reproduced on CD-ROM or microfiche for about $500 (under 50 cents per book). Includes the *Appropriate Technology Sourcebook,* which functions as

the index. Available from VillageEarth.org, or contact:

Village Earth
P.O. Box 797
Fort Collins, CO 80522, USA

*Appropriate Technology Sourcebook: A Guide to Practical Books for Village and Small Community Technology.** Ken Darrow and Mike Saxenian. Appropriate Technology Project, 1993. Available free online, or in hard copy, from VillageEarth.org. Reviews over 1,050 books, pamphlets and papers from around the world to bring you the best ideas and information. Most of the reviewed materials are part of the *Appropriate Technology Library,* which includes many hard-to-find and out-of-print items. The hard copy *Sourcebook* includes hundreds of illustrations from the reviewed materials to inspire your inventiveness. Developing-world applications are often far ahead of what's common in the US. Highly recommended.

Cradle to Cradle: Remaking the Way We Make Things. William McDonough and Michael Braungart. North Point Press, 2002. Rethinking design and manufacturing to make products more ecological and people-friendly.

*Design for the Real World: Human Ecology and Social Change.** Victor J. Papanek. Pantheon, 1971; 2nd edition, Academy Chicago Publishers, 1985. Explores how design affects ecology and people's quality of life. Includes techniques that can help you make sure your design is addressing the right issues in effective ways. A classic.

Direct Use of the Sun's Energy. Farrington Daniels. Yale University Press, 1964. The best primer on solar energy ever published, it covers all the basics.

ecoDesign: The Sourcebook, revised edition. Alastair Fuad Luke. Chronicle Books, 2006. Lists a wide variety of earth-friendly designs and products, including furniture, buildings, lighting, vehicles and more.

Ecological Design: Inventing the Future. Brian Danitz, 64 minutes. Ecological Design Project, 1994. [DVD/videocassette] A documentary about design pioneers in architecture, energy systems, transportation and industry. Order online.

*Electric Vehicles: Design and Build Your Own.** Michael Hackleman, 1977. Out of print. Within two months of getting this book, Phil built his first electric vehicle. Some of the information on motors and controllers is out of date, but the charts are very helpful.

How Buildings Learn. Stewart Brand. Penguin, 1994. The first book we've seen that explores what happens to buildings *after* they're built, and why various features do or don't work.

The New Electric Vehicles: A Clean and Quiet Revolution. Michael Hackleman. Home Power, 1996. Out of print. One of the most comprehensive books ever published on EVs. Covers bikes, trikes, cars, planes, boats and more. Includes technical information about many of the vehicles, plus chapters on the design and installation of the electric parts of the EV. Hundreds of photos.

The New Science of Strong Materials or Why You Don't Fall through the Floor, revised edition. J.E. Gordon. Princeton University Press, 2006. *Structures: Or, Why Things Don't Fall Down,* revised edition. J.E. Gordon. Da Capo, 2003. Delightful explorations of how and why structures and materials work—or don't.

Nomadic Furniture 1. James Hennessey and Victor Papanek. Pantheon Books, 1973. *Nomadic Furniture 2.* James Hennessey. Pantheon Books, 1974. Both out of print. Ingenious ideas for furniture suited to mobile lifestyles. Most designs disassemble for moving, and many can be adapted to grid beam.

Passive Solar Energy: The Homeowner's Guide to Natural Heating and Cooling. Bruce Anderson and Malcolm Wells. Brick House Publishing Co., 1996. Passive solar avoids pumps, fans, gizmos and fancy electronic controls in favor of simplicity, reliability, durability, low cost and user involvement. Covers the basics for temperate climates in simple, understandable language, with lots of pictures.

Pedal Power. James C. McCullagh, ed. Rodale Press, 1977. Out of print. Everything people pedal *except* bicycles: lathes, potter's wheels, sewing machines, grain grinders, electric generators, plows and more. Most could be built with grid beam.

Real Goods Solar Living Source Book- Special 30th Anniversary Edition: Your Complete Guide to Renewable Energy Technologies and Sustainable Living. John Schaeffer. Gaiam Real Goods, 2007. An easy-to-understand introduction to alternative energy.

Solviva: How to Grow $500,000 on One Acre and Peace on Earth. Anna Edey. Chelsea Green Publishing Company, 1998. Some of the best thinking we've seen on solar design, sustainability and waste treatment. Read this before you design, build or retrofit a home, workshop or greenhouse.

Systems of Living Space. Joseph Provey. H. Regnery, 1977. Out of print. Many aspects of Provey's system adapt easily to grid beam. Ingenious details include modular work surfaces, hanging shelves and bed platforms, and much use of fabric, rope, netting and plastic tubs.

Wind Power, Revised Edition: Renewable Energy for Home, Farm and Business. Paul Gipe. Chelsea Green Publishing Company, 2004. The definitive text on small-scale wind technologies.

Shop books

We are still looking for the ultimate how-to book for the shop novice. Most shop books are poorly organized, assume you already know a lot, or both. We suggest exploring your local library. Find and read the books that are easy for *you* to understand. Rigging handbooks may be purchased at bookstores or rigging supply shops.

Global issues

Critical Path, revised edition. R.

LARRY TODD

Buckminster Fuller. St. Martin's Press, 1982. *Operating Manual For Spaceship Earth.* R. Buckminster Fuller, Plume, 1978. We recommend anything by Fuller. Bucky was a true futurist, and discussed resource management decades before most people realized there would be problems.

The End of Suburbia. Gregory Greene, 78 minutes. The Electric Wallpaper, 2004. [DVD] A documentary exploring possible negative consequences of declining oil production. Buy from endofsuburbia.com.

Priority One: Together We Can Beat Global Warming. Allan J. Yeomans. Biosphere Media, 2007. Topsoil is the only carbon sink that humans can easily access and utilize, using proven technology we already have to rapidly reduce atmospheric carbon.

Short Circuit: Strengthening Local Economics for Security in an Unstable World. Richard J. Douthwaite. Green Books, 1998. Describes various methods for making local economies more robust, and separating them from the destabilizing effects of globalization. Based on real-world projects, this book explains what has and hasn't worked.

Magazines

These magazines are outstanding resources for the do-it-yourselfer.

Electrifying Times
Cutting-edge electric vehicles, experiments and prototypes.
63600 Deschutes Market Road
Bend, OR 97701 USA

(541) 388-1908
electrifyingtimes.com

Home Power
Definitive information on home energy systems and alternative energy, including power generation and storage, buildings and building designs, electric vehicles, and product reviews. And it's published off-grid! Regular articles on electricity basics help newcomers.
P.O. Box 520
Ashland, OR 97520 USA
(916) 475-3179
homepower.com

Make
Do-it-yourself technology projects of all kinds.
O'Reilly Media
1005 Gravenstein Highway North
Sebastopol, CA 95472 USA
(707) 827-7000
makezine.com

Popular Mechanics
What's new in mechanics and mechanical inventions. Full of interesting ideas.
P.O. Box 7170
Red Oak, IA 51591 USA
(212) 582-8369

Popular Science
What's new in applied science and technology. Many products and ideas can be adapted for home use.
P.O Box 5096
Harlan, IA 51593-2596 USA

ReadyMade

ReadyMade Magazine

How-to information for making and modifying a wide variety of projects and products.
817 Bancroft Way
Berkeley, CA 94710 USA
readymademag.com

Organizations

Need some real people to talk to? Here's a smattering of organizations to help you.

American Solar Energy Society
Has chapters in many US states.
2400 Central Ave., Ste. A
Boulder, CO 80301 USA
(303) 443-3130
(303) 443-3212 fax
ases.org

Electric Auto Association
Has chapters in the US and Canada.
eaaev.org

Electrathon America
Want to see electric vehicles race? Want to build your own Electrathon racer? Get the rule book and race schedule from these folks.
electrathonamerica.org

International Human Powered Vehicle Association (IHPVA)
Improved bicycles, human-powered boats and aircraft.
ihpva.org

Willits Economic Localization (WELL)
One of the first economic localization groups in the US, WELL inspired the creation of many more.

willitseconomiclocalization.org

Worldwatch Institute
Takes the pulse of the planet and forecasts long-term trends. It makes a point of blowing through all the hype and getting at the real truth about what works.
1776 Massachusetts Ave., N.W.
Washington, D.C. 20036-1904 USA
(202) 452-1999
(202) 296-7365 fax
worldwatch.org

Events

Maker Faire
Wild and wonderful home-built technology, from battling robots to Tesla coils, furniture, do-it-yourself recycled clothing and more. Held annually near San Francisco, California, and in Austin, Texas.
makerfaire.com

Midwest Renewable Energy Fair
Held the third weekend in June in Custer, Wisconsin. Workshops by some of the best people in the alternative energy field, plus many renewable-energy and alternative-technology vendors. Midwest Renewable Energy Association sponsors workshops throughout the year and puts out a quarterly newsletter.
Midwest Renewable Energy Association
(715) 592-6595
the-mrea.org

Solfest
Exhibitors and vendors showcase solar, wind, hydroelectric and other renewable energy technologies, plus ecologically

friendly clothing, agriculture and more. Held yearly in Hopland, California.
Solar Living Institute
13771 S. Hwy. 101
P. O. Box 836
Hopland, CA 95449, USA
(707) 744-2017
solarliving.org

Tour de Sol

Sponsored by the Northeast Sustainable Energy Association (NESEA), Tour de Sol is a US auto race rewarding high vehicle efficiency and low pollution. In 2007 a new race called the 21st Century Automotive Challenge pitted battery-powered cars, hybrid cars, bio-diesel and regular gasoline-fueled cars against each other to gather real-world performance data. Check their website for race information.
nesea.org

Grid beam online

exercise-desk.com
Treadmill and bike desks.

gridbeamers.com and **grid-beam.com**
Our grid beam websites.

recliner-workstation.com
Recliner workstations.

synergyii.com
Reinhold Ziegler's website features some grid beam designs.

Websites of grid beam vendors are listed in the "Suppliers" chapter.

Grid beam designers

Michael Hackleman
P.O. Box 2205
Willits, CA 95490 USA
michael.hackleman@gmail.com

Phil Jergenson
P. O. Box 1029
Willits, CA 95490 USA
(707) 459-4240
phil@gridbeamers.com

Richard Jergenson
P. O. Box 1577
Willits, CA 95490 USA
(707) 459-6362
rick@gridbeamers.com

Wilma Keppel
gridbeam@renewfrontier.org

Reinhold Ziegler
Synergy California L.P.
P.O. Box 3171
Sausalito, CA 94966, USA
(415) 290-4490
(425) 459-6210 fax
synergyca@earthlink.net
synergyii.com

For updates, check our websites at grid-beamers.com and grid-beam.com.

Suppliers

Using local materials minimizes the waste in packaging, fuel and money that goes with ordering long-distance. We recommend that you shop at locally owned stores whenever you can. That keeps money in your community instead of siphoning it off to some distant locale. Buying locally lets you check your suppliers' business practices for yourself. Avoid companies ripping off their employees and the environment, and vote for the good ones with your wallet.

What if you can't get what you want locally, and making it yourself isn't practical? The following list of suppliers can sell you most of the parts you need. We buy from most of them ourselves. If you know of a better source, or a good supplier we're not aware of, please write or call so we can post it on our website and include it in the next edition of this book.

Grid beam
Wooden grid beam
QuikStix™
P.O. Box 1029, Willits, CA 95490 USA
(707) 459-3959
gridbeamers.com
Phil and Richard's company is the only commercial source of wooden grid beam that we know of. They also sell joint connector bolts, weld nuts, adapters; and other grid beam–related products.

Aluminum grid beam

80/20 Inc.
1701 South 400 East
Columbia City, IN 46725 USA
260-248-8030
260-248-8029 fax
8020inc.net
Makes 1½-inch plain and flanged aluminum grid beam, plus hardware and accessories that work with the system: brackets, wheels, casters, feet, leveling legs, hinges, etc. Parts are listed on the website under "HT Series Framing". Click "Distributor Lookup" to find a supplier near you, or order from McMaster-Carr. 80/20 sells their (non-metric) tubes throughout North America, and in Australia, New Zealand, Costa Rica, Puerto Rico and the United Kingdom.

McMaster-Carr Supply Company
(404) 346-7000 Atlanta, Georgia
(630) 833-0300 Chicago, Illinois
(330) 995-5500 Cleveland, Ohio
(213) 692-5911 Los Angeles, California
(609) 689-3000 New York/Philadelphia
mcmaster.com
Mail-order source for 1½-inch aluminum grid beam, plus a limited selection of brackets, feet and other accessories. Also sells steel grid beam and a huge variety of useful accessories.
QuikStix™
Contact information on page 245.

Steel grid beam

Allied Tube & Conduit
16100 S. Lathrop Avenue
Harvey, IL 60426 USA
(800) 882-5543
(708) 339-1610
(708) 339-2399 fax
alliedtube.com
Makes Telespar and Qwik-Punch steel highway sign posts, plus Square-Fit, which is identical to Telespar but sold to other markets. Also sells locking pins, brackets and other specialized hardware that works with their tubing. They market through several separate networks of dealers. Call Allied to locate the Square-Fit and Telespar dealer nearest you.

McMaster-Carr Supply Company
Contact information at left.
Mail-order source for 1-inch and 2-inch electroplated steel tubing with 1-inch hole spacing in 6-foot lengths. Sells Telespar in lengths up to 12 feet. Also sells 80/20's aluminum grid beam, and many parts that work with grid beam.

Northwest Pipe Company
(800) 369-5009
(713) 863-4300
(713) 863-4313 fax
pozloc.com
Makes POZ-LOC Performance Posts, a brand of steel highway sign posts.

S-Square Tube Products
5495 East 69th Avenue
Commerce City
Colorado 80022-1952 USA
(888) 267-6463
(303) 286-7051
(303) 287-0109 fax
s-squaretube.com

Makes S-Square steel highway sign posts. Will ship small quantities virtually anywhere in North America. Expect to pay more for small orders.

Unistrut Corporation
4205 Elizabeth
Wayne, Michigan 48184 USA
(800) 521-7730
(734) 721-4040,
(734) 727-4000
(734) 721-4106 fax
unistrut.com
Another network of dealers selling Telespar steel tubing and components. Call for a catalog and the dealer nearest you.

Ultimate Highway Products
10680 Fern Avenue
Stanton, CA 90680 USA
(800) 730-4939 sales
(714) 484-4254
(714) 761-2965 fax
info@uhp-inc.com
Makes Ulti-Mate steel highway sign posts, plus various brackets and specialty hardware.

Hardware

QuikStix™
Contact information on page 245.
Mail-order source for joint connector bolts and weld nuts. Also sells grid beam and related products.

8020/Inc.
1701 South 400 East
Columbia City, IN 46725 USA
260-248-8030

260-248-8029 fax
8020inc.net
Sells brackets, bolts, feet, wheels and other components that work with 1-½-inch metal grid beam. Some also work with 1-½-inch wood

Fastenal Company
2001 Theurer Blvd.
Winona, Minnesota 55987 USA
(507) 454-5374
(507) 453-8049 fax
fastenal.com
Most grid beam fasteners other than joint connector bolts and weld nuts are available from Fastenal in plated or stainless steel. Order online, or visit walk-in stores in major US, Canadian and Mexican cities.

Panels

Buy most plastics from your local plastics dealer — we use TAP Plastics, a West Coast chain.

Alcan Composites
55 West Port Plaza, Ste. 625
St. Louis, MO 63146 USA
(800) 626-3365 (US)
(270) 527-4200 (International)
alucobondusa.com
Sells Alucobond and Dibond worldwide. Call to find a dealer near you.

Consolidated Plastics
1864 Enterprise Pkwy.
Twinsburg, Ohio 44087 USA
(800) 362-1000
Plexiglass, Filon, glass rod, industrial and laboratory plastics.

LARRY TODD

Finishes

Build It Green
builditgreen.org
Online database of nontoxic building products and their sources includes wood finishes.

Components and tools

Alternative Energy Engineering (AEE)
P.O. Box 339
Redway, CA 95560 USA
(888) 840-7191
(707) 923-2277
(707) 923-3009 fax
www.aeesolar.com
A good source of solar energy components at reasonable prices. Wholesale only.

Azusa Engineering, Inc.
1542 W. Industrial Park St.
Coving, CA 91722-3487 USA
(818) 967-4167
(818) 966-4071
(626) 967-4167
azusaeng.com
Parts for go-karts, mini bikes and ATVs, including industrial roller chain, sprockets, suspension components, wheels, axles, cables and throttles. They also make custom sprockets. Phil uses some of their brakes.

Bailey Sales Corporation
P.O .Box 19805
Knoxville TN 37939-2805 USA
(800) 800-1810 from US and Canada
(65) 6862-5556 from Europe and Asia
(865) 588-6000 from other locations
baileynet.com
Wholesale only. Bearings, tires, wheels, axles, transmissions, hydraulics. Very inexpensive; a lot of their stuff is close-outs.

C & H
2176 E. Colorado Blvd.
Pasadena, CA 91107 USA
(800) 325-9465
(213) 681-4925
(626) 796-2628
(626) 796-4875 fax
candhsales.biz
Military surplus motors, gearboxes, electronics, wire, meters, fans, solenoids, switches, etc.

Constantine's Wood Worker's Catalog
Constantine's Wood Center
1040 E. Oakland Park Blvd.
Ft. Lauderdale, FL 33334 USA
(800) 443-9667
(954) 561-1716
constantines.com
Exotic and hard-to-find woodworkers' supplies mail ordered to anywhere in the US.

Edmund Scientific Company

60 Pearce Ave.

Tonawanda, NY 14150 U.S.A.

(800) 728-6999

scientificsonline.com

The catalog is 500 pages of educational and scientific gadgets. Much is applicable to alternative energy, including instruments, meters, fiber optics and Fresnel lenses.

Electro Automotive

P.O. Box 1113

Felton, CA 95018-1113 USA

(831) 429-1989

(831) 429-1907 fax

electroauto.com

Motors, controllers and other equipment for car-size electric vehicles, plus kits for converting gasoline cars to electric.

Enco Manufacturing Company

400 Nevada Pacific Hwy.

Fernley, NV 89408 USA

(800) 873-3626

(800) 965-5857 fax

use-enco.com

Metalworking equipment such as drill presses and milling machines at good prices via mail order. Much imported stock, but all good quality. We've bought lots from them.

Graingers

(888) 361-8649

grainger.com

Wholesale only. Industrial and commercial equipment and supplies with after-sale replacement parts. They have outlets all over the US. The best source for motors.

They carry a terrific series of cast lightweight pillow block bearings, some with 3- and 4½-inch hole spacing, plus shaft bearing locks, fan blades and, much more. Excellent support services, often a twelve-hour turnaround time. We've never seen anyone as efficient. A bit pricey.

Great Plains

(800) 525-9716

(800) 221-1589 international

(866) 641-2568 fax

2800 Southcross Drive West

Burnsville, MN 55306 USA

gpcatalog.com

Affiliated with Northern Tool + Equipment, very similar and a bit cheaper, but carries fewer vehicle parts.

J.C. Whitney & Co.

(800) 603-4383

jcwhitney.com

Everything automotive, parts and accessories, American and foreign. A huge selection of after-market and customizing accessories for cars.

McMaster-Carr Supply Company

Contact information page 246.

A complete source for commercial and industrial equipment. Tools, motors, pumps, wiring, industrial casters, steel and aluminum grid beam, and much more.

Northern Tool + Equipment

2800 Southcross Drive West

Burnsville, Minnesota 55306 USA

(800) 221-0516

northerntool.com

LARRY TODD

Phil buys most of his vehicle parts here, including Azusa go-kart brakes. They carry hydraulics and parts for small-scale vehicles, plus farmstead and homestead equipment.

Real Goods

Real Goods Solar, Inc.
360 Interlocken Blvd. Suite 300.
Broomfield, CO 80021 USA
(800) 347-0070
realgoods.com
Renewable energy products and installation: solar modules, wind and hydro-electric power, energy efficiency products, books.

Surplus Center

P. O. Box 82209
Lincoln, NE 68501 USA
(800) 488-3407
surpluscenter.com
Garden tractor transaxles, hydraulic parts and more.

West Marine

(800) 685-4838
(831) 761-4800 international orders
westmarine.com
Durable marine hardware and electrical supplies.

Woodworker's Supply

5604 Alameda Pl. NE
Albuquerque, NM 87113 USA
(800) 645-9292
(505) 821-0500
woodworker.com
Woodworking supplies shipped anywhere in the US. Power tools, blades, belts, drill bits, router bits, wooden dowels, pegs, pins, handles, eye and ear protection, roller stands and rollers, plus many hard-to-find items.

If what you're after isn't available locally or through one of the vendors listed above, check the *Thomas Register of American Manufacturers*. The Yellow Pages of the industrial US and Canada, the *Thomas Register* lists thousands of companies by products offered, name, trademarks, etc. Updated yearly. Search it online at ThomasNet.com.

Afterword

We hope you've enjoyed this journey through the wonderful world of grid beam. As you've seen, the possibilities are virtually unlimited.

Grid beam is so standardized that if *you* can build something, other people can too! This book is just the start of something much bigger: a worldwide network of grid beam builders sharing plans and ideas. Modular parts, digital photos and the World Wide Web make it easy.

We invite you to join us in creating this new future — building projects, sharing plans, creating and buying products that work with grid beam.

The more components that work with grid beam, the more projects become possible and the easier they are to build. Imagine cottage industries and factories all over the world creating components and accessories that work with the system. Now imagine hundreds of thousands or even millions of people buying these parts, and incorporating the resulting projects into their lives. All these people can mix and match parts and build custom projects that meet *their* needs — and all can easily share their plans with *other* do-it-yourselfers who want something similar. All of us benefit from each other's experience.

251

Thirty years ago few people imagined that they would ever need or own computers. Today computers are indispensable. Computers, digital cameras and the Web have made people more productive by helping us organize and share information. Now it's time to reprogram our physical spaces so we can develop better ways of living.

Please join us online at gridbeamers.com and grid-beam.com, and share *your* projects, photos, grid beam stories. Find out what other people have done, and improve on it. And have fun!

Remember, with grid beam, if you can imagine it, you can build it!

Glossary

Many items in this glossary are described more fully in the text. Check the index.

Units of measurement

While most of the world has adopted the metric system of measurement, the US still uses the **US Customary System** (also called **American Standard**) for building materials such as lumber and most metal tubing. Figure 25.1 and Figure 25.2 compare common units of measurement in both systems. **US units are often different from Imperial (British) units with the same name.**

Units of measure — US Customary System

US Measure	Symbol	Abbreviation	Measures	US Equivalent	Metric Equivalent
inch	"	in.	length	$1/12$ foot, $1/36$ yard	2.540 centimeters
foot	'	ft.	length	12 inches, $1/3$ yard	0.305 meter
yard		yd.	length	36 inches, 3 feet	0.914 meter
mile		mi.	length	5,280 feet, 1,760 yards	1.609 kilometers
ounce		oz.	weight	$1/16$ pound	28.350 grams
pound		lb.	weight	16 ounces, $1/2{,}000$ ton	453.592 grams
ton		tn.	weight	2,000 pounds	907.20 kilograms
gallon		gal.	liquid volume	16 cups, 231 cubic inches	3.785 liters
cup		c.	liquid volume	$1/16$ gallon, 14.44 cubic inches	0.237 liter
cubic inch		cu. in.	volume	0.0693 cups	16.387 milliliters
foot-pound		ft.-lb.	torque	12 inch-pounds	0.138 newton-meters
horsepower		hp.	power	33,000 foot-pounds per minute	745.7 watts

Units of measure — metric system				
Metric Measure	**Abbreviation**	**Measures**	**Metric Equivalent**	**US Equivalent**
millimeter	mm	length	$^1/_{10}$ centimeter, $^1/_{1,000}$ meter	0.039 inch
centimeter	cm	length	10 millimeters, $^1/_{10}$ meter	0.394 inch
meter	m	length	1,000 millimeters, 100 centimeters	39.370 inches, 1.094 yards
gram	g	weight*	$^1/_{1,000}$ kilogram	0.353 ounce
kilogram	kg	weight	1,000 grams	2.205 pounds
ton		weight	1,000,000 grams, 1,000 kilograms	1.102 US tons
liter	l	volume	1,000 cubic centimeters	0.264 gallons
newton-meter	Nm	torque	1.02 kilogram-meter	0.738 foot-pounds
watt	W	power	1 newton-meter per second	0.00134 hp
ampere	A	electric current		
volt	V	voltage	watts per ampere	

* Actually mass, which remains identical whether the object is on Earth or floating weightless in space.

abrasive blade: A disk of abrasive used as a metal-cutting blade in an **abrasive cut-off saw.**

abrasive cutoff saw: A special kind of high-speed **chop saw** for cutting steel. It uses **abrasive blades.**

AC Abbreviation for **alternating current.**

accessory: Any component that can be used with grid beam and which is not a stick, panel, fastener or adapter. Accessories include wheels, axles, motors, gears, transmissions, batteries, wire, rope, plumbing parts, windows and lamps.

adapter: A part used to attach accessories that don't bolt directly to grid beam.

alternative energy: Alternatives to the concentrated sources of energy currently popular in industrial nations, such as fossil fuels and nuclear power. We look forward to the day when today's "alter-

native" energy sources such as solar and wind have become mainstream, and today's mainstream sources are obsolete.

ampere-hour: The unit used for rating battery capacity. A battery rated for 10 ampere-hours can theoretically provide a 1-amp current for 10 hours, or a 10-amp current for 1 hour. In practice, draining batteries fast (like electric vehicles do) yields fewer amp-hours, and draining lead-acid batteries more than 60 to 70 percent damages them.

appropriate technology: Technology that is friendly to people, society and the environment. This generally requires it to be simple, affordable and user-maintainable.

ATV: An all-terrain vehicle designed to operate in rugged or wet terrain such as hills, swamps and creeks. ATVs usually have four (sometimes three) wheels fitted with wide knobby tires.

beamer: A grid beam user or fanatic.

bearing: A part that supports and guides moving machine parts while reducing friction. The parts inside may be metal balls (ball bearings), cylinders (roller bearings), or cones (tapered roller bearings). Compare to **bushing.**

blade guide: A guide for a power saw that helps you make straight cuts. Also called a fence.

blocking: The tendency of a surface finish such as paint to stick to other finished surfaces. Blocking inside a tri-joint can pull paint off sticks when the joint is disassembled.

bogie steering: Steering with wheels mounted on an axle that pivots in the center. Children's wagons use bogie steering. See diagram in Figure 21.1.

bottom bracket: The part of a bicycle where the crank arms attach. (The pedals mount on the crank arms.)

box beam: 1. A wooden **box truss.** 2. The name the Jergensons used for grid beam in their first book, **Box Beam Sourcebook.**

box frame: A type of grid beam frame that resembles the outline of a box. Compare to **offset frame, stem frame.**

box truss: A structural beam constructed like a long, hollow box.

breakout: Splintering that sometimes occurs as a drill bit exits wood or plywood.

bushing: Also called a plain bearing. A round sleeve inside an opening in which some other part will ride. Bushings commonly reduce friction in a rotating shaft, or guide a part that moves. A bushing can also decrease the size of a too-large hole, or protect a soft material from wear.

Button Shelf™: A round wooden shelf attached by one bolt.

camber: Tilting the top of a vehicle wheel toward or away from the center of the vehicle as viewed from the front. Proper camber improves handling and reduces tire wear.

carbide: A super-hard material used in saw blades and drill bits.

caster: 1. A small wheel on a swivel, designed to attach beneath objects and make them easy to move. 2. Tilt in the **steering axis** (Figure 21.12). 3. The amount of this tilt.

center punch: A tool with a sharp point used to make dimples in metal where a hole will be drilled. The dimple keeps the drill bit centered while you start the hole.

check: 1. A small split in wood grain that has little effect on strength. 2. To split by checking. Compare to **split.**

chips: The waste material produced when you drill a hole.

chop saw: A power saw on a pivoting arm. Types include the **abrasive cutoff saw, miter saw** and **cold saw.**

chuck: The part of a drill or drill press that holds the bit.

cold saw: A low-speed chop saw for materials that must stay cool. It turns about 10 rpm and uses a carbide blade.

compression: A force tending to compress something (squeeze it together).

contact patch: The part of a wheel or tire that touches the ground.

counterbore: 1. A bit that makes a square-bottomed, recessed hole (Figure 2.14). 2. To counterbore a hole.

countersink: 1. A hole with the top enlarged so that the tapered head of a screw will lie flush with or below the surface. 2. To enlarge and taper the top of a hole.

cross cut: To cut wood across the grain.

cross bracing: Diagonal bracing designed to keep a structure from **racking** or collapsing.

cutting fluid: A lubricant for drill bits and saw blades that keeps the cutting edges from overheating and helps the chips escape the cutting area.

dead load: The weight of a structure or vehicle. The dead load of a roof is only the weight of the roof itself, and doesn't include snow, carpenters, pigeons and wind. Compare to **live load.**

differential: Gearing used in an axle to permit paired wheels to maintain power while turning at different speeds. This is necessary because during a turn, the outside wheel travels a longer arc than the inside wheel, and must turn faster to keep up. Differentials improve vehicle efficiency and reduce tire wear.

double A-arm suspension: A **double wishbone suspension.**

double wishbone suspension: A type of suspension using two A-shaped arms one over the other, commonly used for automobiles. It is known for its good handling.

drift: A tapered pin for aligning holes. Also called a drift pin.

drill rod: Round metal rod of very hard steel, available in many sizes. It is used to make drill bits.

drive shaft: A shaft that transmits motion or power.

drive wheel: A powered wheel.

drywall: A type of panel used for indoor walls. It has a mineral core sandwiched between sheets of heavy paper. Also called wallboard, plasterboard, gypsum board or sheetrock.

dynamic load: A variable load, such as the weight of a child bouncing in your lap. Compare to **static load.**

Electrathon: A type of racing in which electric vehicles powered by identical battery packs compete to see which can go farthest in one hour.

electroplate: A thin layer of metal used to coat an object made of a different metal. Most silver-colored nuts and bolts are steel electroplated with zinc or cadmium to protect them from rust.

emery cloth: An abrasive similar to sandpaper. Its cloth backing makes it more flexible.

energy density: A measure of how much energy you can cram into a given weight or volume of storage medium. The energy density of a fuel determines how much of it a vehicle can carry.

A typical 64-pound (39-kilogram) lead-acid car battery stores roughly the same amount of energy as ½ cup (.01 liter) of gasoline weighing about ⅕ pound (90 grams). Gasoline thus has over 320 times the energy density of the battery — which is why Hollywood uses gasoline rather than batteries to produce movie explosions.

farm jack: A hand-powered jack that walks a clamp along a perforated steel beam using a pair of moving pins. It can be used for lifting, clamping, pushing and winching. Also called a handyman jack or high lift jack.

Filon: A brand of **UV-stabilized** sheet fiberglass.

finish: 1. Paint, varnish, oil or other coating material. 2. To apply a finish to something.

floor stand: An adjustable-height work support.

foot-pound: A US measure of **torque.** See "Units of measurement" at beginning of glossary.

forged: A metal part made by heating and hammering. Forged hooks and eye bolts are much stronger than **turned** hardware.

fork: A two-pronged mount for a steered wheel, such as the front wheel of a motorcycle or bicycle.

galvanized: Coated with zinc for protection from rust and corrosion. **Hot-dip galvanized** finishes are more durable than **electroplate.**

gear wrench: A wrench with a ring-shaped ratchet at one end.

gin pole: A pole with one or more pulleys, used for lifting or lowering loads. A gin pole on the base of a windmill is used to drop the tower to the ground for servicing.

glazing: Any window or skylight material, such as glass or plexiglass.

grade: 1. A measure of bolt hardness, indicated by a pattern of lines (US sizes) or numbers (US or metric) on the bolt head. 2. A measure of the steepness of a slope. Percent of grade equals the number of units (feet, meters or whatever) of rise for every hundred horizontal units. A road that goes up 15 units for every 100 units forward has a 15 percent grade. A vehicle climbing a 15 percent grade uses about 15 percent more power than traveling level ground at the same speed.

grain: The direction or arrangement of fibers in wood.

green: Lumber that has not yet dried. It is still heavy and wet from being inside the tree.

grid beam: 1. The generic name for any square, perforated beam capable of creating a tri-joint. Sometimes referred to as sticks, struts, members, mainframe or matrix. 2. A building system or project that uses grid beam for its main structural members.

grid beam component: A standard grid beam stick, panel or connector, or any accessory that mates directly to grid beam.

grid power: Electricity from the public power network.

gusset: A small board or panel, usually triangular, used to brace a corner or joint.

hand screw: A type of woodworking clamp that has wooden or plastic jaws.

hardboard: A panel material made by compressing wood fibers, and usually a binder, at high temperatures. It is smooth on one or both sides, and available in solid sheets and pegboard. The solid sheets are sometimes called masonite (after the name of the original brand), fiberboard, pressboard or beaverboard.

hardware: Fasteners and building parts such as bolts, nails, hinges and locks. Most hardware is metal.

head tube: The tube at the front of a motorcycle or bicycle frame where the front fork assembly attaches.

helical rotor: A vertical axis wind turbine design similar to the Savonius rotor, but using spiral rather than scoop-shaped blades.

horizontal axis wind turbine: A wind turbine in which the shaft is parallel to the wind direction, and the blades spin at right angles to the wind. Horizontal axis designs must reorient when the wind direction changes. Compare to vertical axis wind turbine.

horsepower: A US unit of power, abbreviated hp and equal to 745.7 watts. See "Units of measure" at beginning of glossary.

hot-dip galvanizing: A coating process that uses zinc to protect steel from rust. It is more durable than electroplate.

inverter: A device that changes direct current to alternating current. Inverters allow DC power sources such as batteries to run equipment that requires AC.

jackshaft: An intermediate shaft between a motor and what it drives. Gears or pulleys on the jackshaft gear the power up or down, allowing very low or very high gear ratios.

jig: A device for guiding a tool, holding work pieces in place, or assembling something. Jigs are most often used when you're making or doing a lot of the same thing, such as drilling holes in grid beam. A jig can be as simple as a stop against which pieces can be pushed.

jointer: A woodworking tool for making the edges of boards flat and square.

joist: One of the horizontal beams that holds up a floor or ceiling.

kerf: 1. The slot made by a cutting tool such as a saw blade. 2. The width of this slot.

kingpin: The steering axis around which an automobile's wheel pivots. Some designs have a steel pin there.

ladder truss: A type of **truss** that has two parallel outside rails (like a ladder) connected with diagonal members (Figure 18.11).

leading link: A type of front suspension in which the axle rides ahead of the forks on arms or a pivoting yoke.

liquid thread locker: Liquid plastic that hardens on bolt and nut threads to keep them from unscrewing. Thread locker works only on metal-to-metal joints. Use in place of lock washers.

live axle: An axle that spins with the wheel. Compare to **stationary axle.**

live load: The moving or variable loads a structure or piece of equipment is subject to in addition to its own weight. The live load on a roof might include wind, dead leaves, snow and people cleaning the gutters, but would not include the weight of the roof itself. Compare to **dead load.**

Living Structure: A type of furniture invented by Ken Isaacs in the 1940s. A three-dimensional skeleton supports elements such as tables, seating, storage and beds, all of which can be moved and recombined as needed. Ken built most of his Living Structures from grid beam.

Loctite: A brand of **liquid thread locker,** available in various types.

machine screw: A bolt with a screw head.

MacPherson strut: A type of suspension often used in automobiles because it is easy to fabricate.

matrix: Ken Isaacs's name for the frames of his **Living Structures.** Only some were made from grid beam.

member In construction, a beam, plate or built piece meant to become part of an assembled frame or structure.

mineral spirits: A petroleum distillate, often used as a paint and varnish thinner.

miter box: A blade guide for a hand saw that keeps the cut square.

miter saw: A type of **chop saw** used for cutting precise angles.

modular: Designed with standard units or dimensions that make the parts interchangeable.

momentary switch: A switch that returns to the off position once released.

motor controller: An electronic control for regulating the speed of an electric motor.

National Coarse thread: The coarser thread on non-metric US bolts and hardware, abbreviated NC. We use it because it is the commonest US thread size. Compare to **National Fine thread.**

naphtha: A petroleum-based solvent and paint thinner.

National Fine thread: The finer thread on non-metric US bolts, abbreviated NF. Since fewer types of hardware are available with this thread, we use **National Coarse thread.**

nominal size: The stated size of a piece of material, which may differ from its actual size. The nominal size of two-by-four lumber is two inches by four inches; the actual size is approximately 1½ inches by 3½ inches.

nut driver: A tool similar to a screwdriver, with a hex socket on the end.

off the grid or **off-grid:** Not getting electricity from the public power network.

offset frame: A variant of the **box frame** that has the posts offset from the frame corners. This allows standard-size panels to be used as shelves with no notching. Compare to **box frame, stem frame.**

pallet: A movable shelf/bench/desk surface stiffened by lengthwise grid beam rails underneath. Ken Isaacs used pallets in many of his Living Structures.

parabola: A type of curve used in headlights and solar concentrators to direct light. Solar concentrators use parabolas to direct parallel rays of sunlight *to* one point or strip. Headlights use parabolas to spread light *from* one point into parallel rays.

parabolic: Shaped like a **parabola**.

parallel circuit: An electrical circuit having two or more paths where current can flow. Vehicle lights should be wired in parallel so that each bulb will stay lit if others burn out. Compare to **series circuit, series-parallel circuit.**

pegboard: A panel with holes in a grid pattern, usually made from **hardboard**. Many manufacturers make hooks, shelves, racks, drawers and more that plug into the holes.

piano hinge: A very long hinge used for joining two edges that require support all along their lengths.

pillow block: A bolt-on metal block that supports a bearing or rotating shaft.

pilot hole: A small hole that guides a screw, nail or drill bit. Pilot holes prevent fasteners from splitting brittle materials.

plane: 1. To smooth the surface of wood by shaving the surface with a sharp blade. 2. A hand tool that planes wood.

planer: A power tool to **plane** wood.

plumb line: A string holding a suspended weight, used to find vertical.

post-and-beam construction: A centuries-old method for framing buildings that uses big timbers notched and pegged together at the joints. The frame is stiff enough to stay straight without diagonal braces or panels.

pulley: A wheel with a V-shaped groove around the outside edge, used with a V-belt to transmit power between rotating shafts. Also called a sheave.

QuikStix: 1. Jergensons' brand of grid beam, available in wood or aluminum. 2. The name of Jergensons' company, which sells grid beam components.

racking: 1. A type of distortion typical of projects knocked out of square. 2. The forces that cause racking. See Figure 19.4 and Figure 19.5.

rebar: Also called re-rod. Steel reinforcing rod with a ridged surface, used to strengthen concrete.

regen: Short for **regenerative braking.**

regenerative braking: Also **regen**. A method of recapturing and storing the mechanical energy of braking. Spinning an electric motor mechanically generates power. Regen uses the speed of the vehicle to spin its motor and charge the battery. The resulting drag slows the vehicle. Regen has the most braking force at high speeds or very low gearing. A road vehicle with regen also needs conventional brakes.

rigger: A professional who does **rigging.**

rigging: 1. Ropes, chains and cables used to support, position and control equipment or materials. 2. Using rigging.

rip: To saw wood along the grain.

rod end: A metal loop that screws onto the end of a threaded rod or shaft. Compare **rod end bearing.**

rod end bearing: A **rod-end** whose loop contains a bearing. Also called a **hime joint.**

rout: To shape with a **router.**

router: A power tool for shaping edges and cutting slots in wood. We use routers to round the edges of wooden grid beam.

rpm: Revolutions per minute.

S4S: Abbreviation for "Surfaced 4 Sides," which means lumber planed smooth on all four sides.

Savonius rotor: A **vertical axis wind turbine** with two or three scoops. The scoops are sometimes made from split 55-gallon oil drums.

scratch-build: To build from components (bought or fabricated) rather than from a kit or by modifying an existing object.

SEER: Solar Energy Expo and Rally, an alternative energy fair held in northern California in the 1990s.

series circuit: An electrical circuit in which two or more components are connected so that electricity flows through one before it flows through the next. Compare to **parallel circuit, series-parallel circuit.**

series-parallel circuit: An electrical circuit in which components can be connected either in a **series circuit** or in a **parallel circuit.** Used to supply current to a motor, this wiring provides more than one speed without a transmission. A vehicle with two 12-volt batteries can use the series circuit to supply 12 volts for low speed, and a parallel circuit to supply 24 volts for high speed.

shank: The non-threaded portion of a bolt's shaft.

shear: 1. A machine that uses scissors-like action to cut something. 2. Force pushing parts of a project to slide past each other in opposite directions (Figure 19.4). Shear causes **racking.**

shear wall: Panels used for cross-bracing, so called because they resist **shear** forces.

sheathing A layer of boards or panels on the outside of a building that strengthens the structure and provides something to attach shingles or siding to.

sheet stock: Any panel-type building material that comes in standard-size panels, such as plywood and **drywall.**

shoulder: A projection on the underside of a bolt head, such as a carriage or elevator bolt, designed to bite into wood and keep the bolt from turning.

signboard: A type of exterior plywood with a smooth, paintable surface, used for outdoor signs. Also called Medium Density Overlay or MDO.

solar tracker: See **tracker**

solenoid: A special kind of switch for powering heavy electrical loads. A light-duty switch turns on the solenoid, and the solenoid completes the circuit.

Solman: Any of several portable power sources designed and sold by Phil Jergenson. They consist of a solar panel, charge controller, battery and optional inverter. Some versions can be hand-carried; larger versions have wheels.

speeder: 1. A small, motorized railroad work vehicle that rides the tracks. 2. A small, motorized rail vehicle used for recreation. 3. A person who drinks too much of Richard's coffee.

spindle: 1. A shaft that turns, especially the main shaft of a drill press. A **chuck** on one end holds the drill bit. 2. The part of a vehicle that a wheel hub attaches to.

split: A deep separation in wood grain that weakens the board. Splits can go completely through a board. Compare to **check.**

static: 1. Not moving. 2. The hassle you get from your mate when you take over the living room to build grid beam projects.

static load: A load that is constant, such as a book on the floor. Compare to **dynamic load.**

stationary axle: An axle that doesn't turn. The bearings are in the wheel. Compare **live axle.**

steering axis: The imaginary line around which a steered wheel turns. On bicycle or motorcycle, it runs down the center of the **head tube.** See Figure 21.12.

stem frame: A type of grid beam frame that uses a minimum of sticks. Compare to **box frame, offset frame.**

step drill bit: A special bit for drilling sheet metal and thin plastic.

stick: A piece of grid beam frame material.

sticker: 1. A board or other spacer used to keep materials off the ground or to separate layers of drying lumber. 2. To stack on or spaced with stickers.

straight edge: A straight piece of something stiff, such as angle iron or grid beam, used to mark straight lines and cuts.

stressed skin: A strong construction method that uses the project's skin as part of the structure for strength. The most common type is a rectangular frame of wooden or metal sticks attached to a stiff panel skin on one or both sides. The sticks resist **compression,** and the panels resist **tension** and **racking.**

sun: A measure of sunlight intensity. A solar furnace concentrates 10 suns when it puts 10 times more light on the target than would fall on the same target in direct sunlight.

swing arm: A fork or arm hinged on one end. Simple and light, swing arms are used for motorcycle rear wheels.

tap bolt: A bolt with threads all along the shaft.

tempered: Treated to be harder, stronger or more resilient.

tempered hardboard: Hardboard impregnated with oil to help it resist moisture. It is smoother and harder than untempered hardboard.

tension: 1. A force tending to pull or stretch something. 2. To apply tension to something; pull it tight. Compare to **compression.**

tension element: A part of a structure that resists **tension** (pulling) loads.

test bed: A reusable chassis used to test components.

thimble: A metal fitting that protects the end of a cable from crimping and wear.

threaded rod: Bolt threads with no head. It is sold in pieces several feet long. Also called all-thread.

torque: A turning or twisting force. Amount of torque = (amount of force applied) x (length of lever). Long beams in projects act as levers that magnify torque, which is why bigger projects are more likely to need cross-bracing. Torque is measured in foot-pounds or inch-pounds (US) or Newton-meters (metric).

torsion: The stress caused when one end of an object is twisted while the other end is held motionless or twisted in the opposite direction. Torsion is caused by **torque.**

torsional racking: A type of racking that twists a project's frame (Figure 19.5).

track: 1. The distance between wheels on opposite sides of a vehicle, measured from the center of the tires' **contact patches.** 2. To follow the path of the sun, pointing directly at it throughout the day. See **tracker.**

tracker: A device for keeping a solar collector aimed directly at the sun throughout the day.

trail: The distance between a wheel's **steering axis** at ground level and the center of its **contact patch.** See Figure 21.12.

transaxle: A combination **transmission, differential** and axle.

transmission: The gearbox of a vehicle, by which engine or motor power is transmitted to the wheels. It usually has two or more gears, used for matching the load to the motor power and speed.

tri-joint: A grid beam joint in which three bolts connect three pieces of grid beam that cross at right angles (Figure 1.6). Tri-joints are strong, rigid and automatically self-squaring.

triple clamp: An assembly that attaches motorcycle forks to the frame.

truss: A structure consisting of straight sections connected at the joints into triangular units. Common examples include metal and wooden railroad bridges, TV and radio broadcast towers, and the Eiffel Tower. Trusses are very strong for their weight.

turnbuckle: A device for tensioning cables and threaded rod. It has a central body with a threaded hook or eye in each end. One set of threads is reversed, so that twisting the turnbuckle body screws both ends in or out without twisting what they're attached to.

turned: Hooks, eyes and other hardware formed by bending steel rod. **Forged** hardware is much stronger.

untempered: Not strengthened or made more resilient by special treatment. Compare **tempered**.

UV stabilized: Plastic or fiberglass made to resist damage from the ultraviolet light in sunlight.

V-belt: A belt used to transmit power between rotating shafts. See **pulley**.

vertical axis wind turbine: A **wind turbine** with scoops or blades that travel toward and away from the wind. Its center shaft is at right angles to the wind. Usually the shaft is vertical, so that wind from any direction will power the rotor. Some "vertical axis" turbines are mounted with the shaft horizontal and at right angles to the prevailing wind. Compare to **horizontal axis wind turbine**.

web truss: A wooden I-beam.

wheelbase: The distance from front to rear wheels, measured from the center of the tires' contact patches.

Index

About the Authors

Phil Jergenson is an artist and systems designer who enjoys building solar powered machines. "I enjoy chasing dreams and testing new ideas. I am a trained model maker and self-taught machinist and metal fabricator. I have lived off-grid for 30 years, and spent 15 of those years building and living in micro-houses in remote locations. I have scratch built more than a dozen small solar-powered vehicles, some which are tractors and work vehicles." Phil is a co-founder of the Renewable Energy Development Institute (REDI), a 19-year-old nonprofit in Willits, California.

A 30-year resident of Willits, California, Richard Jergenson started a number of successful businesses in the 70s and 80s, including his favorite, running the local cinema. *The Whole Earth Catalog* and *Mother Earth News* fueled his life-long interests in technology, energy, transportation (especially railroads), and alternative lifestyles. A cultural archivist and 20-year member/officer of the Mendocino County Railway Society, he is a member of Roots of Motive Power and active in the Little Lake Grange. One of the builders of the world's first solar-electric rail vehicle, the Sol Train, Richard has been grid beaming since 1977.

A professional welder and metal fabricator in the mid-1980s, Wilma Keppel switched to grid beam in 1995. "I am interested in anything that works exceptionally well — whether grid beam, regenerative land management, or mental performance." She writes on environmental topics and is a site editor for ManagingWholes.com. Since 2003 Wilma has done research in practical psychology — real things we ordinary people can do to improve our lives. She teaches life enhancement and mental performance skills through Peak Performance Preparation in Oakland, California (PeakPerformancePreparation.com).

Phil Jergenson

Richard Jergenson

Wilma Keppel

If you have enjoyed *How to Build with Grid Beam* you might also enjoy other

Books to Build a New Society

Our books provide positive solutions for people who want to make a difference. We specialize in:

**Environment and Justice • Conscientious Commerce • Sustainable Living
Ecological Design and Planning • Natural Building & Appropriate Technology
New Forestry • Educational and Parenting Resources
Nonviolence Progressive Leadership • Resistance and Community**

New Society Publishers

ENVIRONMENTAL BENEFITS STATEMENT

New Society Publishers has chosen to produce this book on Enviro 100, recycled paper made with **100% post consumer waste**, processed chlorine free and old growth free.

For every 5,000 books printed, New Society saves the following resources:[1]

61	Trees
5,549	Pounds of Solid Waste
6,106	Gallons of Water
7,964	Kilowatt Hours of Electricity
10,087	Pounds of Greenhouse Gases
43	Pounds of HAPs, VOCs and AOX Combined
15	Cubic Yards of Landfill Space

[1]Environmental benefits are calculated based on research done by the Environmental Defense Fund and other members of the Paper Task Force who study the environmental impacts of the paper industry.

For more information on this environmental benefits statement, or to inquire about environmentally friendly papers, please contact New Leaf Paper – info@newleafpaper.com Tel: 888 • 989 • 5323.

For a full list of NSP's titles, please call **1-800-567-6772** *or check out our website at:*

www.newsociety.com

New Society Publishers